RT
RARY
CRAGSTAN

Textile design

Simon Clarke

introduction

1. Context

2. Printed textile design

3. Woven textile design

4. Mixed media textile design

5. Design principles

6. Creating a collection

7. Education and employment

Related study material is available on the Laurence King website at **www.laurenceking.com**

Published in 2011 by Laurence King Publishing Ltd
361–373 City Road
London EC1V 1LR
Tel: +44 20 7841 6900
Fax: +44 20 7841 6910
e-mail: enquiries@laurenceking.com
www.laurenceking.com

This book was designed and produced by
Laurence King Publishing Ltd, London

A catalogue record for this book is available
from the British Library.

ISBN: 978-1-85669-687-6

Designed by Lizzie Ballantyne
Portfolio series design concept by Jon Allan

Printed in China

Author's acknowledgements
Thanks to University College Falmouth for its support
and to all the designers, design studios, manufacturers
and businesses who contributed to this book. Thanks
also to my publisher Laurence King and his team,
especially Helen Evans, Anne Townley, Susie May,
Claire Gouldstone and Srijana Gurung.

Front cover image: Tree of Life by Timorous Beasties, www.timorousbeasties.com
Back cover image: Hussein Chalayan – Autumn Winter 2007/Catwalking.com
Frontispiece: Robot Fish Sea by Anna Glover

Introduction

A textile design is a piece of cloth made by weaving yarns spun from natural and/or artificial fibres. While this process forms the textile, other processes contribute to its decorative and functional qualities. Principally, these are printed textile design, where the cloth is printed and finishes are applied to it; and mixed media textile design, which includes embroidery and fabric manipulation. This book describes how printed, woven and mixed media textiles are designed and produced, and explores how they are used for products and in specific market contexts. Historical and cultural references, design principles and methods, and approaches to developing a textile collection are also key themes, as is technology, which plays a pivotal role in enabling new aesthetics and product forms to be realized.

Textiles have evolved alongside mankind to transform the material world, and textile design is the primary element in clothing and interior decoration – and is also prominent in other fields from fine art to architectural engineering. Some of our most innovative achievements are represented by textiles, and this is reflected in the extravagant designs in haute couture, whether these are innovatory or new interpretations of classic recurring designs like animal patterns. Although regional geographies and related traditions have contributed towards its rich diversity, trade between these regions means they have seldom been truly isolated and has led to remarkable innovations in hybrid textile design.

Far left
The animal pattern – a recurring design classic – receives a new interpretation by Dries Van Noten in Look 35 from his autumn/winter 2009/10, women's collection, shown at Lycée Carnot.

Left
This all-white garment captures the creativity in textile design that can result from innovative collaboration, in this case between Karl Lagerfeld at Chanel and François Lesage, who has transformed fabric manipulation and embroidery to the level of art forms. Chanel, 2009 summer collection, haute couture.

Who this book is for

Textile Design is a broad and informative overview of textile design and provides insights into a wealth of aesthetics, production techniques and textile products – both historical and the latest cutting-edge innovations – to give a real sense of the potential offered by textile design. It is primarily for undergraduate, degree and pre-degree art foundation students who want to pursue a career in textile design: its aim is to introduce them to, and impart a real flavour of, what is now a multifaceted, multibillion-pound industry. It is also accessible to enthusiasts who simply wish to know more about textile design and production practices.

Above
Detail from the patchwork, wax-print patterns for the Binta chair designed by Philippe Bestenheider (2009). The patterns are reminiscent of those on fabrics worn by women throughout the African continent.

Below
The form of Bestenheider's Binta chair was influenced by African wood-carved seating. The difference, though, is that the polyurethane rubber form provides a more comfortable experience.

How to use this book

While *Textile Design* can be read from start to finish, it does not necessarily need to be read in a particular order. The intention is that students will find it useful at different stages in their studies as they develop interests in specific aspects of design and production, and that it will be a source of inspiration for further investigation. It will give a sound knowledge and understanding of the textile industry and the design and production methods – and language – used within it. It also describes the skills of a textile designer and the activities involved in the design and manufacture of a textile collection.

Historical and cultural textiles are a recurring source of inspiration for many textile designers, and **chapter 1** is a broad historical and cultural overview of their design, from the ancient world to the twenty-first century. It is not a comprehensive survey; rather, it gives a sense of how creative thinking and technology have developed over the passage of time.

Chapter 2 discusses printed textile design and examines how a design moves through the stages of preparation and manufacture in screen printing, digital design and digital inkjet printing, along with other finishing methods. Printed patterns from the figurative to the abstract suggest the range of subjects that may be drawn upon. Relationships between design and science, as well as environmental and eco-design issues, are introduced. Examples of

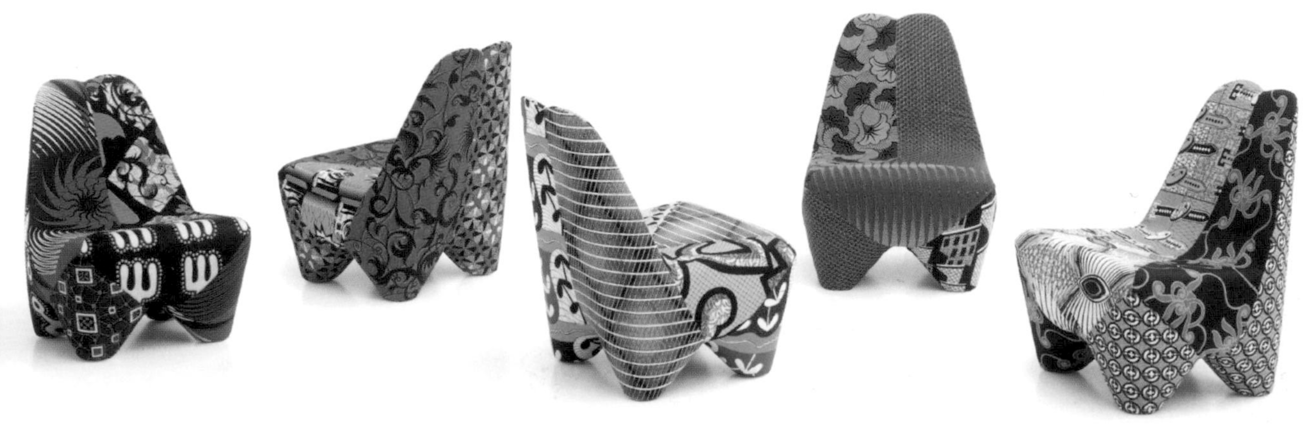

Clouds, a modular room-dividing system which absorbs sound, made from textile pieces held together by elastic bands. Conceived by innovative furniture, product and interior designers Ronan and Erwan Bouroullec in 2009 for textile manufacturer Kvadrat.

designers, design studios and manufacturers of printed textile design provide the context for particular design and printing topics.

Chapter 3 examines the creative and technical attributes of woven textile design, from weaving on a hand loom to using digital design and powered jacquard techniques. References to designers, design studios and manufacturers, and their design work contextualize creative and manufacturing approaches.

Chapter 4 follows a similar format to chapters 2 and 3, but the subject is mixed media textile design and its focus is the creative and technical potential of embroidery and fabric manipulation. Both areas are in a state of flux as designers take advantage of the burgeoning range of technologies that has developed in recent years. Embroidery techniques using hand, machine and digital techniques are examined, and are contextualized in relation to innovative artists and designers, and traditional and new ways of fabric manipulation are discussed.

Chapter 5 introduces ideas and different perspectives on a range of key design principles and methods used by textile designers. The main themes are design tools, concept/trend predictions, colour, drawing/imagery, pattern, and visualizing textiles in the context in which they will be used.

Chapter 6 explores the design process and how it leads to a collection of finished designs.

Chapter 7 examines what is involved in studying for a degree in textile design and there is also information about the career directions open to graduates, with references to textile design products and markets discussed in earlier chapters.

Textile design presents unique opportunities for individuality once the basic design and technical knowledge have been acquired: two designers working on the same project brief invariably come up with two different interpretations of a theme because of their differing perspectives and perceptions. This is the magic of textile design.

1. Context

Within a concentrated time scale of just over 200 years a remarkable diversity of thinking and creativity has evolved in textile design. While this is certainly the result of developments such as the technological innovations of the Industrial Revolution, the invention of synthetic fabrics in the twentieth century and, most recently, the digital revolution, the inspiration that fuelled this evolution – and continues to inspire modern textile designers – is firmly rooted in the remarkable variety of imagery, design styles, patterns and techniques that has been created over the past 4000 years.

This chapter looks at the historical and cultural contexts in which textile design has evolved, and provides insights into the creative and technical capabilities of its early craftsmen, as well as highlighting the work of key twentieth-century designers. It also describes the complex trade relationships that have existed and, in some cases, continue to exist in the field of textiles, and discusses the environmental and ethical challenges that textile designers face in the twenty-first century.

This opulent Sunni textile is an example of a complex geometric pattern based on mathematics, an art form for which the Islamic world is renowned.

Early history

Ancient Egyptian wall paintings that show figures wearing patterned and embroidered fabrics indicate a developed textile infrastructure – a view supported by the discovery of funerary models of weave workshops that date from 1950 BC. The most famous of these, the Meketra, contains figures preparing **yarns** and weaving at looms. It suggests a workshop space in a building, perhaps in the lower floor of a house and slightly below ground, a location that would have helped to maintain the level of humidity necessary for weaving fine linen. Also in Egypt, but more than 2000 years later, Christian iconography was a prominent feature of textiles designed for the Church, which subsequently established itself as a source of influence and patronage for textile designers throughout Europe. During the expansion of Islam in the eighth century the figurative textiles of the Shi'ia Fatimids and the geometric patterns of the Sunni reached new creative heights. The range of styles and production techniques from these and other early civilizations is extensive and many contemporary textiles have evolved from this rich resource.

Above
The Meketra tomb model gives an insight into how textiles were woven in ancient Egypt. Three young women crouch behind platforms preparing roves for splicing, and in front of them three women are spinning, each with two spindles. There are two horizontal ground looms with two weavers; a woman crouches at the far end of one of the looms. Two women unload two spindles to transfer the spun yarns on to a group of three pegs set into the wall.

Left
Coptic textiles typically feature decorative borders and a large central motif portraying a priest or devotee who seems forever youthful. In this design the border includes mythical beasts and flying angels.

Cultural interchanges: African cloths and beads

The influence of trade on African textiles is apparent in two unique cloths, one of which is found in West Africa and the other in the east. The **kente** cloth of Ghana is designed from strips of woven fabric which are sewn together to produce a length of fabric – a strip-weaving technique that is likely to have been introduced into the country by trans-Saharan caravans that brought textile craftsmen, some of Arabic descent, to Ghana along with trade items. With the rise of royal patronage and the increasing purchasing power of the Ashanti people, local weavers began to construct kente cloth made entirely of silk, and the fabric became established as the regalia of the Ashanti aristocracy and royal court. Colours and patterns are bold and symbolic, and often relate to Ashanti proverbs. The most complex pattern is Adweneasa, which means 'My skill is exhausted' or 'My ideas have come to an end', and announces that there is no room on the cloth for any more pattern. While kente cloth is traditionally made of silk, contemporary versions are woven from cotton and **rayon**/viscose yarns.

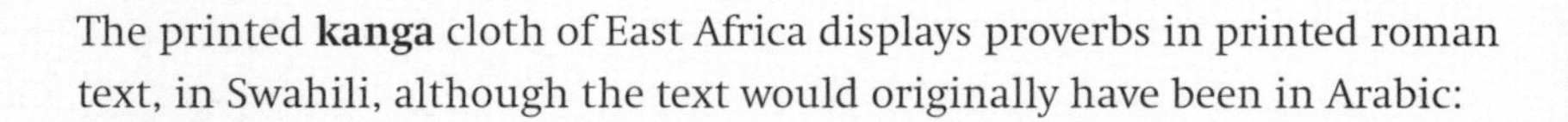

The printed **kanga** cloth of East Africa displays proverbs in printed roman text, in Swahili, although the text would originally have been in Arabic:

both formats reflect trade influences in this part of Africa. The design content in kanga cloth is broad and shows regional and external influences introduced by mercantile traders and colonialism in the late nineteenth century and earlier. One group of designs displays political and commemorative themes that refer to contemporary African events. However, they probably have their origins in designs produced to mark the coronations of George VI and Elizabeth II. They also show stylistic traits from Chinese iconography: China was, and remains, a supportive trade and development partner in East Africa's textile sector, and the Chinese revolutionary graphic style and typical related themes are notable in a design that celebrates 20 years of the Tanganyikan African National Union (1954–74) and was printed in 1974.

Bead decoration has a similar history to cloth in Africa in that it was originally introduced as a trade item in exchange for ivory, slaves and animal skins. Beadwork continues to have aesthetic and cultural significance among the Masai in East Africa and the Zulu of South Africa, who continue to rely on imported plastic beads. Among the most dramatic examples of beadwork design are the headdresses and garments worn by Zulu rickshaw pullers on the Durban beachfront, who once provided the city's main means of transport. Beadwork is still important in KwaZulu-Natal, where successful co-operatives run by women are making a key contribution to regional economies.

Above, left
Chinese and Tanzanian textile designers developing kanga designs at the Urafiki Textile Mill in 1968. The collaborative venture between Tanzania and China continues.

Above, right
Photograph of a Zulu rickshaw puller on the Durban waterfront in South Africa. The bold use of colour and pattern with large amounts of beadwork is indicative of traditional Zulu culture.

Opposite, top
Ashanti noblemen wearing strip-woven kente cloth.

Opposite, bottom
This kanga design was first produced in the late 1960s, and celebrates the modernizing and industrializing of Tanzania. Its style suggests a Chinese revolutionary graphic – unsurprisingly, given that the Urafiki Textile Mill employed Chinese textile and graphic artists.

The textile trade

Trade led to the transfer, interchange and assimilation of ideas from one culture to another, and was central to the development of textile design. Merchants who travelled along the Silk Road, the ancient caravan route that linked the eastern Mediterranean with central China, introduced silks and other Chinese products to Central Asia and Europe. The trade in silk was at its height during the Tang dynasty (618–907), a relatively stable period in Chinese history, but eventually declined because of tribal politics. In about 1500, the Spanish and Portuguese, followed by the English, Dutch and French, opened sea routes to, and developed trade links with, the East Indies. Conversely, the Chinese seafarer Zhang commanded maritime expeditions to Southeast Asia and India, and as far as Arabia and the east coast of Africa, and established textile trading networks that still exist today.

The remarkable interchange between cultures as a result of trade instigated the creation of some of the world's unique textiles. This is particularly apparent in Africa, where overland caravans and mercantile trading along sea routes has been a major influence. Examples are woven kente cloth from the Ashanti kingdom in Ghana, printed kanga cloth from East Africa and Zulu beadwork from South Africa.

The Silk Road was a major caravan route between the Far East and the West and took its name from the trade in silk, cultivated and manufactured in China, which was highly prized in Europe from as early as the Roman Empire.

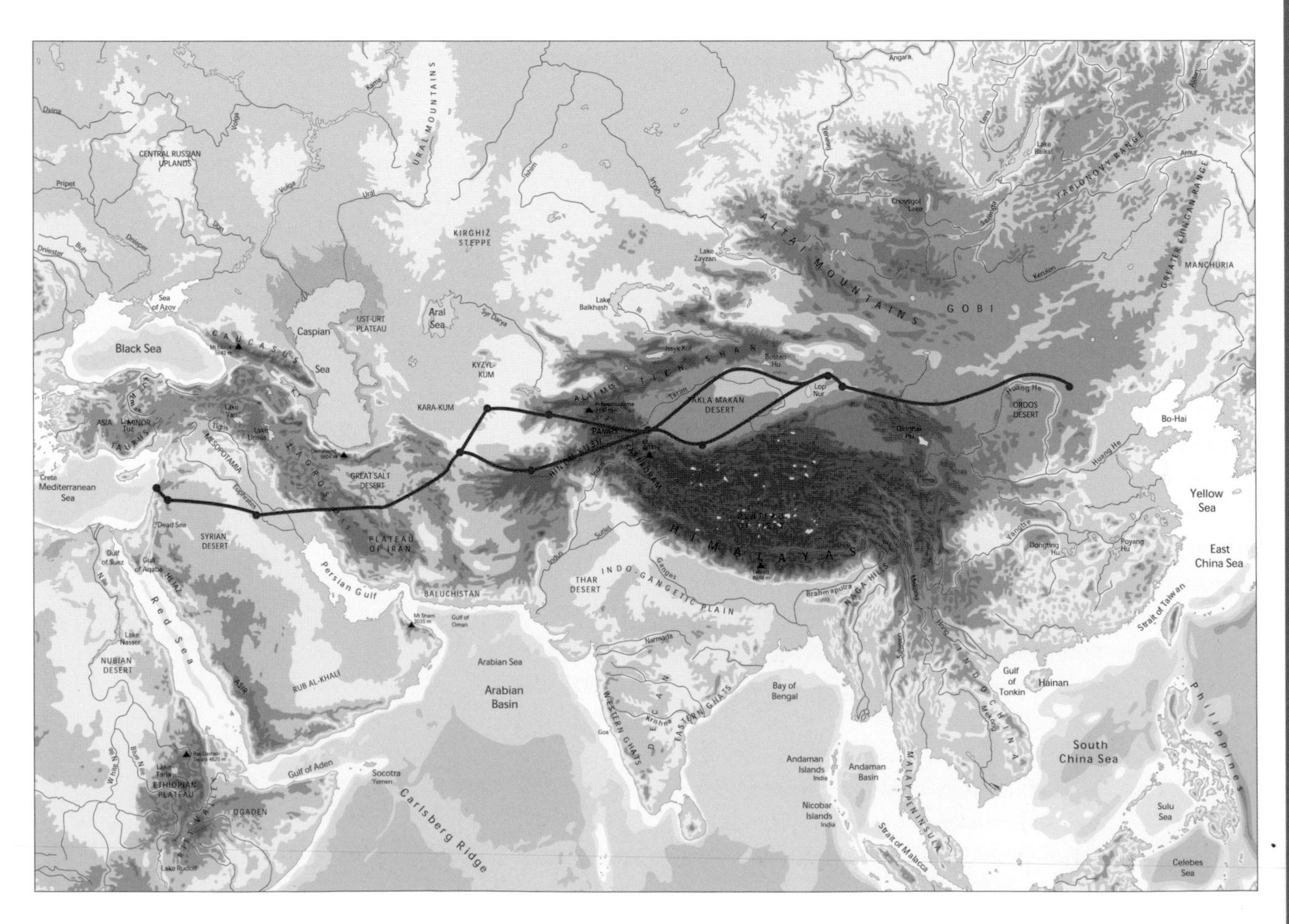

Today, the volume of the textile industry is huge – global figures in 2008 for textile imports were $262,863,000,000 and for textile export $250,198,000,000. While there are exceptions, such as haute couture textiles, in the majority of cases textile design, sourcing, production and distribution will involve a series of worldwide participants and activities driven principally by the need for textile companies to be competitive within their particular markets. It is now increasingly common for a textile company, in the United Kingdom for instance, to conceive the original design, after which subsequent sourcing and production of the textile occurs in one or more countries.

Common locations for manufacturing are China and India because of low manufacturing costs, countries which at the same time have improved production standards by having to adhere to international trade requirements and customer expectations regarding quality. Even with the shipping costs connected with manufacturing away from home, finished textile goods remain the most competitive option. The final distribution of the textile goods will often involve their return to their country of conception, or they may be distributed throughout a number of countries, depending on the company's wholesale and retail outlets.

The management of this process, with expectations for rapid turn-around times from conception to market, demands thorough monitoring and requires efficient communication between all participants, wherever they may be in the world. While quality control can be monitored by visits to the textile manufacturer and through the evaluation of **samples**, intelligently managed digital technologies, bespoke software and communication networks play a major role.

A figurative design on silk from the Tang dynasty, China.

Industrial and technological innovations

From the twelfth century to the eighteenth the design and manufacturing of textiles in Europe, Asia and the Far East was a cottage industry whose products reflected in the eighteenth century regional aesthetic styles and manufacturing capabilities in fabrics that were made from silk, linen, cotton and wool and used a range of woven, embroidered and dyeing techniques.

However, in England in the eighteenth century a shift towards mechanical production methods triggered a series of innovations that led to the Industrial Revolution. The **flying shuttle** created by John Kay in 1733 led the way to powered weaving, although its productive use was held back until yarn strengths had improved. It threw the **weft** thread through the **warp** threads mechanically, which meant that the operator no longer had to bend over the machine to pass the **shuttle** from one side of the loom to the other by hand and, more importantly, meant that two operators were no longer required for wider fabrics, one to throw and one to catch.

The spinning jenny, invented by James Hargreaves in 1764, increased productivity in spinning, and in 1771 Sir Richard Arkwright built Cromford Mill,

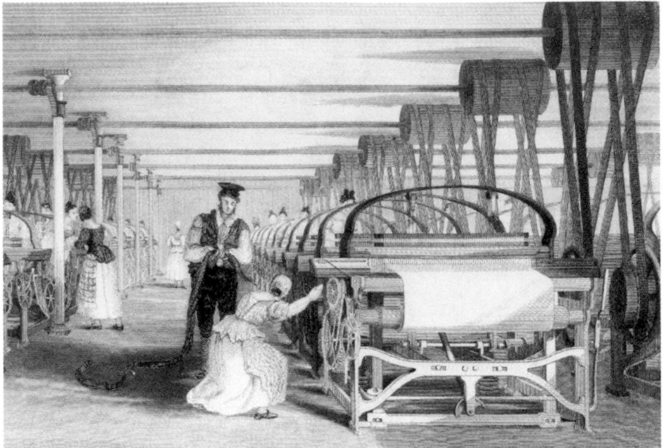

which incorporated the water frame, an automatic, water-powered spinning machine capable of producing yarn strong enough to make a warp. The homes he built around the mill for his employees were the first planned workers' village. The final stage in the mechanization of spinning was the invention of the **mule** by Samuel Crompton, in 1779. This hybrid machine combined the **roller drafting** – the use of rollers to draw out the thread – of the water frame with the **running twist**, or continuous twisting of fibres into yarn, of the spinning jenny, enabling fine yarns to be produced consistently.

The first practical **power loom** was designed by Edmund Cartwright in 1787, but was superseded a couple of years later by a steam-driven weaving mill in Doncaster which had 400 power looms – or mechanized versions of the hand loom. Flaws in these machines initially limited their widespread use, but by the 1820s the technical problems were resolved and weaving was transformed. Kenworthy Bullough had made the operation completely automatic by 1850 with the introduction of the Lancashire loom which was superseded 50 years later by the Northrop loom that could reload the shuttle with yarn. By 1927 highly efficient shuttleless looms were introduced. With further advances in technology to maximize production other types of loom were introduced into the textile industry, such as **air-jet** and **water-jet looms**. In France too, technological textile innovations were taking place, and in 1801 Joseph Jacquard invented a loom that incorporated a series of punchcards to control a complex pattern of warp threads, the forerunner to the contemporary **jacquard loom** (which is discussed further in chapter 3).

The mechanization of sewing techniques was significant for all forms of sewn textile design. In 1830 Barthélemy Thimonnier, a French tailor, patented a sewing machine that sewed straight seams using a chain stitch. By 1841 he had a factory that boasted 80 of the machines but it was destroyed by rioting French tailors who were afraid that they would lose their livelihood. Thimonnier's invention set in motion the steady development of mechanized embroidery that has led to today's electrically driven and digitally influenced industrial techniques.

Above, left
In 1771 Richard Arkwright established Cromford Mill where machinery and production methods for water-powered cotton spinning were pioneered. *Cromford Mill by Moonlight*, painted by Joseph Wright in 1783, captures the atmosphere of the 'dark satanic mills' of the Industrial Revolution.

Above, right
An example of power-loom weaving from the 1820s.

Opposite page
Le ballon de Gonesse, a toile de Jouy of 1784, illustrates the flight of the aerostatic machine built by the Robert brothers in 1783. The manned balloon flew from the Tuileries in Paris to the nearby village of Gonesse, where it came down and was destroyed by angry locals.

Left
Nylon parachute, c.1955. Nylon is far superior in strength and durability to silk, the original material used for parachutes.

Opposite
This design by William Morris (1834–96) is indicative of the quality he brought to textile design at the end of the 19th century. He believed in craftsmanship rather than mass production, and drew inspiration from Persian, Turkish and Italian Renaissance textiles in London's Victoria & Albert Museum.

Similar innovations were taking place in printed textiles, and particularly in their design. The name Oberkampf is synonymous with the finest **copperplate** and **roller-printing** techniques, which resulted in the printed textiles known as **toile de Jouy** in England – a reference to the Oberkampf factory's location near Paris. The fine drawings and high-quality engravings of Jean Huet, the chief designer, set new standards of creativity in printed textile design. The themes he portrayed included classical mythology as well as ancient and modern history, and popular patterns of the time commemorated important events.

The Industrial Revolution made the mass production of textiles possible. In the case of printed fabrics, thousands of metres of low-cost designs could be produced in the time it would take to make one length of hand-printed cloth. In England, this high-volume printing tended to compromise the standard of the designs, with the few quality-conscious printed textile factories following trends in France. William Morris took up the challenge to remedy the situation by producing fabrics inspired by naturalism and the patterns in the Persian, Turkish and Italian Renaissance textiles in the Victoria & Albert Museum. However, his most significant contribution was his ideas and theories, which influenced the thinking behind the Arts and Crafts movements in Britain and the United States.

Innovations in textile manufacturing continued to revolutionize the industry during the twentieth century. A significant example is the invention of **nylon**. The result of earlier breakthroughs in fibre technology, such as rayon, it was developed during the 1930s and in 1938 its manufacturer, du Pont, publicized it as the miracle fibre, stronger than steel and as fine as a spider's web. This first man-made textile was engineered from coal, water and air, and was initially developed for the hosiery market because of its strength and stretch characteristics. However, with the outbreak of the Second World War its

versatility as a high-performance textile was recognized and nylon fabric was subsequently used for products such as parachutes. In 1959 du Pont developed another major synthetic fibre: **spandex**, also called **elastane**, is known for its elasticity and strength. It revolutionized many areas of the clothing industry and is significant in garment manufacturing today, where spandex, often blended with nylon, is used in swimwear and for high-performance sportswear.

Synthetic **dyes** include **acid**, **Procion™**, **disperse**, and **azo** or **direct dye** types. They have a longer history than synthetic fabrics and have been equally revolutionary in transforming textiles and their design. In 1856 the British chemist William Perkin discovered the first commercially viable synthetic dye – mauve – a development that marked a decline in the use of natural dyes. The azo dyes were invented in 1884 and became the first synthetic ones that would adhere to cotton without a fixing agent – the reason why they are known as direct dyes. The advantages of synthetic over natural dyes, which still apply despite the resurgence of natural types, are that they are cheap to produce, yield brighter colours and are more colourfast and easier to apply to fabrics. The downside was that when they were first used, at a time when there was little regard for the health of dye workers, they were toxic and carcinogenic. Today, improvements have been implemented through government legislation.

Technological innovation persisted in the late twentieth and early twenty-first century with advances in digital design and manufacturing. One example is the integration of the digital in jacquard weaving, which has enabled photographic quality imagery to be woven. All-out experimentation and fine craftsmanship are essential elements in the methods used by the Dutch textile

Above, left
These striking 1960s-inspired swimsuits with oversized silver buttons are a mix of polyamide with elastane. Agent Provocateur, Janine collection (2009).

Above, right
Innovative fashion designer Karl Lagerfeld fused an acute sense of textiles with form and aesthetic to achieve dramatic and functional beachwear inspired by the 1970s rock 'n' roll era in his Cruise collection for Chanel, 2009. The first preview took place by the curvilinear swimming pool side at the Raleigh Hotel in South Beach, Miami.

Opposite page, left
DollFace2 (2007/08) is an example of how Lia Cook draws on the technology of digital jacquard weaving to create powerful contemporary art pieces.

designer Eugene van Veldhoven, who fluctuates between ultra-modern and traditional printing and coating techniques for both interior and fashion fabrics. He applies patterns to cloth using a range of techniques from inkjet printing to machine embroidery. The ideal outcome is an ensemble of pattern, technique and cloth, which he puts into a portfolio and takes to trade fairs and individual clients such as Jakob Schlaepfer and Schoeller in Switzerland or Maharam, Macy's and Calvin Klein in the United States.

Digital inkjet printing has not only revolutionized the scope of textile design; it is also extremely efficient in controlling the management of dye-use in printing and reducing dye wastage during manufacturing.

Top
Innovative textile designer Eugene van Veldhoven stands alongside one of his textiles – a black-and-white striped fabric that features patches of dangling strips – during production, 2007.

Above
While digital inkjet printing was a significant breakthrough in textile design, this technology is also linked to a positive environmental factor: a reduction in dye wastage during printing. Matthew Williamson, 2009 winter collection, ready-to-wear.

Twentieth- and twenty-first-century textile design

In the twentieth century, conceptual and aesthetic shifts in the visual arts alongside technological innovations in textile manufacturing extended the creative boundaries of textile design. The Art Nouveau and Art Deco movements, as well as Modernist and Post-Modernist art groups, inspired new aesthetics in textile design. In this very creative period designers and design studios developed philosophies that melded the traditional craft of textile design with the demands of a commercial world, functioning in an era of huge and rapid technological change.

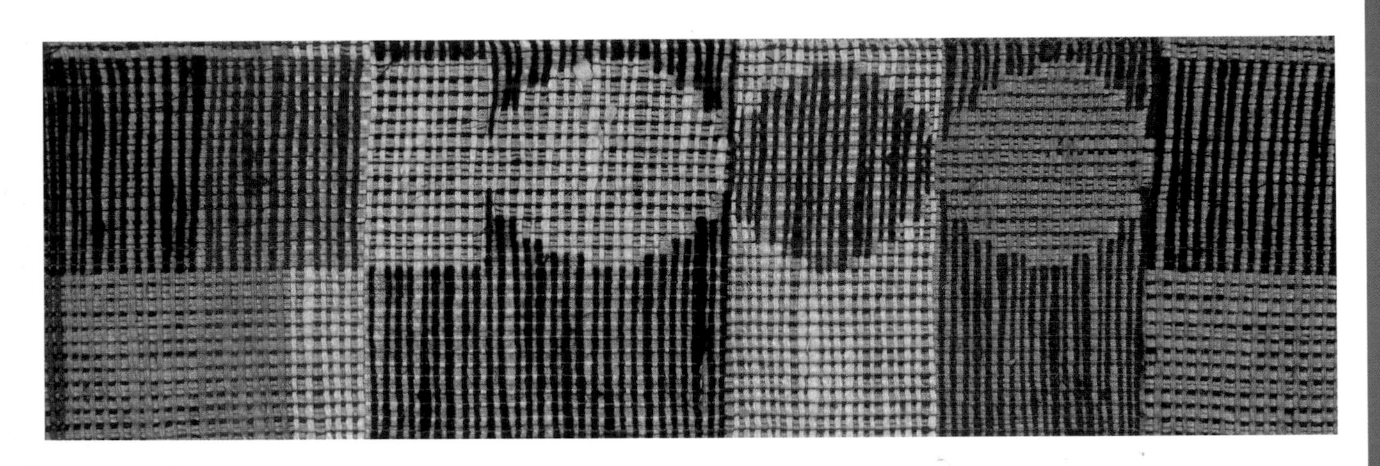

The Bauhaus was a unique twentieth-century phenomenon committed to educating a new type of designer for industry, and remains an influential model today. Its underpinning philosophy was to improve society through the integration of art and design. The weavers Gunta Stolzl and Anni Albers were key figures and exceptional designers and educators. Stolzl maintained a balance between hand weaving and craft as sources of individual expression and experimentation with new materials. Albers was both a hand weaver and an industrial designer, who believed in industrial production supported by craft-based design. She was the first weaver to be given a solo exhibition at the Museum of Modern Art in New York in 1949. When the Bauhaus was closed by the Nazi regime in 1933 Anni Albers and her husband Josef Albers, the painter and colourist, were invited to teach at Black Mountain College in the United States where the Bauhaus ideals were maintained.

Above
A sample of a design for weave by Gunta Stolzl (1897–1983).

Opposite
A hand-painted design for weave by Anni Albers (1899–1994).

1.

Above
The fabric for this coat was designed by Sonia Delaunay (1885–1979). With her husband Robert Delaunay (1885–1941) and others she founded Orphism, an art movement that was characterized by a strong use of colour and geometric shape. Sonia Delaunay's work embraced painting, textile design and stage sets, and her work has been a recurring source of inspiration for textile designers.

Right
Raoul Dufy (1887–1963) was a Fauvist painter whose progressive outlook on design provided genuine direction for textile designers in the early 20th century, particularly through his collaborative projects with the innovative fashion designer Paul Poiret.

Art and textile design

In the early part of the twentieth century a number of fine artists, in particular Sonia Delaunay and Raoul Dufy, made major creative contributions to textile design and this has continued into the twenty-first century as artists perpetuate the relationship between fine art and textile media with refreshing results.

During the 1960s the boundaries between art and design were questioned by Pop artists Andy Warhol and Roy Lichtenstein, who used designed media in their artworks, and the Hungarian-French painter Victor Vasarely developed Op Art from the Constructivist designs of the Bauhaus. In this climate of change the designer Verner Panton collaborated with Mira-X, which set out to be identified as an exclusive international textile design studio, and was originally part of the Swiss furnishing company Möbel Pfister. Panton was an important innovator for Mira-X because he thought of design in broad terms. He was its chief designer, responsible for both its fabrics and the creation of space with the aid of textiles. Mira-X image became largely synonymous with that of Panton himself. Mira-X Set, the company's first textile design collection in 1971, was based on a radical and very methodical concept.

Collection Diamond, produced in 1984, was Panton's last important contribution to Mira-X. It was based on a single module recurring in numerous forms, in this instance the triangle. Surfaces of a triangular grid were filled with colour, and a process of translation, rotation and reflection gave rise to structures that varied from strict rows and small or large hexagons to completely free forms. By exploring all avenues within this project of a lifetime, Panton pursued a strategy that traditionally belongs almost exclusively to the fine arts. His designs were based on the system and rigour characteristic of an extremely clear method, which he applied innovatively without falling prey to fleeting fashions. Panton was an 'ideologist'. His method of constantly working on one theme and extending a single system is a radical technique rare in the field of textile design and is probably what makes his work so unique. His method could stand as a classic model of design.

Experimental and innovative creative ideas remain central to the ethos of good textile design, which is inspired by both classic themes and influences engendered by modern society. Urban art is motivated primarily by the artist Jean-Michel Basquiat, graffiti artists and, more recently, stencil artists like Banksy and Blek le Rat have influenced contemporary design.

The artist Desiree Palmen brings a distinctly individual interpretation to urban art through her inventive adoption of camouflage in her Streetwise

Below
Furnishing fabrics from Decor 1, the first Mira-X Set collection, by designer Verner Panton (1971).

Bottom, right
Rubin furnishing fabric for Collection Diamond (1984) in the Mira-X Set collection series by Verner Panton.

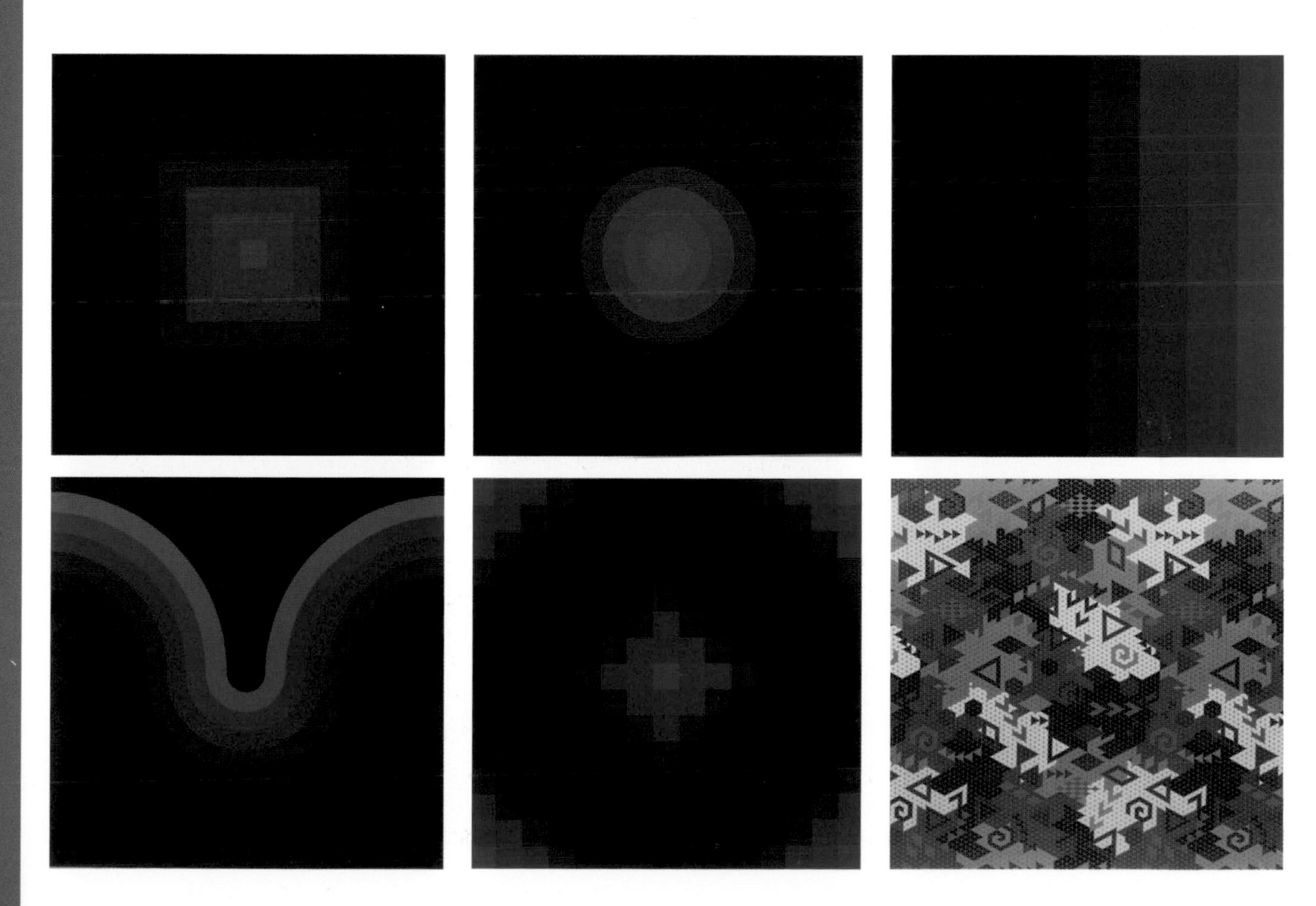

Tram, from the Streetwise series by Desiree Palmen (2002), explores the conceptual realm of urban camouflage patterns. Acrylic on cotton.

series, which explores human mimicry in urban environments and uses garments painted to resemble their background. The series was influenced by the installation of police surveillance cameras in so-called dangerous areas of Rotterdam: Palmen's concern about surveillance and the escalating use of identity-based electronic information systems triggered the idea of wearing camouflage in public spaces. In her painted clothes Palmen explores the potential for the wearers to dissolve or even disappear into their surroundings. Urban art such as Palmen's reflects individuality – a characteristic of niche textile markets, such as skatewear, where being different and associated with alternative design aesthetics is paramount.

Tradition and innovation

The fine arts have provided major influences in the development of textile design, but it is when traditional crafts receive the same status and appreciation that some truly innovative ideas emerge. At the NUNO Corporation in Tokyo, a pioneering company in the field of techno-fabrics formed by the Japanese designers Junichi Arai and Reiko Sudo in 1984, the design philosophy stresses the importance of the relationship between

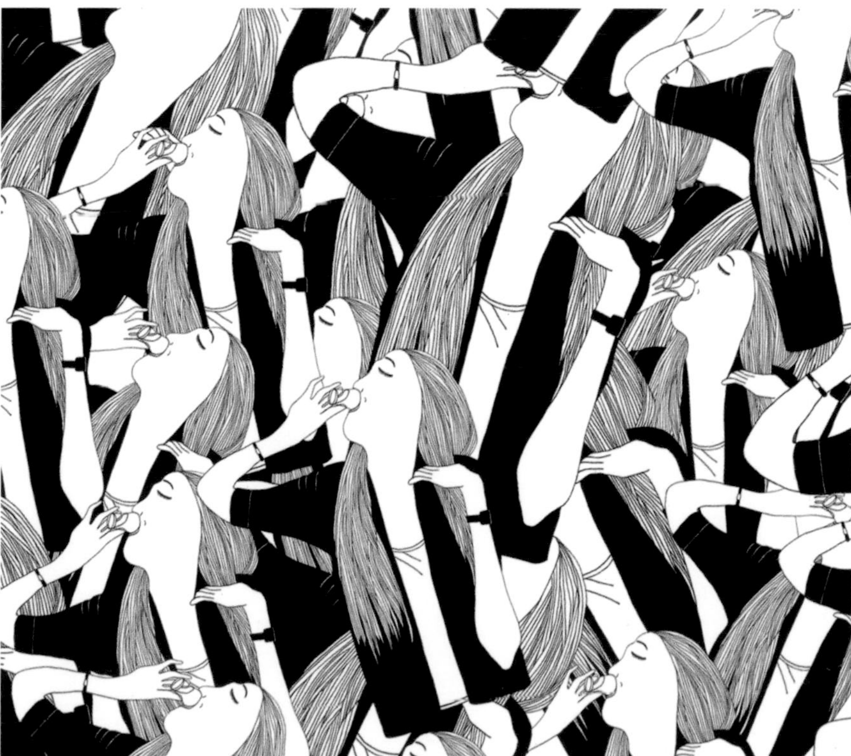

Above
The printed textile designs from the Fancy Dress Optional collection by Kay Stanley (2008) are here used on garments worn in a nightclub setting – the original source of inspiration and the intended market for the designs.

Left, top
Fancy Dress Optional 1, a printed textile design by Kay Stanley (2008), draws inspiration from first-hand experiences of street and youth culture to create a bizarre festival atmosphere. In this kaleidoscopic design many of the characters wear striking animal masks which hint at the personalities behind them.

Left, bottom
Fancy Dress Optional 2, a black-and-white printed textile design by Kay Stanley (2008), captures the energy and vitality of club culture in the single repeated motif of a girl in a little black dress knocking back her drink.

craft and new technology. Reiko Sudo, the present director and head designer, has maintained this vision and the company is respected worldwide for its innovative fabrics. This reputation is a result of the aesthetic sensibilities employed in the development of NUNO's fabrics, which incorporate a very inventive approach towards textile materials.

Metallic yarns are traditionally used in Japanese textiles: for example, washi (slit gold-leaf yarns) have been used in *nishi-jin* weaving to produce the obi sash worn around a kimono. *Nishi-jin* weaving is a style of weaving which dates back over 1200 years when it was developed to meet the demands of the imperial court in Kyoto. The main characteristic of this process is the use of coloured, gold and satin yarns. A new interpretation of this process by NUNO, spattering stainless steel on the surface of a **polyester** fabric to establish a metallic coating, is an innovative response to this traditional practice.

Like the founders of NUNO, Alexander Girard, who led the textile division of famous furniture manufacturer Herman Miller between 1952 and 1973, looked to the past for inspiration. But in his case it was to the traditions of the folk art he collected from Mexico, which he used to infuse colour, whimsy and humour into modern design. Girard was an intelligent designer who believed in good design. He recognized that this lay in a designer's self-belief and that he or she should design what they believed to be right. At Herman Miller

Above, left
Stainless-steel gloss design from the 1989 Spattering series by NUNO. The designers borrowed secret spray-plating techniques from the automotive industry for the innovative textiles in this series.

Above, right
Patchwork textile designed by Yuka Taniguchi and produced by NUNO for the 2004 Tsunagi Patchwork series. It is made by patching together chips from different NUNO fabrics.

Below, left and centre
Alexander Girard's (1904–93) Jacob's Coat, a woven striped fabric upholstery, was used on Charles and Ray Eames' folding chair, Sofa Compact (473), for Herman Miller.

Below, right
Girard drew inspiration for his designs from Mexican folk art. In this photograph Girard is surrounded by an array of folk art. Like many artists and designers he was an avid collector.

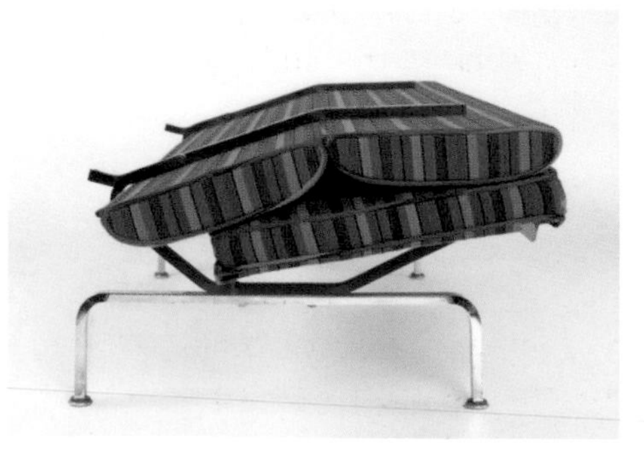

Small Hours, a printed textile design by the British designer Lucienne Day (1917–2010) for Heal's (1952).

Girard brought colour and light to the furniture designs of George Nelson and Charles and Ray Eames. He saw himself as a reasonable and sane Functionalist tempered by irrational frivolity, and provided textiles that worked with moulded plastic and metal, and the new furniture styles of the mid-twentieth century. His ethos was that interior décor should be accessible, affordable and functional.

Heal's furniture store had a similar design philosophy to that of Girard, while maintaining a solid craft philosophy, and found a star designer in Lucienne Day. She and her husband Robin emerged from the post-war Festival of Britain era and were brought together by a passion for modern design: their first collaboration was when Robin helped Lucienne to set up her exhibition at the Royal College of Art in 1940. His advice on presenting furnishing fabrics on furniture to show how they might be used resulted in an armchair produced to his design by Heal's and upholstered with her block-printed fabric, Bushmen. The store was astute in commissioning new work from Lucienne Day on an annual basis and promoted her as a star designer by printing her signature on the selvedge of their fabrics.

The bold designs created by the Italian designer Emilio Pucci, a key European figure in fashion and textile design who was known as 'the prince

Far left
A classic Pucci textile design (2009).

Left
The Florentine design house Pucci collaborated with marine designers Wally Yachts to create a distinctive aesthetic for the Wally 60 yacht (2009). The design for the sail captures the essence of the Pucci style, which also features in textiles in the cabin areas.

of prints' by the international fashion press, were inspired not so much by tradition as by the natural landscapes of the Mediterranean and exotic cultures. He set up his company and studio in the family palace in the heart of Florence in the late 1940s, and began developing his signature prints of brightly coloured kaleidoscopic abstract designs in the 1950s. Pucci had a straightforward design philosophy: he believed all designers should offer products of great creativity and artistic inspiration, and that these should bring joy into peoples' lives. The Pucci label still maintains a distinct design identity under the direction of Laudomia Pucci, the daughter of Emilio Pucci. Although Pucci is renowned historically for its bold fashion prints, the company was involved in other types of design, and this remains the case with projects that include furniture and a 90-metre (300-foot) hand-painted sail for the marine design company Wally Yachts.

Rather than tradition, innovation is a constant thread in the philosophy of many textile design companies and studios. In 1953 Vuokko Nurmesniemi joined Marimekko, established in Finland in 1951, to design clothing and printed fabrics for garments and interior decoration. She devised the company's design philosophy of setting rather than following trends, which remains a core belief enshrined in its philosophy – a belief that is firmly embedded in many university textile design departments.

Nurmesniemi followed in the footsteps of Maija Isola, the visionary head designer of Marimekko's interior fabrics until 1987. Isola helped to establish the company's international reputation with brightly coloured printed fabrics and simple design styles, and in 1963 created the iconic textile design Melooni.

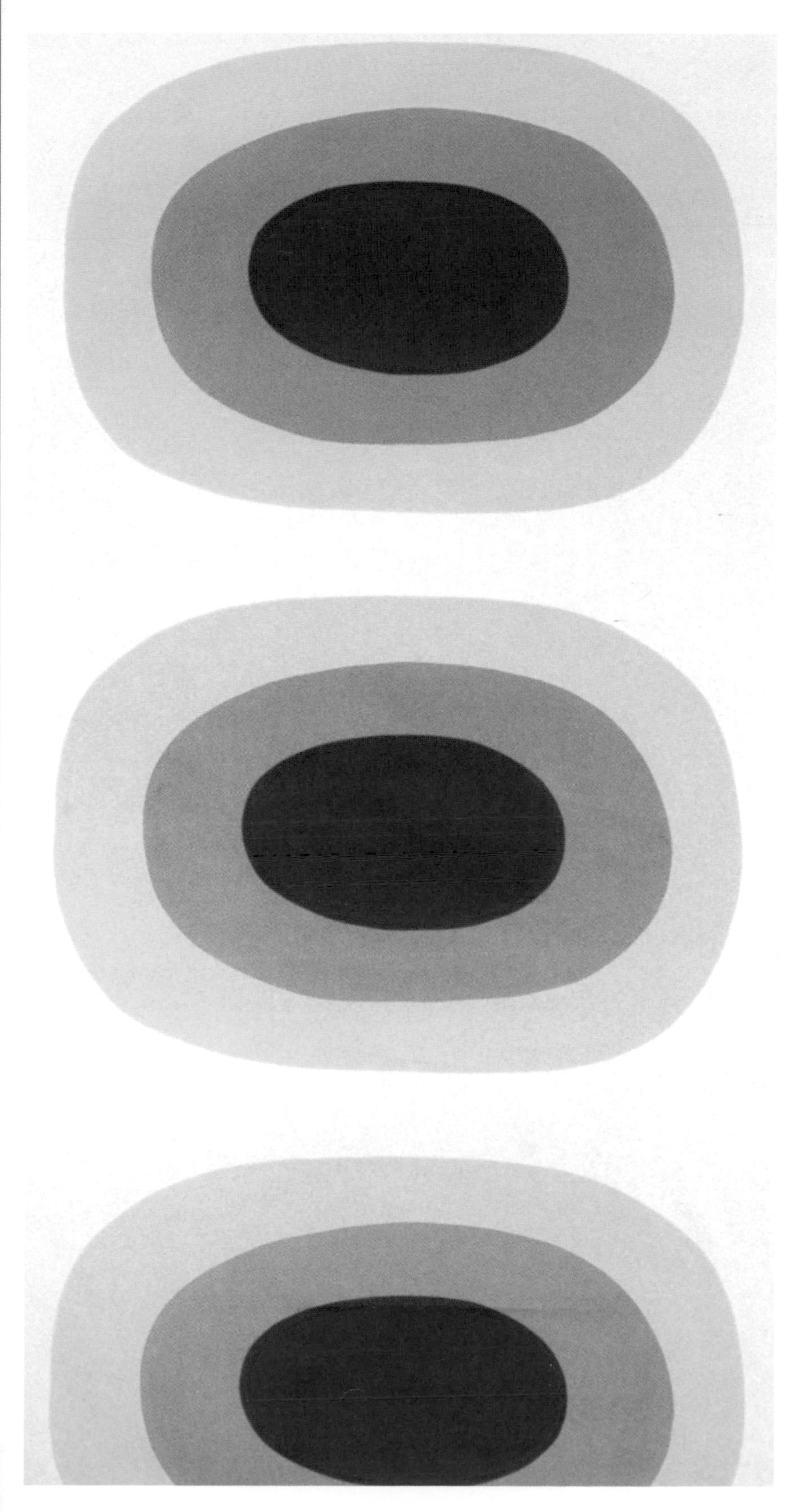

Above
In this contemporary printed textile collection by Marimekko the designs continue to provide a progressive edge while reflecting the essence of the company's earlier classics.

Left
Melooni was designed by the Finnish printed textile designer Maija Isola (1927–2001) in 1963, and has become a classic. Isola created her first designs in 1949 for Printex Oy, Marimekko's predecessor, and was subsequently head designer of Marimekko's interior fabrics until 1987.

Environmental concerns

How a textile is manufactured and how the products that are used to make it have an impact on the environment, and are consequently key considerations for textile designers. This applies especially to many industrial dye processes where fabrics are basically dipped in a vat and then washed. The result is dye-contaminated water that has to be treated before it is returned to its source, which is often a river. The treatment consists of separating the water from the dye to create a dye sludge and cleaner water, which is returned to the source – leaving the problem of what to do with the sludge.

On one occasion in China, a river downstream from a factory that manufactured dyed textiles ran deep red and investigators later discovered that untreated dye effluent was being dumped into it – even though the discharge levels of dye waste were regulated by law. This disregard for environmental legislation is not unique to China, and is often caused when international textile markets demand low-cost fabrics and trigger manufacturers to look for opportunities to save money.

Another environmental disaster created by textiles occurred in Central Asia when the two main feeder rivers for the Aral, the world's fourth largest inland sea, were redirected to irrigate cotton fields and the fishing fleet was marooned in a landscape of sand.

The response to environmental and ethical problems like these has been a steady and growing move towards ecological and sustainable textile design, which is increasingly motivated by consumers wanting to see evidence on textile products that the materials used in their production are appropriately sourced and that manufacturing methods use minimal energy. Textile design students frequently request environmental and sustainable issues as design and research topics, indicating an awareness of their importance and a desire by the next generation of designers to instigate change.

The plight of the Aral Sea in Kazakhstan was brought to the attention of the world in Al Gore's film *An Inconvenient Truth*. Fishing boats are marooned because the Soviet Union has redirected the rivers that feed it in order to grow cotton.

The balance between ecology and economics is a key issue, with legislation in many developing countries undermining the potential to produce **eco-textiles**. The textile designer is without doubt aware that a product is designed for a specific purpose, but the **eco-textile designer** also has to be aware of how the product will be manufactured, used and eventually disposed of. Perhaps the most logical step towards a safer future is for designers to redesign the way they design. If this were done on a global scale, it would transform industries, societies and cultures. Eco-design is effectively a fresh start, a way to do things differently – and education is paramount.

Above, left and right
Throughout her career, textile designer Vibeke Riisberg has explored a range of ideals, aesthetics and production processes with highly creative results. Her interest in sustainable textiles, used in the clothes shown here, is not necessarily visually apparent. But factored into her designs from the outset are considerations of function, user needs, durability, environmental impact and the use of resources.

Below
The Wheel, a design by Ollie Wolf for Howies®, spring 2009. Howies® has an ethical philosophy that is reflected in the concepts and processes used in the design and production of its casual clothing.

Textile design by Jack Lenor Larsen (b. 1927) for his African collection, 1963, referencing West African Adinkra and Adire cloth.

Summary

Using historical and cultural themes in textile design requires a range of creative approaches: drawing and photographing sources of inspiration, writing notes on production techniques and collecting textile samples are examples. Throughout his career, the American textile designer Jack Lenor Larsen has been inspired by research trips to other cultures. His approach has been to work closely with traditional designers and craftsmen in order to understand and reinterpret the aesthetic and technical elements in their textiles. And he is far from alone in drawing on other cultures for inspiration.

2.

Printed textile design

Printed textile design has produced a wealth of styles and imagery in the more than 2000 years since patterns were first applied to cloth, and today it is a highly creative and ever evolving area of **textile finishing**. The main catalyst in this is the designer, who creates innovatory design styles, motifs and patterns inspired by conceptual and visual open-mindedness, along with a receptive attitude towards new technologies: developments in digital textile design and digital inkjet printing have stimulated growth in the field of printed textiles, providing new opportunities for design as well as flexible production methods.

Many printed textiles are currently mass produced in Asia or the Far East, where labour costs are low, using **rotary** or **flatbed screen-printing** methods. However, some Western textile printers remain competitive; examples are niche design and **hand screen-printing** companies like Eley Kishimoto and Timorous Beasties, whose success is due to the individuality of their designs.

This chapter looks at key developments in printed textile design and production, and describes the processes used in screen and digital inkjet printing. Motifs, patterns and styles, from the figurative to the abstract, illustrate the breadth of printed textile imagery, and scientific, environmental and eco-design issues are considered in relation to printed textile design.

Above
Bunny Dance shirt dress from the Bonnie Bunny collection by Eley Kishimoto, 2008 autumn/winter collection. This printed rabbit pattern suggests there are few boundaries when it comes to the motifs that can be used in fashion textiles.

Opposite
Iguana, a digital print realized in 2004, captures one aspect of the striking graphic style of Timorous Beasties, established by Alistair McAuley and Paul Simmons in Glasgow in 1990. The company – named after Robert Burns' poem 'To a mouse' – designs printed textiles for furnishings, and is well known for its blending of traditional textile design styles with surreal and contemporary imagery.

Historical background

It is probable that the earliest method used to produce printed textiles was **block printing**, a process that involves using a fine chisel to cut out a motif or image on a wooden block. Ink is applied to the block, which is pressed on to a length of cloth to make a printed impression, and the process is repeated to create an overall pattern. Block printing was practised in ancient Egypt before 1000 BC, with evidence to support this provided by way of printed remnants found in tombs. Resist printed Coptic textiles from the fifth and sixth centuries AD have also been found in Egypt. India and China have an equally rich early history in printing. In Europe printed woollen textiles, with designs depicting warriors and goddesses, have been found in Greek graves in the Crimea dating back to the fourth century BC. In the Lower Rhine region in Germany samples of printing on linen and silk from the twelfth century show another creative response to printing which reflected Byzantine and Middle Eastern influences. In the South American country of Peru printing was also an established method of decorating textiles before the Spanish conquest of the sixteenth century.

In the seventeenth century, as trade with Asia increased, traditional hand-painted and block-printed Indian calico prints were imported into Europe. Their patterns contained a variety of brightly coloured flowers, fruits and small animals, and the prints reflected an accumulated knowledge that spanned two millennia of textile dyeing and printing. This refreshingly new design aesthetic and production expertise could not be matched by European textile producers, who were predominantly weaving heavy silks, woollens and rough linens, and the popularity of the Indian prints undermined textile production in

France and England. In France this led to a ban on their import in 1686 and in England an Act of Parliament in 1720 banned the wearing and domestic use of imported **Chintz**. By 1759, however, the ban was lifted after European mills perfected the manufacture of copies, known as 'Indiennes'. At first these were block-printed but in the mid-eighteenth century, with the introduction of new manufacturing technologies at the start of the Industrial Revolution, block printing was replaced with mechanized roller printing. This development marked the mass production of printed textiles. Modifications in the design of Indiennes to meet the requirements of European customers coincided with mechanization. Although the original calico prints were produced for the seventeenth-century fashion market, Indiennes are today recognized as interior design classics and are manufactured in both Europe and India.

After the late nineteenth century block-printed textiles became a niche market; producing them was labour-intensive and they were unable to compete with their industrially manufactured counterparts. However, Liberty Fabric in London produced small quantities of expensive block-printed silks and wools until the 1960s.

Above, left
The decorative Indiennes printed in England at the outset of the Industrial Revolution undermined and mimicked the traditional Indian calico print.

Above, centre
This block-printed paisley design on cotton by Liberty Fabric shows the quality and detail that could be achieved using this traditional printing process.

Above, top right
Indian wood blocks: the paisley and other Indian motifs are stained with blue dye.

Above, bottom right
The traditional process of hand block-printing.

Screen-printed textile designs

The invention of flatbed **screen-printing** in Lyon, France, in the 1930s transformed textile printing. A fine silk-gauze mesh was stretched around a frame and **lacquer** was applied to it to create a **stencil** – the unlacquered areas formed the motifs or pattern to be printed. The frame was placed on the fabric, and a specially designed implement, a **squeegee**, was used by hand to force a dye paste through the mesh. The fabric would then be allowed to dry in between the printing of each different colour. Hand screen-printing still functions like this today, but the equipment is much improved. For example, lacquered stencils have been superseded by stencils created with light-receptive photosensitive film, discussed in more detail in a following section on design and production (see page 40).

Synthetic fibres, polyester in particular, made it possible to manufacture screen meshes that, unlike the early silk-gauze versions, maintained tension. Their high-tensile strength enabled the mesh to be stretched more tightly over the screen frame, which enhanced the accuracy and quality of the printing: the **screen**, and hence the stencil, no longer had a tendency to expand and contract when the fabric was washed and dried between colour applications. The introduction of metal screen frames further improved production as wooden frames tended to warp when exposed to regular washing and drying. These innovations contributed to effective multicoloured screen printing.

Flatbed screen-printing was mechanized in the 1950s, with the development of semi- and fully automatic production methods. And in 1962 rotary screen-printing, based on the same principles as the flatbed process, was launched. In brief, this uses a nickel cylinder which is microperforated to create the stencil, and which rotates continuously while it is in contact with the fabric, ensuring consistent printing. The dye paste is forced through the

Below, left
This unusual fish-eye photograph shows dye being applied to a screen in preparation for using a squeegee in the flatbed screen-printing process at the Marimekko factory. The design in production is the 1964 bold floral 'Unikko' by Maija Isola. Like Melooni, it has become a classic because of its continuing popularity.

Below, right
The flatbed screen-printing process.

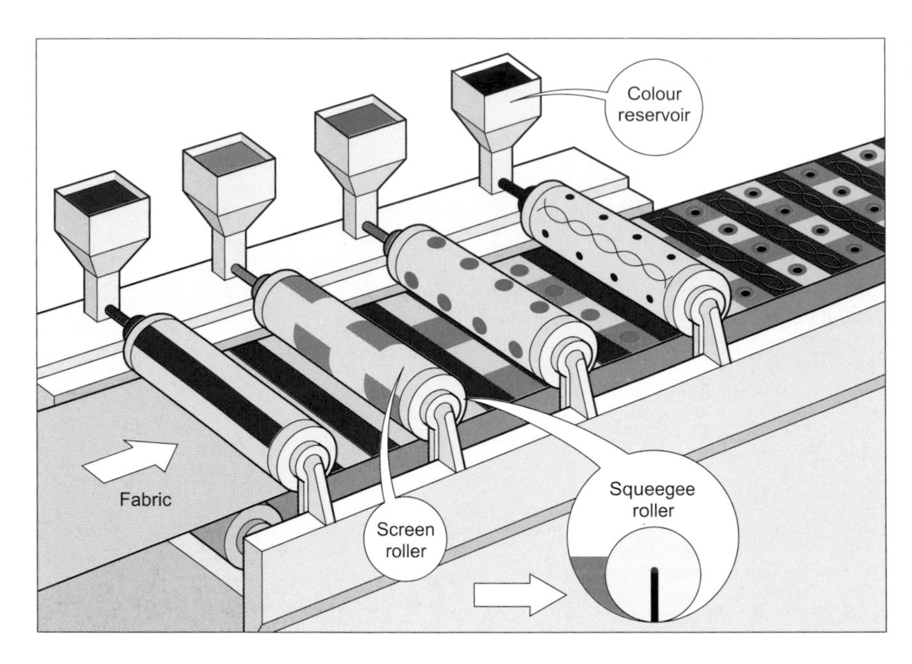

The rotary screen-printing method is extensively used in textile printing. The process involves the continuous rotation of a series of cylindrical screens that are each fed with ink from the side. Each cylinder contains a squeegee which, as it rotates over the fabric passing beneath, pushes the ink out through the stencilled design.

stencil with the aid of a stationary squeegee inside the cylinder. Twenty-four cylinders can be used to print a multicoloured design, with each one applying a different colour. Rotary screen-printing is constantly being refined and is widely used in the textile industry.

Design and production

When a design is chosen to go into production, the first of a number of steps is to decide on the type of fabric to use.

Fabric considerations

If a design has a coloured **ground** it is necessary to dye the cloth, the type of dye depending on the fabric. If it contains **cellulosic fibres**, such as cottons, **Procion™** dyes are good colour solutions. For **protein fibres**, such as silk and wool, **acid dyes** yield the best results. Synthetics like nylon require the use of **disperse dyes**. Fabric shrinkage is common during dyeing and must be factored into the process. In some printing methods the dyed ground is itself printed and its colour may well be the last one to be applied.

Fabric plays a key role in the aesthetic and functional outcome of a design and vice versa, and these elements need to be considered at the early stages of the design process to ensure that a textile is appropriate for its intended function and market as well as for the design. **Silk georgette**, a sheer luxury fabric, normally looks translucent when printed with dye pastes. This fine-quality fabric, and the subtle print design it creates, is traditionally well suited to the high end of the fashion industry. Heavy cotton twills, which can absorb more ink or dye than silk georgette because of their weave structure, produce a bold print design. They are hard-wearing and therefore suitable for use as furnishing fabrics. Innovative ideas and subtle shifts in thinking regarding the relationship of print design, printing processes and fabrics to their functional contexts is driven by designers who want to challenge and explore established traditions.

Design preparation

There is a series of pre-production stages before a design is printed. The finished **repeat** design must be accurately transferred to film, a process that involves **colour separation** and subsequently exposing the screens to ultraviolet light; it also incorporates their **registration**. Once the screens have been prepared for printing and the print table has been set up, the printing process can start. Finishing processes, and printing inks and dyes also play a key role in hand screen-printing.

Repeats

Traditionally, the repeat size of a motif or design varied depending on whether the fabric was intended for fashion (smaller repeats) or furnishings (larger repeats). While this no longer applies to all textile printing, due to innovative designers and breakthroughs in digital technology, the convention persists in many commercial fashion and furnishing markets.

Critical constraints on the size of the repeat motif continue in mechanized and hand screen-printing because of the manufacturing equipment and tools used. The major technical parameters within which the motif forms a repeat pattern are the width and length of the fabric and the size of the screen.

Below, left
A horizontal half-drop repeat pattern.

Below, right
A traditional printed textile design by Liberty Fabric, with cut-through and production notes on repeat size, fabric width and colours.

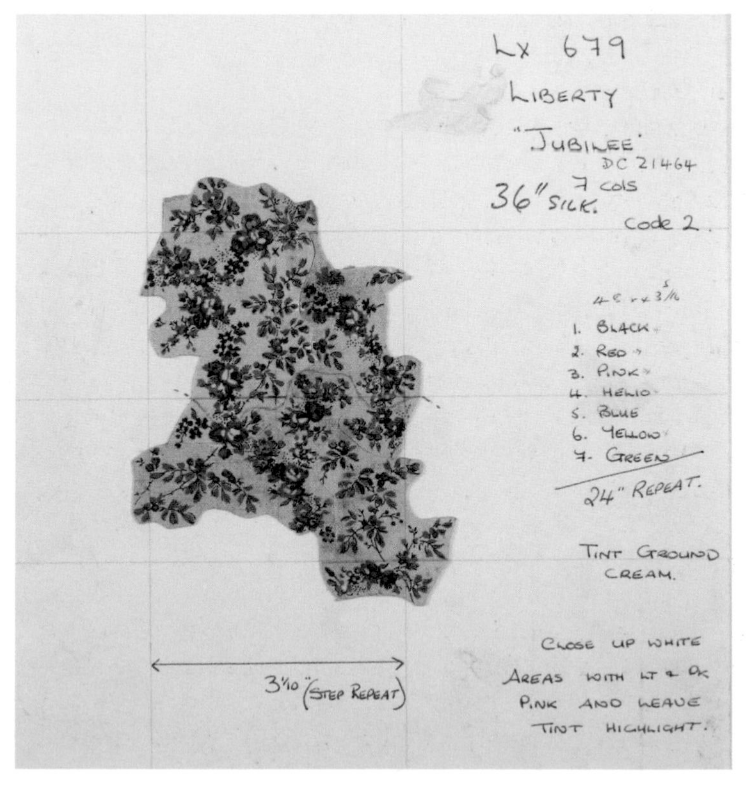

Although digital inkjet printing (see page 64) means designers are no longer constrained by screen-frame sizes when designing repeat patterns, they should still be aware of the parameters of screen sizes when designing, since many digital print samples will subsequently be mass produced using established industrial printing methods.

It is possible that the initial design, often called a **croquis**, may not be suitable for repeating, and to take it towards the stage of screen printing it has to be developed into an actual repeat. The key factor is to redesign its four edges to achieve harmony and rhythm between the repeated areas. Multiple repeats are combined when the design goes into production. The **half-drop repeat** is the one that is most frequently used and is discussed and illustrated, along with variations, in chapter 5. The **cut-through** – an organically drawn line that ideally goes through the **negative space** of the design where no design elements are to be printed, usually the ground colour of the cloth – ensures good design continuity from one repeat to the next. It can occur on the horizontal or vertical edge of the design, and often on both, depending on the size of the motif or image to be repeated. The purpose of the cut-through is to camouflage the repeat joins.

The finished design, in actual repeat with completed cut-through, then goes to the next pre-production stage: separating the colours and making a film of each one.

Opposite page
Sheona Quenby's digital printed textile design for interiors won awards in the 2006 Royal Society of Arts student design competition. Inspiration drawn from exotic imagery was combined with cityscapes. The half-drop repeat pattern is clearly evident. Quenby is now a studio designer at Liberty Fabric.

Colour separation

The colours in the design are separated either manually or digitally. If working manually the designer, or separation artist, will place the first film over the design and paint the first colour area in the design on to the film with an opaque medium. The same is done for all subsequent colours, except the areas where it is possible to achieve a colour in the design through **overprinting**. Here the same area is painted twice on two different films to enable the overprint to occur. In industry, this process is often automated with programmed wide-format scanners translating each colour on to a separate film, which is marked with registration crosses.

Below, left
A film is developed for each colour in a printed textile design – in this instance, for a kanga cloth.

Below, right
Aligning the finished films on a light box provides an overall impression of the design. Accuracy in translating the design elements on to film is crucial as they must be opaque, and the registration crosses on each film must align with the other films in the design. Each individual film is then exposed on to a screen in preparation for printing.

In the photomechanical method a separate screen for each colour is coated with photosensitive emulsion and put in a drying cabinet. When the screen is dry one of the films is attached to it and the registration marks are aligned with marks on the screen, which is then exposed to ultraviolet light. This hardens the areas of photosensitive emulsion that correspond to the non-opaque areas on the film to create a negative stencil from the positive film. The film is removed from the screen and the unhardened emulsion is washed away so that a positive stencil is formed on the screen. The process is repeated for each colour and the registration marks ensure that all the elements in the design will align.

The transfer of the image to the screen can be automated with no films required. In this instance, the stencil is sprayed on to the screen using a very fine wax medium.

Print table: hand screen-printing

Hand screen-printing a textile design on to cloth is done on a flatbed printing table. Although there can be variations, this is normally a solid table covered with a layer of felt over which a canvas-coated neoprene rubber sheet is stretched. The sheet is coated with a water-soluble adhesive – originally gum arabic, which is still widely used in print workshops in university textile departments – which is dried either by fan heaters placed on the table or an overhead heating system, depending on the scale of the printing facility. Once the adhesive is dry the fabric is applied to the coated table; in small-scale print textile workshops this is generally by ironing it down.

An alternative method used for lightweight fabrics and ones that stretch, such as silk and **Lycra**, involves the use of a **backing cloth**: an absorbent cotton fabric that is ironed on to the dried adhesive before the silk or Lycra, which is pinned at regular intervals along the edges of the table. The backing cloth reduces the smudging or loss of adhesion caused by the presence of excessive print paste after printing. It is crucial that both backing cloth and fabric are flat on the print table after they have been ironed down; any creases will affect the quality of the printed design.

Print table: repeat printing

As mentioned above, textiles can be applied to a print table in a number of ways depending on the fabric type and production methods. Once the fabric is attached to the table the screens must be carefully positioned. **Repeat crosses** at one or both sides of the screen are a key part of the procedure and are exposed on to it at the same time as the elements of the design. The area printed by the screen must fit exactly alongside the adjacent one; a slight overlap might be permissible and is better than a gap. An exact fit is not automatically achieved with hand screen-printing, whereas this is possible with rotary screen-printing. The accurate registration of the coloured areas within the design is equally important, though again, a slight overlap might be acceptable. To achieve accurate repeat registration and colour alignment of the design the usual practice is to attach to the screen frame a bracket on a guide rail that runs along the edge of the print table. The bracket rests against fittings known as **repeat stops**, which are spaced exactly one screen repeat apart along the whole length of the table. Two adjustable screws set the distance of the frame from the rail.

As a further aid, a repeat cross is often drawn on the **selvedge edge** of the fabric at the start of the printed area. All screens are aligned with this cross, and often with a corresponding one on the other edge of the fabric for the first full-colour repeat section. Brackets and screws are adjusted accordingly and the first repeat stop is fixed in place. Registration marks are often printed along the selvedge of the cloth, where colour swatches and the designer's or company's name also appear.

Hand screen-printing

The hand screen-printing process consists of forcing a viscous paste through the open areas of each of the screens using a flexible squeegee. The synthetic-rubber blade, which is set into a metal handle, is drawn steadily across the screen at a constant angle and pressure by hand. If a screen is too wide to allow one person to reach across it, two people may work together, one on either side of the table. They need to exert similar pressures or the printing will be uneven. While printing with a hand-held squeegee is common there are industrial variations to this method, including mechanical devices that operate the squeegee and improve output efficiency.

The order of printing often follows the sequence of lighter colours first to darker colours last. If the background colour – on what is called the **blotch screen** – is to be printed rather than dyed the relevant area is usually left until last as the larger amount of colour involved could cause loss of adhesion between the fabric and the table, and affect the registration. Movement of the fabric during printing must be prevented to maintain accurate registration of the pattern.

At the start of the printing process alternate repeats in the first colour are printed along the length of the table and the gaps are then filled in. This allows time for the print paste to penetrate the fabric and partially dry before the screen frame touches the printed area. If this is wet the screen can pick up dye and print a **ghost image** in the wrong area of the design. This problem can be avoided by looking under the screen after printing and using a cloth to remove any dye. If the design includes an outline this is printed first as an aid to accurate fitting. The screen is washed and put into a drying cabinet in preparation for reuse and another screen is selected to print the second colour.

A fine screen mesh is needed to reproduce intricate design details in order to reduce the risk of flooding, which occurs when too much **pigment** ink or dye paste goes into the fabric and affects the look of the design. A fine mesh can hold detail like that in a photographic motif, but it can have disadvantages. For instance, screens may block more easily if pigment inks and **binder**, which are thicker than dye pastes, are used. This problem can be alleviated by washing screens more frequently in between printing.

Field Day puff dress from the Village Fête collection by Eley Kishimoto, spring/summer 2008. The fabric used is hand screen printed.

Design at Liberty Fabric

Liberty Fabric in London is a relatively small wholesale company that has established an international reputation as a world leader in printed textile design and has a unique outlet for their printed textile designs, the Liberty department store. Liberty Fabric design specifically for the fashion market, including fashion houses, top-end designers and high-street labels. The designs are also applied in other product contexts. The company consists of four main groups: design, archive, production and sales, each of which works with the others to provide invaluable input when a new collection is developed. For the design team the advantages are clear: they are able to see every stage of a design's development from concept to final point of sale. And whenever necessary they can access the Liberty archive to view all the design work.

In the textile design studio the designers thrive on a philosophy that emphasizes innovative detailed design on beautiful fabric bases. Intrinsic to this philosophy is individuality and an intelligent use of colour. The independently thinking design team is not heavily influenced by fashions and trends, which enables them to be driven by their passion to create original contemporary design work. Research and inspiration is drawn from an eclectic range of resources, which are often inspired by the lifestyles and interests of the individual designers, such as art galleries and exhibitions, music and film, markets and ornaments, stories and people, photographs, memories, life experiences – everything and anything.

Each season's collections consist of a number of designs on different base cloths. The main fashion range is printed on the classic Tana lawn, a versatile textile that performs well on shirting, dresses and children's wear. It is a fine fabric that is great to wear, and is also excellent for printing as it can accommodate very fine lines and vibrant colours. Poplin, Kingly cord, Middlesen jersey, Lantana and an exceptional range of silks usually feature each season. The silk range is printed across three to four different base fabrics depending on whether they are intended for the spring/summer or autumn/winter collections. The fabrics are exclusively inspired by Liberty's extensive archive, but push the boundaries of textile design with their tasteful, bold and engaging designs. As in many design studios, the fabric ranges are developed two years in advance of the actual season.

Liberty Fabric is seen as a trend leader in the fashion and textile industry and this is reflected in

In Liberty Fabric's silk for the 2009 autumn/ winter collection, an inventive array of styles, motifs and patterns are intelligently connected by an interrelated colour palette.

the fact that they actively participate with Peclers Paris, an influential trends agency that specializes in colour forecasting for the textile industry.

The concept for a design collection is devised by the head designer and introduced into the development of the collection in the form of **design stories**. Each collection contains around 40 designs which are split into four or five different groups – the design stories – each of which has a common source of inspiration that derives from the main concept. This means that even though several different designers work on a collection, each with their own style and design manner, the prints are linked by a common theme and feel. The in-house design team works closely with the archivist, who is a significant source of inspiration and knowledge. Some of their work is based on archival paintings and prints that have never previously been used, which gives the contemporary designs a quintessentially historical flavour.

The early stages of creating a new print are filled with production and printing decisions: how fine a line can be, what colour will sit next to another one, how colours are balanced in a design and how many should be used. Because Liberty's fabrics appeal to a wide range of customers in the fashion industry it's necessary to consider the type of company that would be interested in a specific type of design, the scale and size of its repeat, and its imagery and character.

Every print design emerges from research and sketchbook work, and drawing and painting are consequently fundamental to the process. The designers actively set out to see how far they can push textile design, and use different media and visual sources to create inspiring prints, as well as new methods such as **monoprinting**, collage and photography, and abstract forms of mark-making. Once the designs for all the base fabrics have been identified colour is applied to them using **colour boards** inspired by the initial concept. There are generally the same number of colour boards as there are design stories. For instance, for the 2009 spring/summer collection there were five design stories based on people and the places with which they are associated. The places inspired the colours, so the 'surfer' design story, for example, had a 'beach' colour board, and the 'city workers' a 'city' one. A limited number of colours is used for each story, resulting in designs that are considered and intelligent. The team goes through all the designs to establish which **colourways** work best before they are sent to the printers for sampling.

A period of colour management, sampling and quality checks ensures that the final printed fabrics are of the highest standard. Although the final stages of the design process are in a digital format – a requirement of the printers involved in screen preparation and for the colour processes – flatbed or roller printing is used for all the fabrics.

For the 2009 autumn/winter collection Liberty Fabric worked closely with leading contemporary artists to produce unique designs. Those by Grayson Perry, a huge fan of Liberty fabrics, reflect the recurring themes explored in his ceramic vases, while Paul Morrison created designs that capture his fascination with nature. He has a bold graphic style that he uses to reinvigorate landscape and botanical subjects, and sources from popular culture, fine art, film and science transform familiar images of nature into something uncanny and unnatural. He has skilfully introduced this way of working into his designs for Liberty Fabric.

Below
Grayson Perry's printed textile designs capture themes present in his fine-art works. His teddy bear 'Alan Measles' is a notable presence in one of them, driving a No. 1 classic racing car through a rural English landscape.

Overleaf
Paul Morrison has produced designs that reflect his interests in botany and the landscape. In one of them he creates an uncanny atmosphere by incorporating floral motifs made up of can-openers and other objects.

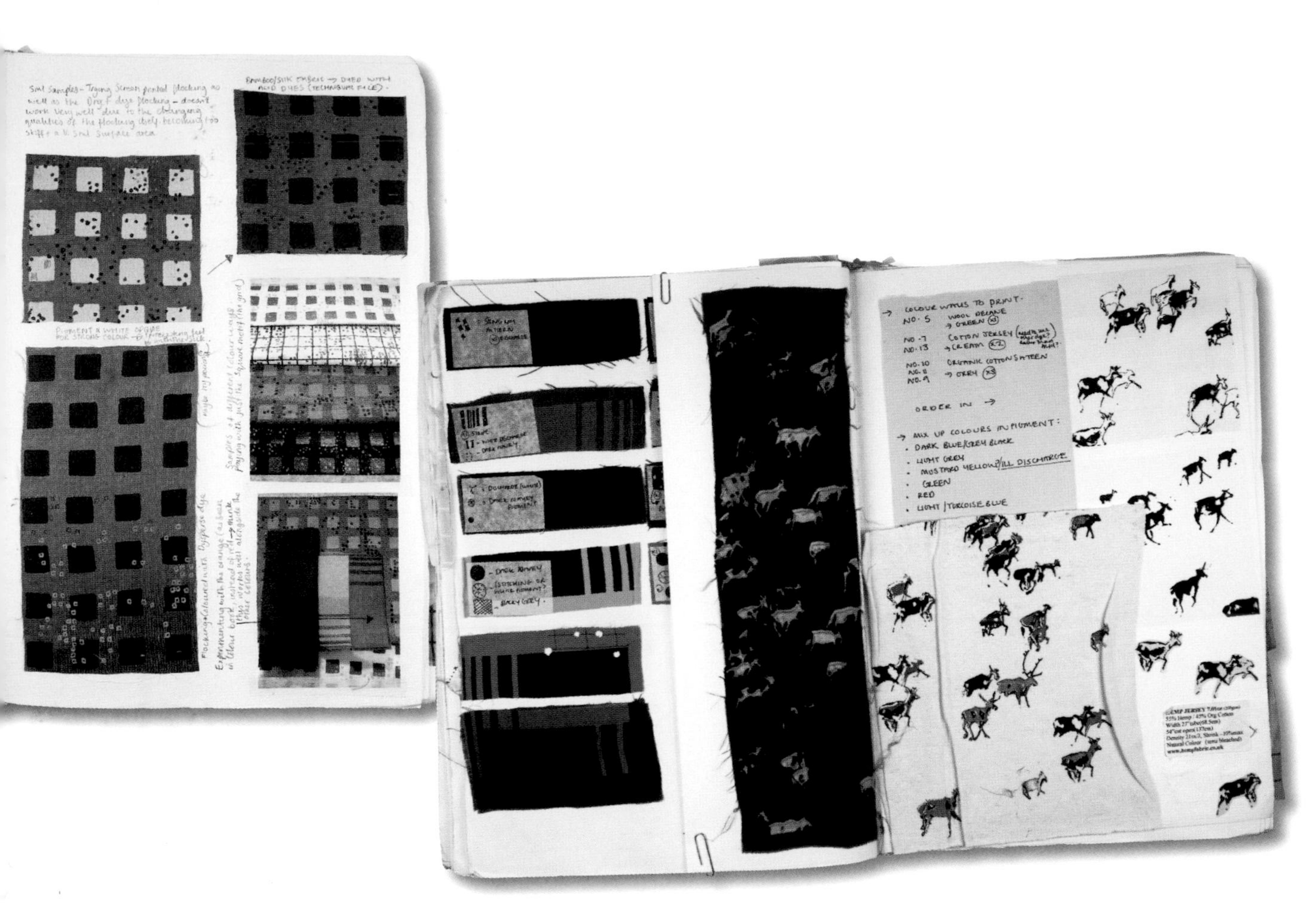

Inks and dyes

Pigment inks and dyes are the main types of printing media and provide a broad range of colour qualities. In the case of the former, a concentrated pigment ink is mixed with a binder **catalyst**, which enables the colour to be transferred on to the fabric. It is popular in the textile industry because of its comparative cheapness and ease of use. Dyes are used to colour cloth in dye vats and in printing. In printing they are mixed with a catalyst, a thickener paste that functions in a similar way to the binder. A baking oven and dry heat are used to fix pigment inks after printing. The pigment inks settle on the surface of the cloth, whereas dyes penetrate it. Dyes provide a better **fabric handle** than pigment inks, although pigment-ink printing has been improved through the introduction of fabric softening agents into the binder.

Both pigments and dyes can be **discharged**, a process that removes the coloured ground of the cloth during printing by bleaching, while simultaneously replacing it with another colour. It is particularly effective in achieving contrasting colours alongside each other or when printing light colours on a dark ground which would otherwise absorb them.

In addition to the basic ink colours there are pigments and binders that can produce effects such as a metallic or pearlescent appearance. **Flocking** and **foiling** processes, as well as glow-in-the-dark and ultraviolet-reactive inks

It is essential to test dyeing and printing processes before manufacturing samples or larger production runs, which involve the manufacturer as well as the designer. Polly Bell carries out extensive tests before producing her samples. She records the results in a print notebook like the 2009 one shown here, and this acts as a clear guide when she produces the final samples. Her notebook becomes a valuable resource that can be referenced in the future when necessary.

Trembath by Alec Walker (1889–1964), founder of the textile company Crysede. A distinctive characteristic of Crysede designs is that they were block-printed on silk using the discharge printing process. This particular design was developed from a painting by Walker, which depicts men working in the violet fields in Trembath in Cornwall, in about 1927.

Shadow on the Wall, Gaza by Norma Starszakowna (2007) exploits the experimental potential of print and dye techniques – a persistent characteristic of Starszakowna's textile pieces.

provide particular textural and aesthetic enhancements. Norma Starszakowna has experimented extensively with printed textile media to produce highly individual print works.

Devoré fabric is popular for both fashion and furnishing textiles. The name devoré, from the French *dévorer*, 'to devour', is a printing method used on mixed-fibre fabrics such as silk/**viscose** velvet. The devoré print paste burns out (cellulosic-) plant-based fibres such as viscose, cotton and linen, and leaves behind fibres like polyester and the (protein-) animal-based fibres silk and wool. With silk/viscose velvet the paste removes the viscose velvet **pile** and leaves the silk backing: the paste is printed on to the cloth which is put into a baking oven that produces controlled dry-heat temperatures. Burn-out occurs at a temperature of over 200˚C (400˚F). For health and safety reasons, because of the fumes the process creates, it is imperative to contain it within a controlled environment.

Expandex is another novelty print paste that becomes effective when it is heated after printing, often in a baking oven: the paste undergoes a chemical reaction to produce a relief surface on the cloth. Designer Nigel Atkinson and artist Grethe Wittrock have been extremely creative when printing with this medium.

Dyes are fixed to cloth by **steaming**: the moisture and rapid heating provided by steam transfer the dye molecules from the thickener paste, to which they have been combined, to the fibres. The time this takes can range from ten seconds to 60 minutes depending on the properties of the dye and fibres. The steamer is in many ways the counterpart of the baking oven as both are involved in fixing inks or dyes on textiles or stimulate chemical reactions in specialist printing pastes. There are industrial and

Obsidian by Grethe Wittrock (2003) was machine woven with nylon and paper yarn, dyed and then hand screen-printed with Expandex paste, which creates a relief surface on the fabric when heated.

batch steamers; the latter are used for specialist items and small amounts of fabric.

Dyed fabrics must be washed after steaming to remove excess dye and thickener pastes. Different types of dye may require slightly different washing processes depending on the fabric. Generally, though, fabrics will be initially washed out in cold water until the water runs clear, followed by warm or hot water washing with a mild detergent, followed again by a final washing in cold water until the water runs clear of the fabric. While it is not necessary to wash pigment printed fabrics, washing will improve the handle of the cloth. With environmental issues high on the agenda, it is increasingly important to improve the extent to which dyes are fixed to a fabric so that there is less discharge of effluents during washing.

Opposite page
This printed textile design by Rupert Newman (2006) shows the complex motif and pattern opportunities that can be harnessed through the creative use of digital design.

Other print processes

There are other print processes that have individual merits and markets. One example is **heat-transfer printing**, a technique developed for printing on to synthetic and man-made fabrics such as polyester and nylon using disperse dyes. Dyes are printed or painted on to the surface of a non-absorbent paper, which under pressure, through the use of a heat transfer press or iron, vapourise and condense on to the surface of the fabric onto which the dyed paper has been placed. Another technique is **wax-resist printing**, a style of printed fabric used by artists and designers in the West and in Africa. Designer Philippe Bestenheider developed an armchair range for Moroso called 'Binta' using a patchwork of manufactured wax prints (see page 7), while artist Yinka Shonibare uses wax-resist prints in his installation pieces. Wax resist prints are fabrics that are printed industrially, using a resin resist, to mimic the aesthetic of **batik**. Wax prints, ranging from national costume to T-shirt design, play an important role in the cultural and economic development of a number of African countries. The South African fashion company Strangelove blends an array of large motif iconography and design styles to create original print concepts that are distinctly African in flavour.

Below
The South African fashion company Strangelove, established in 2001 by Carlo Gibson and Ziemek Pater, crosses the boundaries between design and art. It also collaborates comfortably with like-minded designers. In this placement print design they worked with graphic designer Ian Finch, who drew on Johannesburg buses for the main design motifs.

Motifs, patterns and styles

Throughout history motifs and patterns have been central to the visual identities of cultures and civilizations; how they have been drawn transforms the imagery into a defined aesthetic style. Today, many of the images and styles that are applied to fashion and furnishing textiles are inspired by historical and cultural references.

The **layout** and structural organization of motifs depends on symmetry and asymmetry, the underlying organizational

principle that enables us to understand continuity and variability in pattern. Regular continuity in the layout of a motif to create a pattern is normally referred to as symmetry, and when the layout of a motif to create a pattern is variable, this is described as asymmetry. The actual motif used in a symmetrical repeat pattern can often be asymmetrical like that of the paisley.

How designs from the past are utilized and reinterpreted can be determined by an individual designer's approach to creating a collection. Alternatively, the designer may be asked to incorporate a specific theme and style in a textile design, which will influence its motifs and patterns. Predictions of commercial trends are strong influences. And colour is a vital element in motifs and patterns. The way it is incorporated can radically transform the way a design is seen and how people respond to it. Colour can create atmosphere in interiors and on the catwalk. It can generate a variety of emotional responses to a fabric and is given careful consideration when a textile is directed to a particular market. When a design goes into production it is normally manufactured in a number of colourways to cater for a range of customer tastes.

There are well-established design and pattern types that are intended for either the interior or the fashion markets. However, even though these market-orientated traditions are maintained in some textile design circles because of consumer demand, the boundaries are increasingly ambiguous, with designs intended for fashion finding their way into furnishing contexts, and vice versa. Fashion designer Issey Miyake, and others, recognized that it was not always necessary to use traditional patterns; on a number of occasions this led Miyake to collaborate with highly creative artists to incorporate new visual aesthetics into the fabric of his garments.

The blend of photography, text and virtually generated brush marks in computer-aided design (CAD) for this textile piece by Simon Clarke (2009) demonstrate some of the devices that digital design can contribute to the exploration of new combinations of motifs, visual styles and pattern in printed textile design.

Above, left
The most established and popular design in printed textiles is the floral pattern, which can be redesigned and reinterpreted in a variety of styles. In this fabric, designed for the African market, the stylized floral pattern suggests cultural references from India and Arabia.

Above, right
The paisley pattern has its origins in Indian textile design. It is now used globally in a wide variety of reinterpretations for both fashion and furnishings.

The floral

The most universally successful design category for printed textiles is the floral. Historically, and today, it is popular in both the furnishing and fashion markets.

The designs, sometimes described as botanical designs, cover the wide area of flowers and plants. The portfolio of motifs is extensive, ranging from classic English roses to tropical orchids and alpine flowers, from palms and grasses to a plethora of leaves and fruits. They are represented in many realistic styles that often originate in, and reflect, a variety of visual cultures. From a different perspective, floral and plant motifs and patterns can also be styled on aesthetics developed by artistic movements, such as Pop Art or Expressionism – a design approach that is applied equally effectively in the categories that follow. Many companies produce classic floral designs: Sanderson's reputation was established by the quality of the floral designs in its printed furnishing textiles.

The paisley

A printed-textile design classic, the paisley with its intricate motifs and patterns has been consistently reinvented, leading to hundreds of different interpretations. It originated in India, where it is historically and culturally widespread, but precisely where this happened is unknown. There are various theories about what inspired its creation. One is that it was adapted from an Indian pine cone; another, that it developed from the tree of life or the mango. The motif and pattern arrangements can be simple or extremely complex, and the styling can be very varied. The paisley – it is named after the Scottish town of Paisley where it was manufactured for the European market – is widely used in both the furnishing and fashion markets.

Above
In their Glasgow and London toiles (2004 and 2005 respectively), Timorous Beasties depict uncompromisingly contemporary themes within the traditional design framework of the toile de Jouy. Their modern interpretations convey social and political concerns to raise public awareness of these.

Opposite
This digitally designed and printed textile by Rupert Newman (2006) was inspired by the early twentieth-century Rayonism movement.

Pictorial and figurative designs

Toile de Jouy blends landscape and figurative scenes, often with an underpinning narrative, and has been popular since the mid-eighteenth century. The design work is illustrative and requires excellent drawing skills. Traditionally toile de Jouy was printed in a single colour – most often blue or red – on a plain white cotton ground. The design company Timorous Beasties continues to produce it, but with the significant difference that their thought-provoking designs refer to the urban societies of Glasgow and London. In the early twentieth century the French artist and designer Raoul Dufy produced an example of toile de Jouy that was quite different in style to that of the traditional design (see page 24). Although toile de Jouy has strong interior furnishing traditions, more general figurative designs can also be used in fashion contexts.

Geometric and abstract patterns

Geometric and abstract patterns are inspired by a rich variety of sources, which range from Islamic ornamentation to the motifs and layouts of art movements such as Op Art. After the floral, the circle or polka dot is the most popular printed-textile motif and is widely used in fabrics for both fashion and interior design.

The printed textiles of contemporary designer Rupert Newman are inspired by the Portuguese landscape and the Rayonism art movement of the early twentieth century, which aspired to transcend or float beyond abstraction; the name comes from the use of dynamic rays of contrasting colour to represent reflected rays from various objects crossing each other. This describes the type of abstract/geometric pattern Newman creates but his work has a

Left
Digitally generated printed-textile design by Lillian Farag (2007).

Opposite page
Moth Balls and Sugar Cubes (1927) by Edward Steichen (1879–1973) was based on photographs. It was commissioned and manufactured by Stehli Silks who were well known in the 1920s for producing avant-garde designs by artists, photographers and graphic designers.

contemporary feel, perhaps because it is refined and enhanced on a computer. His designs reflect real knowledge of working with geometric pattern systems and colour, and are perhaps in some ways not far removed from the artworks of contemporary artists like Bridget Riley and Jim Lambie (see page 154).

Conversational patterns

Conversational patterns embrace a large collection of themes which usually incorporate a motif of a creature or object, and a design may depict a whole scene, landscape or cityscape. The motif may be taken out of its familiar context and arranged in a formal layout such as a grid or stripes. Genre paintings, photographs and architectural models can feature. In the first collection of its kind, the American photographer Edward Steichen created a series of ten designs for the Stehli Silks Corporation using photographs of everyday objects, including matches and matchboxes, carpet tacks, thread and eyeglasses. For his 1927 Moth Balls and Sugar Cubes design he photographed the balls and cubes from above with a copy camera that captured silhouettes as well as shadows. Conversational patterns also embrace novelty, commemorative and architectural themes. Lillian Farag has created contemporary digital designs that can be included in this category.

Camouflage

Camouflage is a twentieth-century textile-design innovation that evolved from the natural world, particularly from the way animals conceal themselves within their local environment. Teleo mimetico, the first camouflage pattern printed on to fabric and used to clothe soldiers, was designed in Italy in 1929. Since then, armed forces around the world have produced similar patterns for use on uniforms and accessories. The camouflage patterns will vary in choice of motifs, colours and material depending upon the environment in which it is to be used – jungle, desert or snow – and also from the military forces of one nation to another. The context for military camouflage is broad and extends beyond combat clothing to embrace other military applications such as hardware like helicopters and tanks. Significantly, camouflage has been widely assimilated, with great commercial impact into the fashion industry and to a slightly lesser extent the furnishing textiles markets. Camouflage used in these industries can either be true representations of actual military camouflage or reinterpretations of these designs. Simple design modifications might include retaining a military pattern but changing the original colour to accommodate softer colours such as reds and pinks to embrace a particular womenswear market.

Top
Colourways of the Duckhunter Ape camouflage pattern (1996) designed by Mankey for Japanese clothing company A Bathing Ape.

Above
This second version of the Auscam desert pattern, featuring mint green, was issued to troops in Afghanistan in 2002. Sometimes called 'Ozcam', the formal term for this item of combat clothing is the Disruptive Pattern Camouflage Uniform (DPCU).

World cultures

World cultures is perhaps a more applicable contemporary definition for what has traditionally been called ethnic design. This group embraces textile designs and visual arts from other cultures and usually consists of Western interpretations of motifs, patterns, colours and techniques. This is a rich source from which to design. Africa, India and Arabia are frequently referenced because of their distinctive regional design characteristics, while Eastern Europe provides a wealth of possibilities in the areas of folklore and art. It is important to note that even when designs are reinterpreted for Western markets local textile designers and craft printers, as well as textile manufacturers, perpetuate and develop their own authentic national and regional cultural identities.

The motifs and patterns described above are revisited, redesigned and extended by inventive designers. With today's opportunities to draw upon contemporary themes and imagery and combine them with new technology it seems certain that innovative designs will lead to the establishment of new categories.

Layouts

In addition to repeat patterns there are other layout styles that can be influenced by the context for which a design is intended.

Border patterns are arguably the most significant pattern arrangements after repeats. They present designers with many opportunities while challenging them with the constraints of what is usually a narrow, rectangular strip in which to design. Although they usually run along one, two or four edges of the cloth in a step-and-repeat pattern, they may also feature within a design to enclose a motif. Established contexts for border patterns traditionally include scarves, shawls and sarongs. They also appear on the edge of garments such as shirts, dresses and skirts.

Another alternative to the repeat pattern, and one which has enormous creative scope in printed textiles, is the **engineered design**. In the past, this type of layout was produced by using one screen to create the entire pattern – for example, on duvet covers and towels. With digital technology, it can be printed within the template of a garment shape to ensure there is no loss of design. The digitally printed, engineered design gives designers the opportunity to explore non-repeat patterns and images and has been employed by a number of contemporary designers including Basso & Brooke and Matthew Williamson.

Horizontal or vertical stripes are unique design motifs that stand outside the conventions of half-drop repeats (see page 43). However, the stripes can be repeated. Although vertical stripes have not been easily realized in flatbed screen-printing, as the repeat join can show, digital design and digital inkjet printing have removed this problem and potentially opened a new chapter for the vertical stripe.

Foulard, from the French for scarf or necktie, is a pattern of small motifs that are repeated directly above and below each other at measured intervals.

Ogee is the symmetrical onion-shaped layout used by William Morris and is well used in printed textiles for interiors.

It will be intriguing to see whether these and the many other layouts in printed textiles disappear in the future, and whether a new approach towards layout design will emerge as digital technologies become increasingly effective commercially.

Far left
The Brazilian–British fashion design team Bruno Basso and Christopher Brooke has established an individual identity through its theatrical ready-to-wear garments with bold and complex digitally printed graphics. 2009 spring/summer collection, ready-to-wear.

Left
This printed textile design by Basso & Brooke (2009) shows the creative potential promised by digital design and digital textile printing, in which the quantity of repeats and colour quantity are no longer design constraints.

Digital design and digital inkjet printing

In recent times the biggest impact on printed textile design and production has come from digital design and digital inkjet printing. The creative possibilities in digitally generated aesthetics and motifs have considerably increased the design repertoire; and digital design and digital inkjet printing have enhanced the opportunities to use photographic imagery. The digital design of repeat patterns that do not have to comply with traditional processes is a new development that has emancipated printed textile designers.

Digital design software is, in addition, a critical piece of pre-production technology that contains the design and preparatory functions needed to ensure that all aspects of a particular design translate on to the cloth as intended during digital inkjet printing – a process that has had a major impact in that it enables a design to be produced in an unlimited number of colours. Digital inkjet printing is used to print samples in preparation for rotary screen-printing, or for small production runs for high-end textiles like those used in haute couture. There is also a newly emerging market for personalized, bespoke, digitally designed and printed textiles for both furnishings and fashion textiles – the designer receives an image and instructions from a client and, in consultation with the client, develops a motif into a digital fabric for a specified product context.

Design and production

Improvements in equipment such as inkjet heads and ink dispersion techniques, and the capacity manufacturers now have to facilitate their own 'prepared for print' fabrics – chemically coated fabrics which, when digitally printed and steamed, trigger fixation of dyes to the cloth for digital printing – have stimulated growth in digital textile production. The choice of fabrics is extensive and includes a variety of silk, wool and polyester types. Digital inkjet textile-printing companies can install machinery designed for the pre-treatment coating of most of them. Although production capacities in digital inkjet printing do not match the mass-production methods of rotary printing, new printers like the Robustelli Monna Lisa can produce samples and short production runs. The Reggiani Dream printer is able to produce short production runs and can print 150 metres (490 feet) in an hour. This new technology has the potential to bring about major changes in the textile and fashion industries, from haute couture to the high street, because of its increased speed and production-run capability. Fashion houses can print to order and there is no longer the need for warehouse stock that may be unsold and therefore wasted.

The highly effective Mimaki range of large-format, short-run digital inkjet printers, like the popular TX-2 and TX-3 which are commonly used in design studios for sampling purposes, is the choice for many university textile-design departments. Seen as a revolutionary step forward for the textile industry, such printers became available for general use in 1998 and were cheap enough to be relatively accessible. The chemistry of the inks used in these printers will be fixed through steaming so the resulting fabrics are fully washable. However, unless the printers are in a multiple-machines installation (as in a factory that uses multiple looms), they are limited to producing short runs and are therefore mainly used for sampling or to produce luxury goods. Reducing running costs, including cutting the cost of printers, inks and pre- or post-treatments to enable digital printing to be competitive and acceptable, is now high on the commercial agenda. University textile-design departments recognize the potential of digital technology and have invested in it. Digital design and digital inkjet printing are now integrated in the curriculum of many courses, alongside traditional hand screen-printing methods.

Below, left
In Italy digital printing is seen as a competitive alternative to mechanical screen printing in market areas like fashion. The Robustelli Monna Lisa digital printer can produce samples and short production runs, and can interface with any graphics software.

Below, right
The Mimaki TX-2 digital printer, now widely used in the textile industry, is popular for a number of reasons. It enables quick and effective sampling and short production runs, and is environmentally friendly as there is minimal ink wastage. For designers, it frees them from the constraints of traditional textile printing and provides virtually limitless creative possibilities.

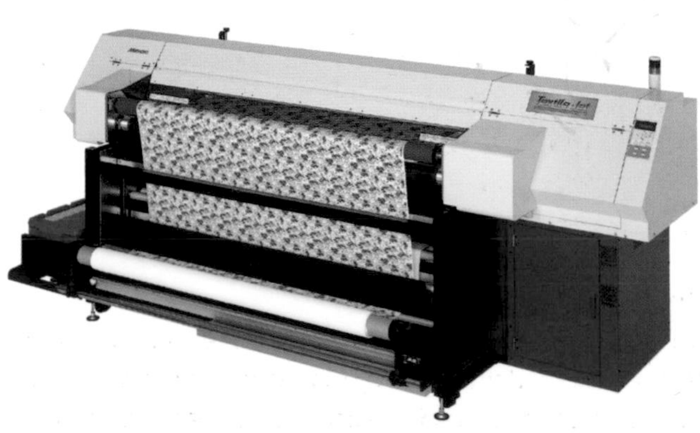

Digital inkjet printing

Digital inkjet printing is a process that builds up the colours and patterns in a design by projecting tiny drops of different-coloured inks, in predetermined micro-arrays, on to the surface of a cloth; each array represents one picture element (pixel) of the design. Usually a set of inks is used, consisting of at least three primary colours: cyan (turquoise), magenta, yellow and, optionally, black – the so-called CMYK inks. To create each of the millions of pixels required involves a vast amount of computation, which continues until the printer has printed a complete design on to a particular fabric type.

The simplest computer-driven printer is controlled by software known as a printer driver. This takes the graphics file data and related information, such as the required **definition**, single or **multipass printing** options, and **substrate settings**, and converts them into output data, which are 'spooled' until they are needed, when the information is sent to the printer's microprocessor/memory for further processing. The final instruction from the onboard processor and its memory module controls the electromechanical devices and the print-head firing systems within the printer.

Design software

Printed-textile design patterns can be produced on many standard graphics-based program. Adobe Photoshop in combination with Aleph Step and Repeat plug-ins is a very effective combination, and software by Lectra Systems, Nedgraphics and BTree are good alternatives. It is normal practice to invest in software that not only gives full design/editing capabilities but can be augmented with many other features, such as an integrated colour management system to enable accurate reproduction of colours within an original design.

In many design studios the traditional mouse has been replaced by the pressure-sensitive stylus and digitizer tablet, which brings the designer closer to drawing with a traditional medium like a pencil or pen.

Jonathan Fuller creates printed textile designs for fashion that exploit the creative potential of CAD software packages like Adobe Photoshop and Illustrator to create a variety of pattern themes. Here, he has developed a design inspired by Bargello embroidery (characterized by upright flat stitches laid in a regular pattern to create motifs), exploring optical and woven repeating effects (2007).

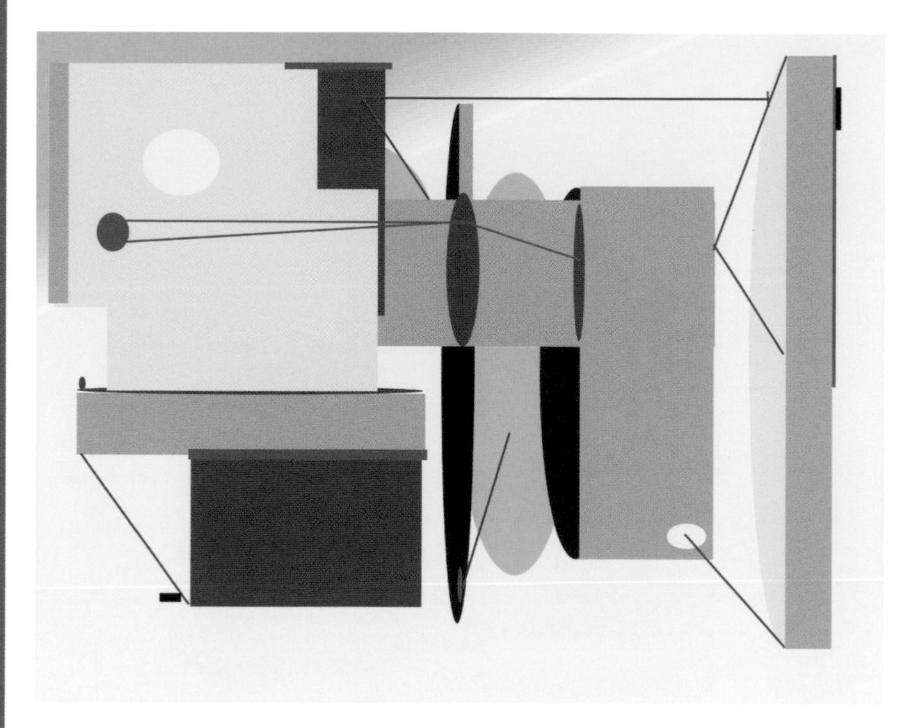

Colour Structure 1 **(left)** and Repeat Colour Structure 2 **(right)** by Simon Clarke (2008). These images reflect a recurring interest in colour and structure. Although abstract, they suggest sculptural and architectural forms. The images have been generated using a blend of CAD software systems including Adobe Photoshop CS3, Aleph-Step-And-Repeat and Treepaint. The images are virtual designs (at this stage) as they have yet to be digitally printed on to cloth, for which Mimaki digital printing will be used.

Even though there is the potential to design purely within the virtual terrain, at least for the moment most designers work initially on paper in a chosen medium or combination of media, whether a design is drawn, painted, collaged or a combination of the three. The designer scans the artwork into the computer, normally using an A3 (16.9 x 12 inch) or larger-format scanner. Scanners capture an image at up to 2000 **dots per inch (dpi)** or more, but for a printed textile design 300 to 600 dpi will produce an acceptable print outcome. Designs are scanned because the initial artwork has aesthetic qualities that for now can only be achieved outside the computer.

The **computer-aided design (CAD)** option is used to refine, modify and enhance a design in the virtual. Its benefits are clear in that repeats can be quickly visualized and, with design modifications, it is possible to achieve total accuracy in a pattern. Consequently, it is no longer necessary to photocopy, cut and paste to visualize repeats. The need to solve the problem of the four edges around a design, to ensure rhythm between repeat areas remains. This redesigning can be done more rapidly on CAD than by hand, giving designers time to generate new designs and increase their creative input.

A new digital vernacular

Working in the virtual provides opportunities to explore a new digital vernacular that can be digitally repeated and printed on to cloth. Another advantage is the way in which photography and video can be used as creative sources when designing. The former is no newcomer to printed textiles but, with enhanced possibilities within CAD and digital printing, there is greater scope for enhanced quality and experimentation. The American

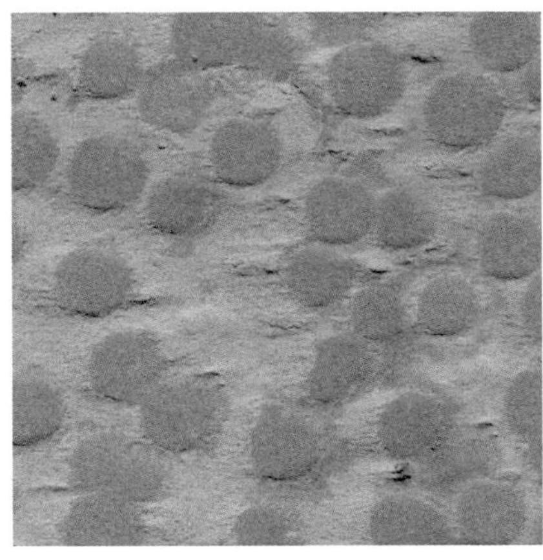

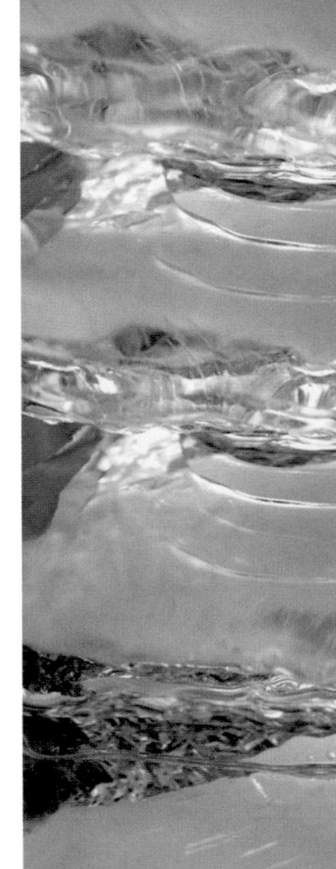

Top, left
Terminus by Mary Stieglitz (2003) is a digitally printed photograph on cotton and depicts the decaying carcass of a cow in the landscape. In terms of atmosphere it is reminiscent of the cattle skull paintings by the artist Georgia O'Keeffe. Photographic art panel, digital print, fibre reactive dye on cotton panel, 66 x 101.6 cm (26 x 40 in).

Top right and above
Kelp and Sand dots by J.R. Campbell (2002) explore the creative potential of photography with an acute sense of the detail that is possible in digital textile printing. In these digitally printed photographs on broadcloth he is additionally experimental with repeat and pattern, which achieve powerful results.

Far left
Flow by Mary Stieglitz (2005) is an installation piece at the entrance of the new cancer wing in the Greeley Medical Center in the USA. Installation 305 x 114.5 cm (120 x 45 in). Photomontage of the Payette River, Idaho, USA.

Left
In Ice Melting (2007), Sheona Quenby uses the melting ice cube as a visual metaphor for global warming. The design challenges the traditional perceptions of repeat by using large motifs that depict three stages of a melting ice cube.

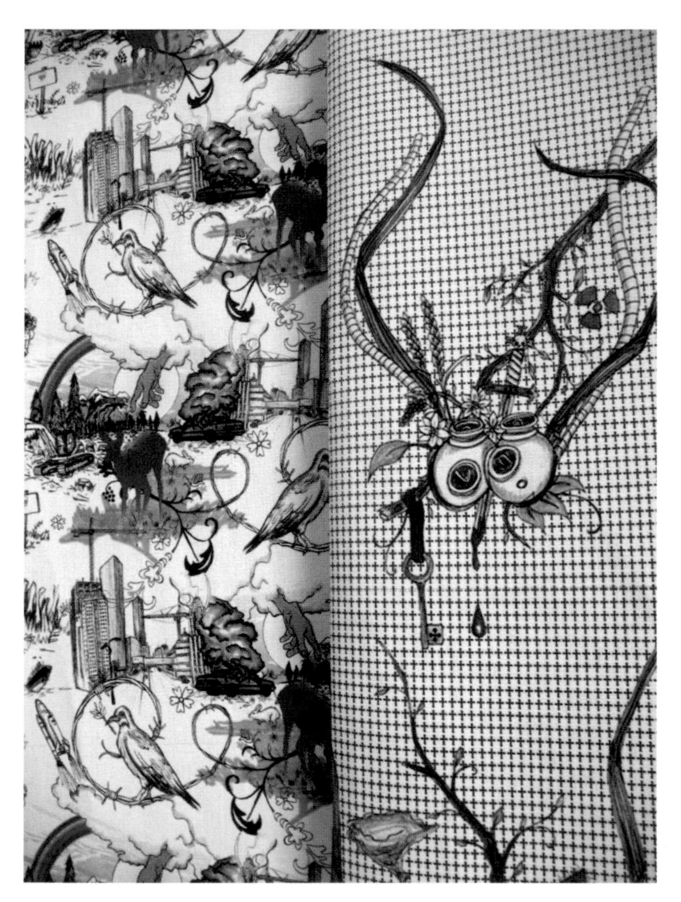

photographer Mary Stieglitz has worked with digital inkjet printing on a number of surfaces, including silk; a choice that raises interesting possibilities for interpretation. The images – subjects range from the surface of water moving in response to a breeze, to animal skeletons – are produced by capturing light, and silk, by its structure, is able to reflect light. The extent to which videos are created and their images captured and redesigned in the virtual to generate digital prints is an area for further exploration. It is already a design approach adopted by experimental, printed-textile design students.

Because of the expanded visual repertoire in the digital design domain, social and moral issues can be effectively communicated, as in the powerful designs of Ed Forster. In Sheona Quenby's artwork digitally manipulated photographs of ice and melting ice cubes function conceptually as a metaphor for global warming, while at the same time possessing distinctly original aesthetics.

Above, left
Ed Forster's digital print designs with symbolic and narrative content were created in 2007, and were inspired by contemporary concerns and events in society. They aim to challenge viewers' moral and ethical consciences.

Above, right
In this idiosyncratic Heartline (2007), Ed Forster blended an ornamental style with a synthetic colour palette. The heart motif in this digital print design is both a religious symbol and in memory of his father's heart transplant.

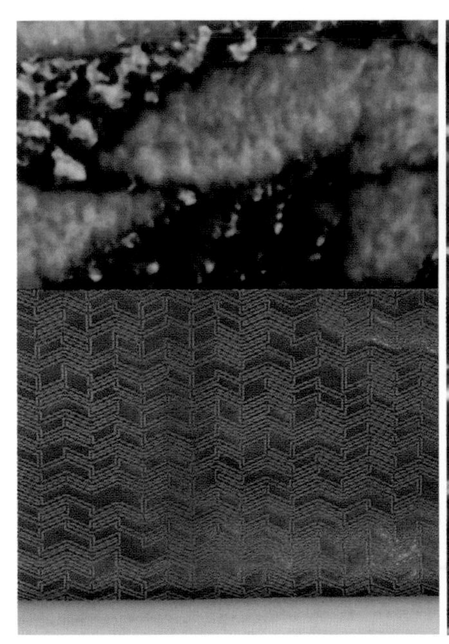

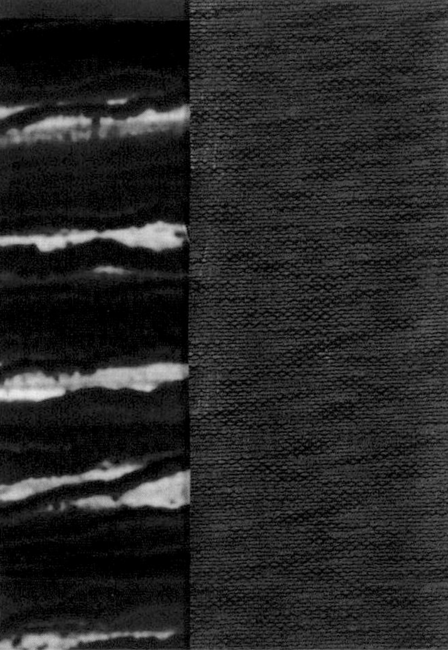

Left
In a project for the Dutch Textile Museum in 2008, Eugene van Veldhoven created fabrics which he photographed and enlarged significantly. From these enlargements he generated unique digital prints. Details of both the original fabrics and the corresponding prints are shown here.

Opposite page
This panel by Hitoshi Ujiie (2006) is digitally printed with textile pigment and disperse dye on polyester. The delicate and expressive leaf motifs illustrate the fine drawing style that can be achieved with digital printing.

Technical emancipation

Digital inkjet printing is revolutionary in many respects. It removes the traditional constraints imposed on the design of repeats. It is no longer necessary to take into account the dimensions of rotary and flatbed screen-printing. And all previous technical constraints are removed, arguably eliminating the need for repetition in a design – a development that has increasingly encouraged designers to create engineered designs to fit specific product shapes. This is apparent in the innovative digital designs of Basso & Brooke (see chapter 6). In conjunction with CAD the creation of new images can be quick while retaining technical accuracy. Digital printing technology in combination with CAD generates printed fabrics with a non-mechanical aesthetic.

Architectural and product design software packages yield opportunities for textile designers to create new aesthetics. Other approaches are also emerging – for example, the creation of sculptural or low-relief pieces that are designed to be photographed and subsequently digitally applied to cloth. Another creative direction is combining digital with hand screen-printing; this could involve digitally printing a design then manually incorporating discharge and devoré elements. The company Jakob Schlaepfer in Switzerland and designer Eugene van Veldhoven experiment creatively with digital inkjet printing.

Digital and traditional print techniques

Designers who have access to digital inkjet printing at the start of the sampling stage can eliminate protracted and expensive screen-printing processes as they are able to control how a design will look as a fabric sample. Without foresight, CAD-generated digital inkjet-printed samples can create problems when a design is prepared for large-volume manufacturing using rotary or flatbed screen-printing processes. If a manufacturer buys a design from a studio, agent or independent designer the image data files on the CD may be difficult to prepare for the production machinery; for example, when they are given to the **computer-aided manufacturing (CAM)** separation artists they could be very complex. This can be rectified by reducing the number of colours in the design on the computer. Alternatively, the fabric sample could be rescanned and the number of colours reduced with CAD in order to produce separated colour films economically. The responsibility lies with the designer, whose imagery, colours and repeat patterns should be in accord with the production methods related to a manufacturer's textile market; he or she should bear these in mind and design appropriately. This is important as, for the immediate future, the digital needs to work with traditional methods. These problems do not apply to small-batch digital-inkjet printing production.

Customization

Digital methods have the advantage of speed. Designs can be emailed to a client as soon as they are completed. Last-minute ideas can be realized and final design adjustments quickly made to colour and pattern, enabling a catwalk or exhibition piece at a trade fair or gallery to be completed just in time – therefore arguably allowing the designer to display the optimum degree of creativity. Matching colours exactly to a client's requirements is possible with dedicated software, such as the Newton colour system which enables precise colour-matching from the artwork on the monitor to the digitally printed design on fabric. A wide range of textiles from silks to heavy cottons and velvets, fine wools and Lycra can be printed using acid, reactive and disperse dyes in the digital printer. Once pigment inks have been perfected for digital inkjet printing growth in this technology should be significant.

Major textile and clothing companies are recognizing the potential of digital technology. For example, Levis uses body scanners to produce individual patterns for garments, based on a customer's measurements. Connect this to CAD textile design and digital inkjet printing, and the fashion industry will be able to establish personalized markets, enabling consumers to be truly individual in their style of dress. Moreover, designs that are digitally stored or archived are easily retrieved for production purposes. Clients can also use the archives to review designs from previous lines or seasons, and update and reorder them as the market dictates.

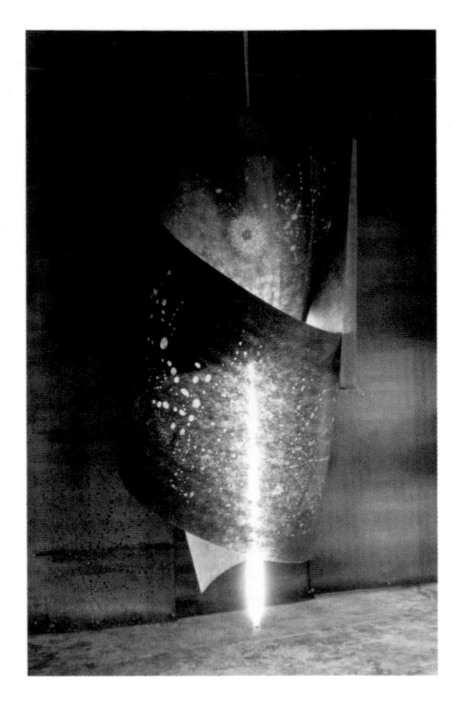

Textile design, the environment and science

It is important that designers are aware of the impact their creative decisions can have on the environment. With 80 per cent of a textile's environmental and economic costs allocated to the pre-production design stages they have a crucial role to play in creating designs that will have the least possible ecological impact.

The environment and eco-design

The Royal Society of Arts (RSA) in London holds annual textile design competitions that require students to show they are aware of what is involved in environmental and sustainable design. Entrants demonstrate this visually in their designs and by selecting manufacturing materials and methods that remove or reduce practices that harm the environment. The aim is to ensure that the next generation of textile designers plays an increasingly responsible role in the preservation of the planet.

Rebecca Earley is a leading innovator in this expanding area of design. Her research is based on the belief that designers can play a key role in enhancing a product's environmental profile. She combines eco-design theories with practice-based applications that culminate in the creation of fashion/textile artefacts that have a limited impact on the environment. In printed textiles she has focused on the use of the **heat photogram** method, a printing process that has a low environmental impact, which she has applied to a number of products, including scarves. She is Senior Research

Above, left
Golden Fern by Rebecca Earley (2006, realized from a photogram of 1994) used the heat photogram technique to produce a new type of printed textile without polluting water and with minimal use of chemicals. This way of utilizing photography to make a printed textile highlights the technique's enormous creative potential for printed textile design.

Above, centre
Earley's Upcycled Shirt (2007) combines recycled polyester with the heat photogram technique.

Above, right
Lantern Grid by Kay Politowicz was exhibited at the opening of the Prato Textile Museum in 2003. This textile installation incorporates a variety of techniques and processes that reflect a particular concern that design should have a mimimal impact on the environment, and reflects an ongoing collaboration between scientist and designer. Materials and techniques used include non-woven industrial nylon/fibreglass filter fabric, indigo dye, walnut and rust, glitter and foil, phosphorescent pigment and pigment paste, magnets, laser cutting and etching, ultrasonic welding, silk-screen printing, tagging, heat gun deconstruction and Shibori dyeing.

Fellow of the Textiles Environment Design (TED) group at the Chelsea College of Art and Design in London, where she has established a physical and conceptual home for researching and developing eco-friendly textile design. TED is a unique collective of practising designers/educators who are concerned with the role textile designers can play in the field of eco-design, and Earley began building its materials resource, now an open access facility, in 2004. Kay Politowicz, also of the Chelsea College of Art and Design, is another pioneer in this cause; her 'Particle Fibres', an experimental installation piece was exhibited at the Prato Textile Museum in Italy.

Design4Science

A collaboration between design and science was successfully forged in the United Kingdom for the 1951 Festival of Britain, when a group was formed to apply certain types of scientific 'pattern' to everyday objects including textiles and ceramics. The patterns, which used structures such as those of haemoglobin, insulin, beryl and mica, were complicated and, before the advent of computers, difficult to replicate accurately. They were submitted to well-known manufacturers, including Warner Fabrics and Wedgwood, and the resulting textiles and ceramics were used in the Regatta Restaurant on the South Bank of the Thames.

In 2007 the innovative Design4Science project reignited this relationship with a national design competition for students. It focused on entrants responding to a series of scientific innovations in molecular biology. The aim of Design4Science was to generate design work that would create a new perception of an area of science that might otherwise be unknown, misrepresented or misunderstood. The intention was to broaden perceptions and create opportunities for discussion. Sarah Jane Bone won first prize in the textile design group for her creative digital designs for printed textiles, which were inspired by cell lineage and cell death, and translated into stylish and relevant laboratory coats for molecular biologists.

Below, left
In 2007, to encourage and promote science through design, the Design4Science project, supported by the Wellcome Trust invited design students to develop work inspired by scientific innovations. Sarah Bone created Worm Repeat, an innovative digitally generated and printed textile that was influenced by the story of cell lineage and cell death.

Below, centre
Digitally rendered laboratory jacket with Bone's Worm Repeat design.

Below, right
This digitally generated and printed textile design by Sarah Bone (2008) is one of a collection inspired by Japanese ghost stories. It was created by combining drawing and photography in CAD using Adobe Photoshop and Illustrator software.

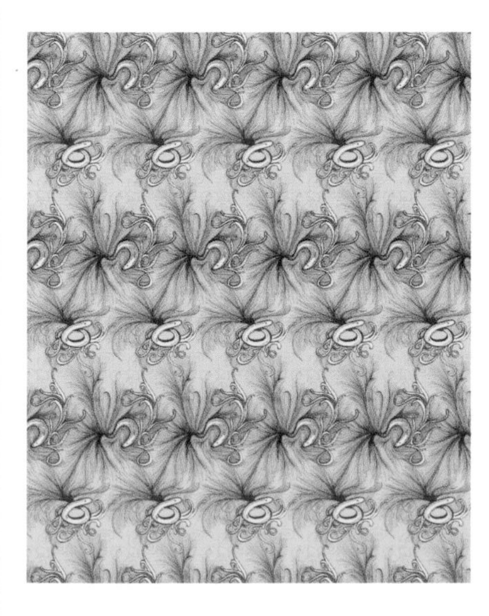

Summary

The classic and the new coexist in printed textile design. While there are established markets for designs like the floral and paisley, there is still plenty of creative scope to reinterpret these classics for both the interior and the fashion markets – and there is an abundance of designers entering the world of printed textile design, bringing the vision and confidence to redefine its aesthetic boundaries. The new draws upon an almost limitless visual source: the world around the designer. The work of designers such as Ed Forster and Sheona Quenby, has shown the creative potential of utilizing contemporary social and environmental themes – a potential that artists commissioned to produce printed textiles frequently capitalize on. This is evident in designs by Henry Moore and, more recently, in designs produced for Liberty department store in London by Grayson Perry and Paul Morrison.

While it is necessary that many designers and studios respond to changing fashions in the printed-textile design market, it is equally necessary that there are innovators who will challenge seasonal trends. These trends are established by political, economic and cultural factors in society, and often reflect the current creative views of innovative leading designers and design studios.

Because of the emphasis placed on their drawing, painting, photography and pattern creation skills, designers working in printed textiles increasingly recognize and utilize their potential to work in other areas. The one that is most obviously, and most closely, aligned to their field is wallpaper design. Abigail Lane at the design group Showroom Dummies works on wallpaper as well as textiles, using large graphic motifs, iconography and patterns to create individual interior atmospheres. British artist Damien Hirst has also produced unique responses to the traditional perceptions of wallpaper for Prada.

Opposite page
The design group Showroom Dummies, under the direction of Abigail Lane, creates printed textiles – for both interiors and fashion – elements of its visually powerful projects. The group's unconventional approach and bold design aesthetic is reflected in Fly in the Sky (2003), illustrated here.

Below, left
Damien Hirst's Skull (2007) was a temporary wallpaper print created for the Rem Koolhaas-designed Prada Epicenter store in New York. It features skulls from the cover of The Hours' album, which Hirst also designed.

Below, right
Vomit (2001), by 2x4 design studio, New York, for the Prada Epicenter store, featured a gigantic floral pattern made up of extremely low-resolution fragments of film stills – some banal, some semi-pornographic – derived from the short film stills shown in the store's ubiquitous displays.

With the opportunities provided by CAM, overlaps and crossovers between printed textile design and illustration are becoming more frequent. This is evident in the unique illustrative work of the design company Eboy, whose work has been applied to textiles.

The traditional contexts of the fashion and interiors markets can overshadow innovations in allied areas, like that of accessories which embraces an array of products, such as scarves, bags and footwear. The innovative footwear designer Jan Jansen has recognized the potential of printed textile design, and has incorporated printed images ranging from simple abstract patterns to busy graffiti in his shoes. Larger companies such as Dr Martens and VANS have also capitalized on the use of print in footwear to change design perceptions of the shoe. For the future, the opportunities for further exploration of printed textile design, aesthetically and functionally, will rest on the imagination and ambition of the designer.

Above
New York Skyline by the pixel art and graphic design company Eboy (2006). Eboy's powerful digital imagery triggered a collaborative project with the fashion designer Paul Smith, which resulted in printed textiles similar to New York Skyline.

Below
Footwear artist Jan Jansen has used the printed image in his designs on a number of occasions. Transparency in the Clouds (1980), shown here, illustrates many of the possible applications for printed textile design. Inspired by John Lennon's 'Lucy in the sky with diamonds', the design uses holes instead of diamonds, transparent plastic with 'flock-print' clouds, metallic goat-leather piping and E.V.A. outsole.

3.

Woven textile design

515.—Jacquard-card making.

Far left
A jacquard loom with punchcards.

Left
Operating the machine that makes the punchcards for the jacquard loom.

The first practical power loom was designed by Edmund Cartwright in 1787, but it was the 1820s before technical shortcomings were resolved and the weaving industry was transformed.

In France, in 1801, Joseph Jacquard invented a loom that represented a major technological breakthrough. A series of punched cards was added to the top of the loom to control a complex pattern of warp threads. This complicated machine later developed into a looped arrangement of cards for creating repeat patterns in cloth and carpets. The jacquard loom enabled intricate patterns to be woven without the continual intervention of the weaver and is widely acknowledged to be a precursor of modern computer science.

Hand-woven textile designs

Anni Albers, former Bauhaus and Black Mountain College weave tutor, took the craft of hand weaving to new levels of creativity during her prolific career spanning the twentieth century. Significantly, this involved breaking down the traditional perceptions of weave, to the extent that her designs were widely seen as art forms full of similar creative content and vitality to that found in fine art and in particular abstract paintings (see pages 22–23).

Albers defined weaving as forming a pliable plane of threads by rectangular interlacing. She described the woven cloth as possessing two key elements: the building material (by which she meant the thread structure and the character of the fibres it contained) and the actual weave or construction. Albers developed her definition by explaining weaving as the process of passing the weft between taut, alternatively raised warps, creating a **plain weave**, or between other combinations of selected warps.

The loom

Although there are a variety of loom types with idiosyncrasies that enable an assortment of woven textile designs to be created, the fundamental components remain similar. In university textile departments hand-operated floor looms, often **dobby** or treadle looms, are frequently used for teaching. In the textile industry some design studios use these for sampling, but if a design goes forward to mass or batch production it is normally manufactured on an industrial power loom. Independent designers generally weave their samples on a hand loom or produce simulated weaves with computer-aided design (CAD), which are printed on to paper. Occasionally they have access to new loom technologies to produce sample and bespoke woven cloth.

Dobby and treadle looms

Dobby and treadle looms operate by the raising and lowering of a system of shafts to which the warp threads are attached. As the threads are raised or lowered a gap is created, called the **shed**, through which the weft thread is passed.

The more shafts, the greater the range of pattern and colour options that can be created, as the order in which they are raised or lowered dictates the way in which the warp and weft threads are interlaced. On a treadle loom, the shafts are 'tied up' to the treadles, which are operated by the weaver's feet. Two shafts and two treadles can be used to make a simple plain weave. The number of treadles that can be operated, however, is limited and so these looms can normally only operate up to 16 shafts with ease.

A dobby loom, however, can operate many more shafts. Instead of using treadles, it uses a dobby mechanism, a chain of bars, usually called **lags**, into which pegs are inserted. The pegs select which shaft is moved. A dobby loom can have an average of 50 bars or lags allowing a much wider variety of weave structures. Dobby mechanisms can be operated mechanically or by

Below, left
The opened warp threads create the shed.

Below, right
Shafts are attached to treadles.

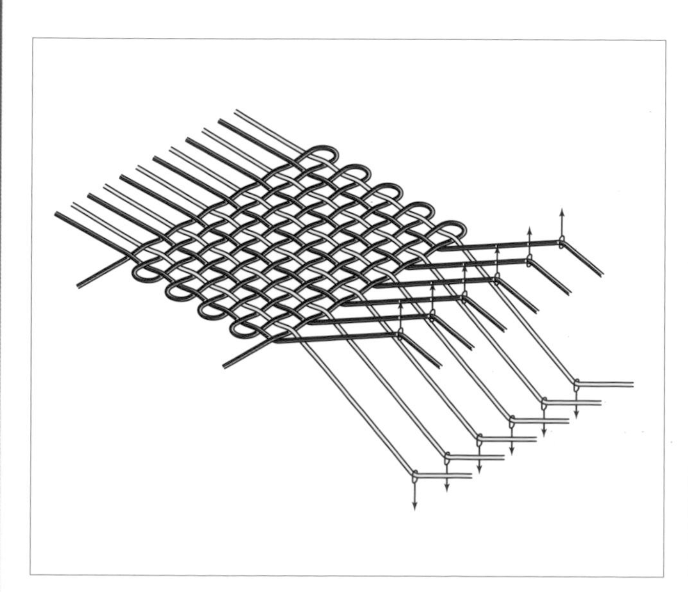

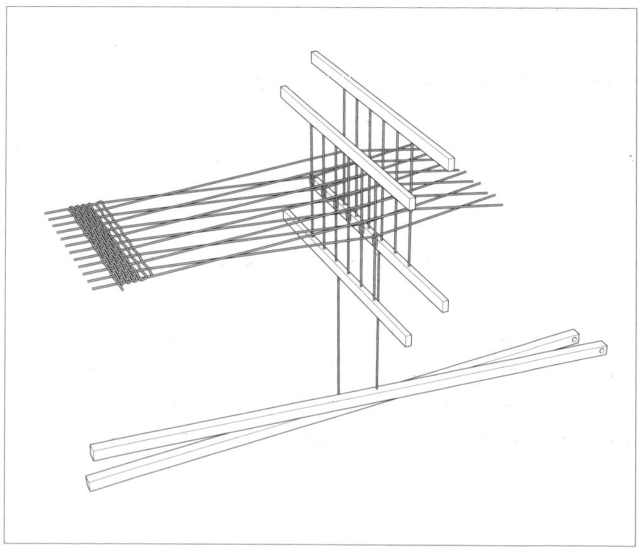

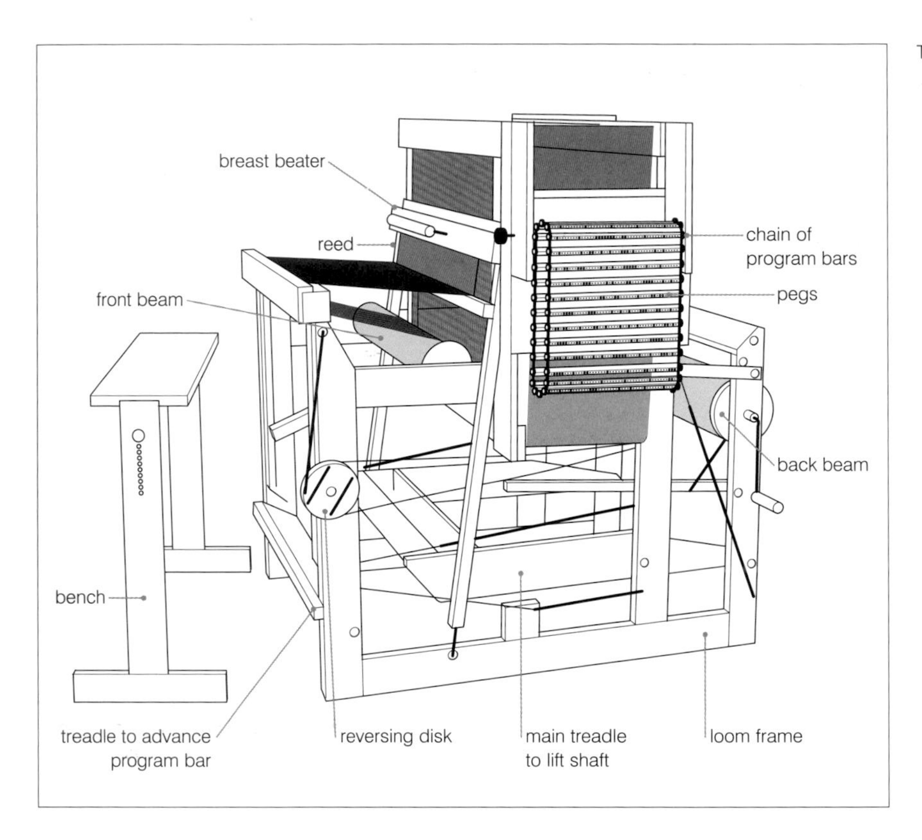

The manual dobby loom.

computer. In each case a pedal triggers the dobby mechanism to select the shaft to be lifted and then moves the chain on to the next lag. The pedal can be moved by leg power, electricity or an alternative power source. On a mechanical dobby the pegs have to be set up by hand, a laborious process, but on a computer-assisted dobby loom solenoids, activated by the computer program used to design the weave, select the shafts. A computer-controlled dobby loom can handle sequences that are virtually unlimited, although not as complex as those that can be achieved on a jacquard loom.

Design and production

Weaving develops from design ideas stimulated by a concept – which may be the result of influences ranging from an architectural style to plant structures, or even a collection of cultural artefacts. It can be necessary to respond to trends, which may last only a season or could be recurring themes like ecological and environmental concerns. Or the concept may be dictated by a customer or a manufacturer. Normally, the designer will be clear about what a cloth will be used for, how it is expected to perform and its proposed price; the visual aesthetic and feel of the cloth in relation to the context in which it will be used are of paramount importance. However, innovative weave companies take the initiative and set rather than follow market trends.

Initial ideas are designed into woven samples, collections of which are generally taken to trade fairs, by manufacturers to fill their order books and by design studios or designers to sell their ideas to manufacturers. Studios and

Linton Tweed: designing for a niche market

Linton Tweed started as Linton Mill, a small business, established by Scotsman William Linton in the city of Carlisle close to the Scottish borders in 1912, whose salesmen travelled the local area with ponies and traps. The tweed the mill produced was of a high quality and led to a fortuitous introduction to Coco Chanel in about 1920. The close association that was established with her fashion house persists to this day: Chanel remains Linton Tweed's most important and prestigious customer, although there are others, including Burberry, Jaeger and Escada. It achieved this stature against stiff competition from the Far East by carving out a niche in the market for its high-quality product and innovative design.

Linton Tweed develops two fabric collections every year, the Linton and the Ullswater, each of which is produced biannually to coincide with the spring/summer and autumn/winter fashion seasons, and showcases them at the twice-yearly international trade fair Première Vision in Paris. The Linton collection comprises textured novelty woven fabrics for the top of the range market and uses fancy yarns, which are more experimental in their twisting and construction techniques than more regular yarn types, sourced from suppliers throughout the world. Classic examples are marl, spiral, snarl and loop yarns. The Ullswater collection is a diffusion range developed in 1995, which retains the quality element but with fewer fancy yarns, and targets the boutique fashion market. The company has recently expanded into the interior furnishing market.

The design team at Linton Tweed ensures that the woven fabrics are at the forefront of fashion trends – hand looms are always busy weaving new samples for customers. Another key characteristic of the company is its continual search for new and innovative yarns from around the world.

Linton Tweed is self-contained in that it is able to control all stages of manufacture. It has its own dye house enabling it to dye its own yarns. A twisting department enables it to make new yarns exclusively for customers and, as well as the hand looms for sampling, there are of course industrial power looms. Traditionally, the manufacturing aim was to supply large, prestigious fashion houses, but today the company will weave short runs in a number of designs to ensure good quality and a wide choice of designs.

Woven tweed garment photographed at Paris Fashion Week, Chanel, 2007/08 autumn/winter collection, haute couture.

Tweed fabric sample by Linton Tweed, 2007/08 collection.

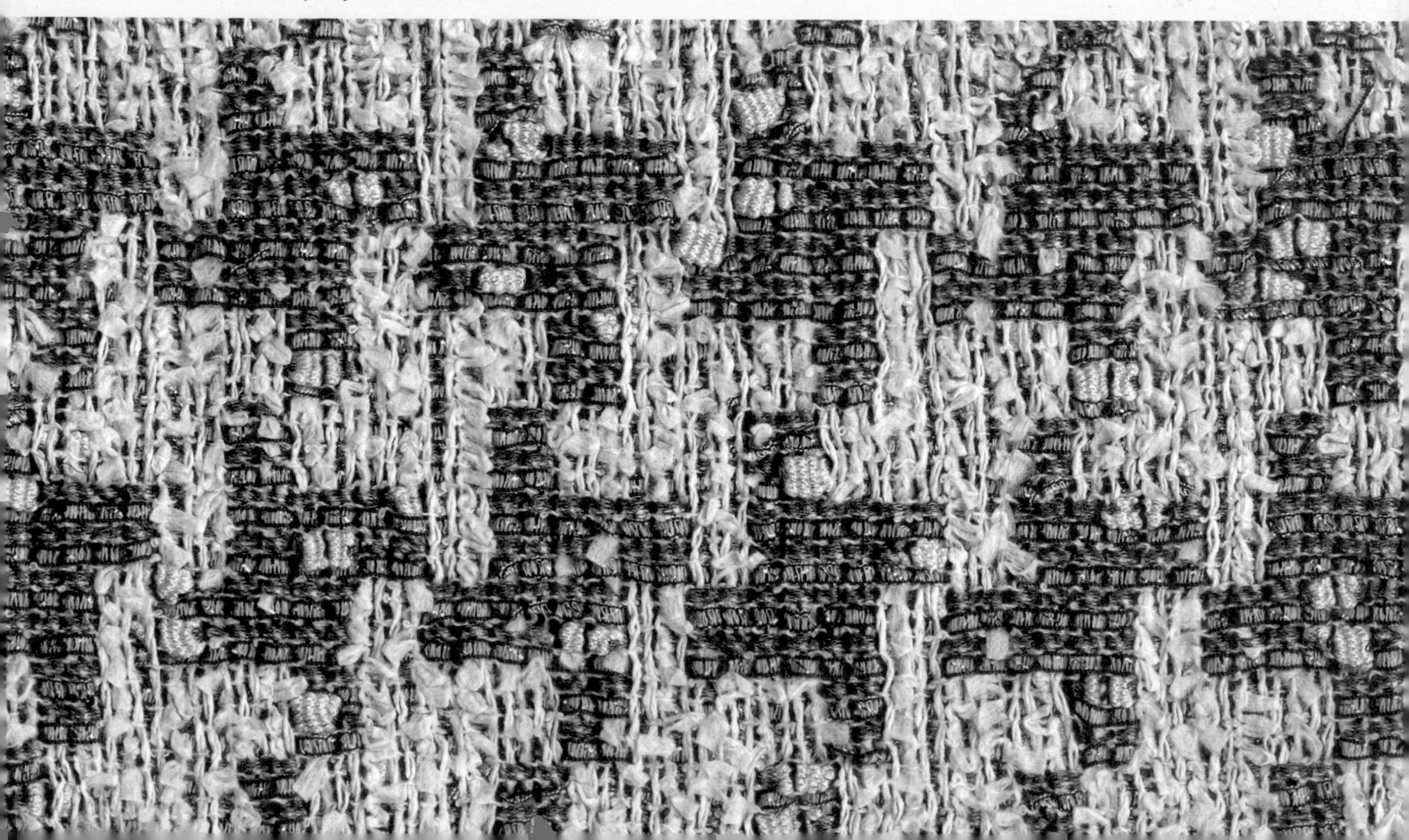

individual designers also visit weave companies, who may have their own in-house design teams. Design concept, design development and design methods are discussed in more detail in chapters 5 and 6.

Yarn, colour and dyeing

The first stage in the weave design is the selection of the yarn. The type of yarn used in a fabric has a great impact on the final cloth. In brief, yarns can be divided into two main groups: **spun** and **filament**. Spun yarns are made of relatively short lengths of fibre that are mechanically twisted or spun so that they hold together, whereas filament yarns are composed of continuous strands of fibre; silk from a cocoon is an example. A wide variety of yarns is available, ranging from classics such as cotton, linen, wool and blended types through to more specialist ones such as **fancy**, **microfibre**, stretch and metallic yarns. Combined with different weaves and structures, this vast pool provides almost limitless possibilities for designers.

Yarns are selected for weaving by designers, design studios and manufacturers who attend international fairs, such as the Pitti Filatti in Florence, where the concentration of yarn manufacturers provides a wide range of qualities and aesthetics at one venue. Predicted trends and developments in yarns are displayed in exhibitions at the fairs, and are also featured in textile publications.

With coloured yarns, the creative opportunities for the designer are significantly expanded. The types of dye used mirror the relationships between dye type and cloth type discussed in chapter 2. To briefly recap, direct and procion dyes are most effective for plant-based yarns, such as cotton and viscose. Acid dyes provide the best colours for protein-based

Below, left
3-D ScotWeave illustration of spun yarn. Spun yarns are made of relatively short lengths of mechanically twisted fibre; cotton, wool and blended fibres are examples.

Below, right
3-D ScotWeave illustration of filament yarn. Filament yarns are comprised of continuous strands of fibre; polyester, nylon and silk are examples.

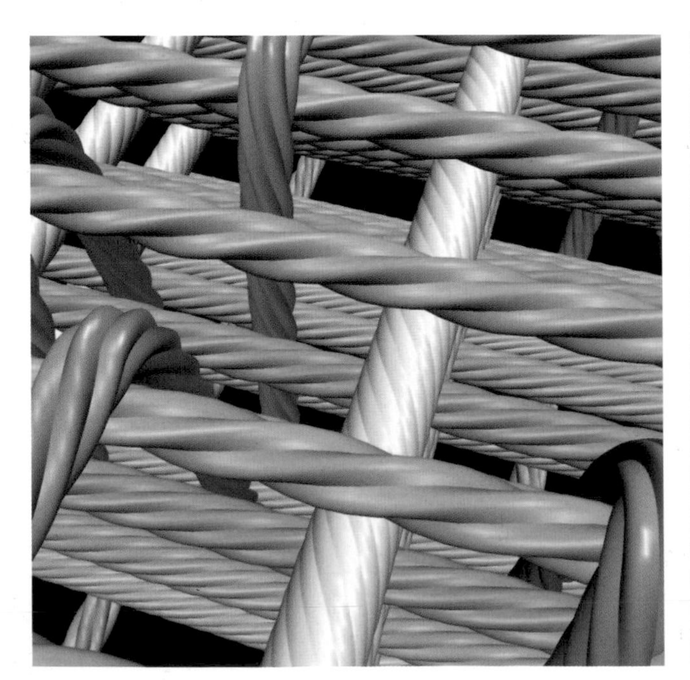

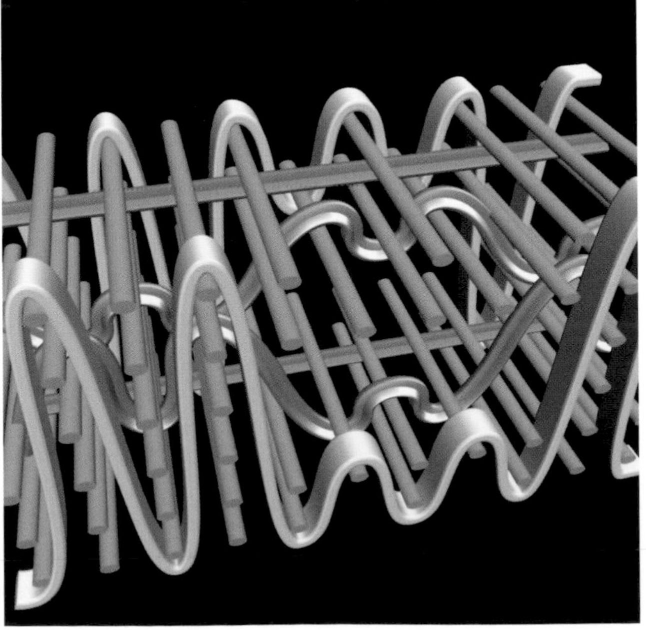

Above
Hanks of dyed wool at the textile design laboratory at University College Falmouth, UK, 2008.

Left
The London-based weaver Mary Restieaux is a leading exponent of ikat, a unique dyeing and weaving technique, based on ancient traditions, still practised in Central Asia, India, Indonesia and Japan. Warp or weft threads, or both, are tie-dyed before weaving.

ones, such as wool and silk, which come from animals. Disperse dyes are most frequently used for synthetics, such as nylon and rayon.

A **hank winder** is used to create **hanks** of yarn for dyeing. In small batch dyeing the hank is tied together to prevent tangling of the yarns. The hank is washed with soap to remove dirt and foreign matter, then dyed using the appropriate dye type. In the case of mass production there are a number of different types of hank **yarn dyeing** machines which can dye up to one thousand kilogrammes of yarn at one time. After dyeing, a **cone winder** puts the dyed yarns on to cones in readiness for weaving, and a **warping mill** is used to set up the warp on the loom.

The colours selected for a design are informed by the weave concept or brief. Consequently, early in the design process designers establish a colour palette; this develops from their visual observations and inspirations, and also takes into account trends seen at trade fairs, in publications and on the internet. Colour selection closely mirrors yarn selection because the two are intrinsically linked.

Yarns and weaving

A yarn and a thread are generally the same thing; however, although it is possible to make specialist threads from yarns the converse is not the case. In weaving, a single warp yarn or thread is called an **end**, often described as a **warp end**. A single weft yarn or thread is known as a **pick** and is usually described as a **weft pick**.

Warp threads support the weft threads and, as a result, are subjected to a lot more tension. Breakages in a warp on an industrial

An example of Central Asian ikat from Western Sinkian, Yarkand or Kashgar, before 1839, silk and cotton (Chinese School).

loom are expensive and disrupt production. If one occurs, it is darned after the cloth has been woven. To reduce the chances of a breakage, warp yarns tend to be superior to, and stronger than, weft ones. When creating samples, designers need to be aware of such potential pitfalls and ensure that their designs are capable of withstanding the demands of industrial manufacturing.

Notation systems

Once the yarn has been selected, the designer creates a **notation system**, a framework developed to describe weaves. Either crosses or marks are used to indicate where the warp thread is uppermost, and this representation of interlacing is marked on graph paper. Each vertical space represents a warp end, and each horizontal one a weft pick. Each square therefore indicates the intersection of one **end** and one pick. Only warp **lifts** or **floats** – a thread that passes over two or more crosswise threads – are indicated by a mark; a weft float is represented by a blank square.

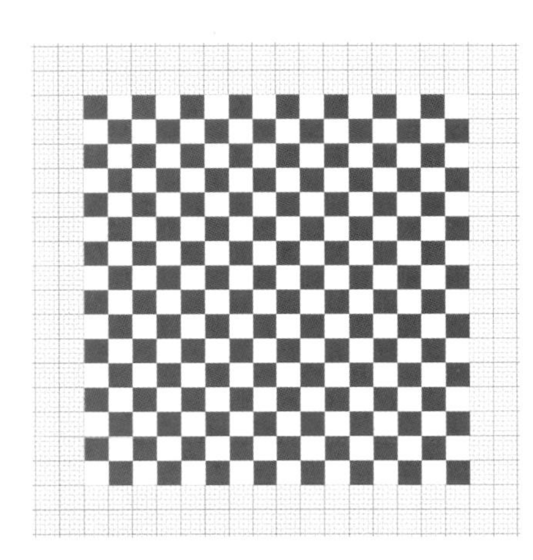

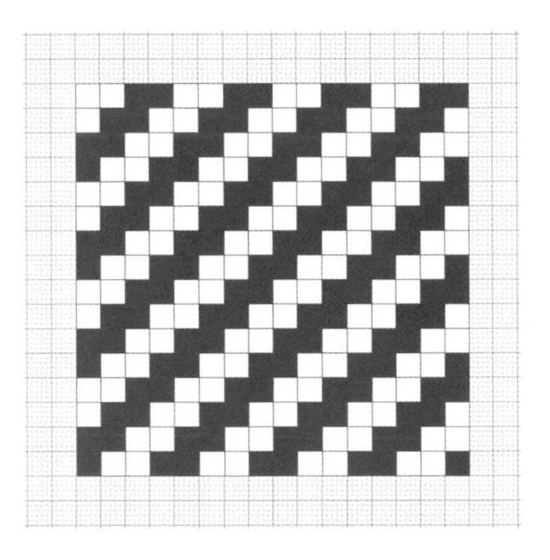

Far left
Notation for a plain weave.

Left
Notation for a twill weave.

The weaving plan

Once the notation system has been created, the designer then needs to consider the weaving plan, which consists of the **draft**, **lifting** and **denting** or **reed plans**. The draft shows the number of shafts and the way in which the warp threads are drawn on to the shafts. It is normally shown at the top of the weaving plan. The lifting plan specifies the order in which the shafts are lifted. On a dobby loom this is called the **peg plan** because the instruction to lift the shafts is determined by the pegs. The lifting plan is shown to the right of the weaving plan.

The denting, or reed, plan refers to the way in which the warp threads are threaded through the spaces, or dents, in the reed, a metal, comb-like device that keeps the warp threads correctly spaced.

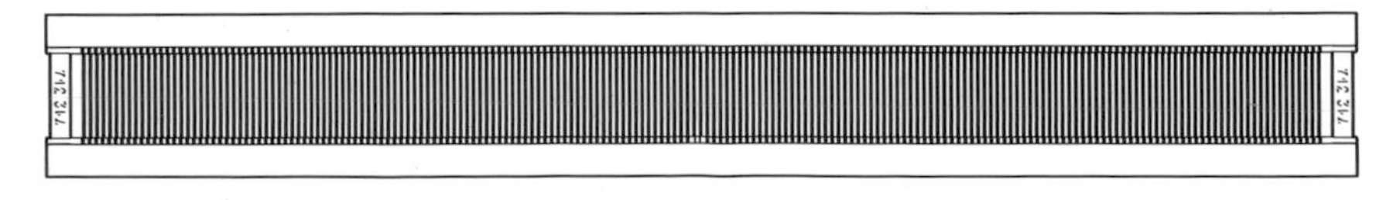

Diagram of a reed.

The number of dents per centimetre determines the **sett** of the warp. Sett defines the spacing of the weft and warp threads in a woven fabric, usually in terms of the number of threads per centimetre. Their density and the relationship between warp ends and weft picks per centimetre affects the type of fabric produced. For example, a low-cost cotton sheeting muslin has a fairly open weave structure so will have fewer warp ends and weft picks per centimetre than a denser cotton-duck canvas. Reeds can have from 6 to 100 dents per centimetre, and so selecting the correct reed for the weave structure is essential.

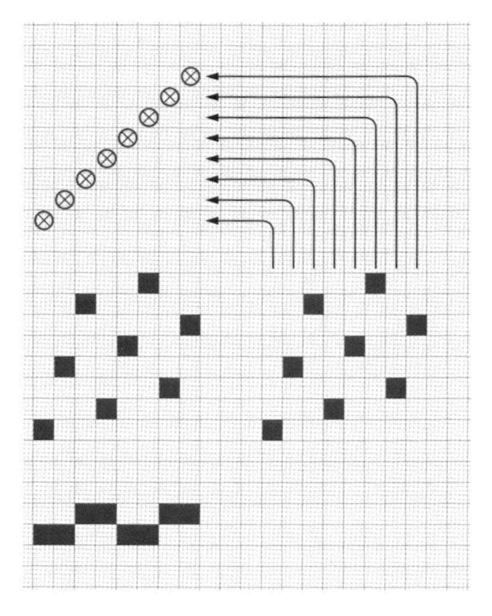

Above
Illustration of the design, lifting plan and reed plan for an eight-end sateen weave.

The weaving process

With the weaving plan drawn up, the loom can then be dressed. In simple terms, the loom operates as a device for keeping the warp threads taut and in parallel order. The warp threads are passed through **heddles** – long needle-like string or metal devices with a central opening called an eye. The heddles are attached to two rods and together they form the shaft.

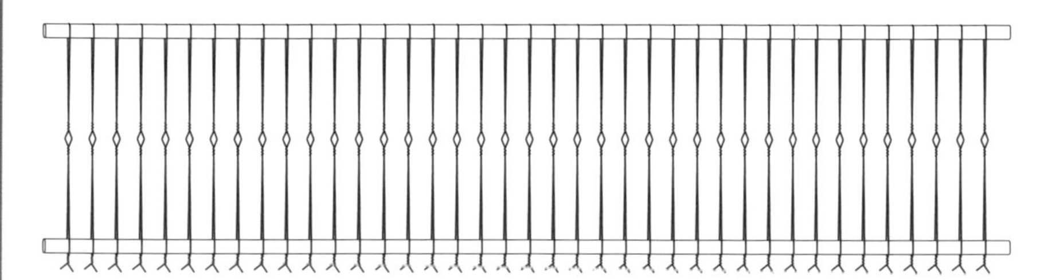

Left
Diagram of a shaft.

As we have seen, a system of ropes and rollers moves the shafts up and down, either by means of treadles using leg power, or by means of the peg and lag system on a dobby loom. As the shafts move up and down an opening is created in the warp threads, called a shed.

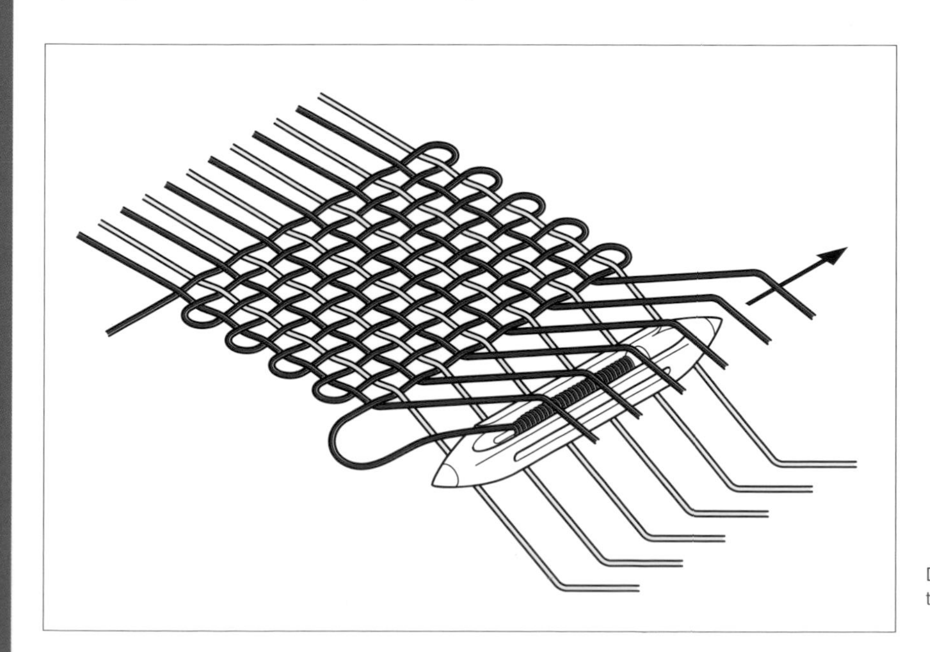

Diagram showing the shuttle travelling through the shed.

Creation Baumann: unconventional textiles

An independent family-owned company in Langenthal, Switzerland, Creation Baumann has set a precedent in interior textiles by using technological expertise to produce the exceptionally inventive and high-quality textiles for which it is internationally recognized. Its ability to sustain its innovative approach is a direct consequence of having design, production and distribution under one roof, which enables textile specialists from the yarn- and piece-dyeing workshop and the weaving mill to co-operate with the design and development.

Although private customers are an important market for Creation Baumann, it also designs textiles that can be used in other contexts, for example to personalize restaurants and hotels. It also produces collections for the healthcare sector, which are developed through consultation with specialists in the field and an interior designer and colour psychologist. Patients and staff in healthcare facilities expect a comfortable, friendly environment and Creation Baumann has responded with colour themes that create uplifting and emotionally engaging atmospheres, and stimulate well-being in patients. Importantly, all the functional contexts and demands of the health care environment are factored into the designs and fabric performance.

Functional characteristics contribute to the aesthetic and atmospheric mood in an interior environment. The company is particularly interested in the light-absorbing characteristics of woven cloth in interiors, and the light absorbency of its fabrics can be tailored to meet the optimum lighting requirements of individual customers. Similarly, the extent to which a fabric absorbs sound is intrinsic to an interior atmosphere and, again, the customer's preferences are factored into Creation Baumann's design approach.

Elux by Creation Baumann (2007) is a digital print on a crinkled metal weave that creates a dramatic abstract collage of blurred rectangles.

Diagram showing the simple components of a loom with the reed/beater in place.

Weft threads are wound on to spools called **bobbins** using a bobbin winder. Each bobbin is then placed in a **shuttle** that carries the thread through the shed. The weft threads run horizontally across the vertical warp.

Once the weft yarns have passed through the shed they are beaten up to the fabric that has been formed using the beater, which is attached to the reed. This process is repeated until the weave is complete.

Weave structures

Before starting the process of translating an idea for a design into the woven fabric it is necessary to decide which weave structure will best realize what the design is intended to achieve. Knowing the principles that govern different kinds of weave allows a designer to adjust his or her draft design to create one that reflects the individual qualities of a specific weave.

Plain weave

In plain or tabby weave the threads in both warp and weft directions interface alternately. Because it has the maximum number of interlacing or binding points, it is firmer and stronger than fabrics that are constructed with the same yarn types but use other structures. It is the simplest and most frequently used weave. **Poplin**, **chiffon**, **crêpe de Chine** and **gingham** are plain weave fabrics.

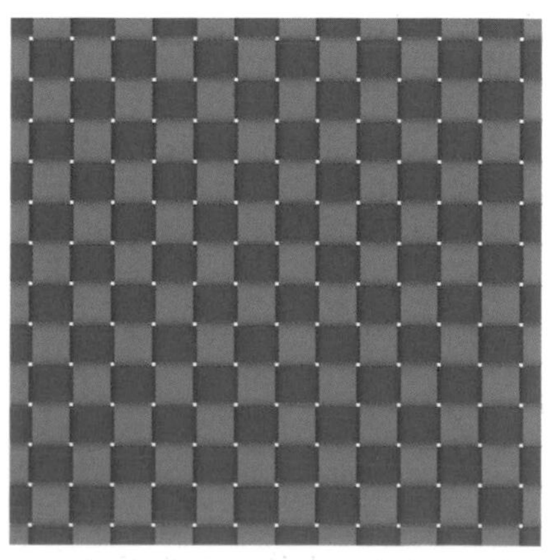

Plain weave.

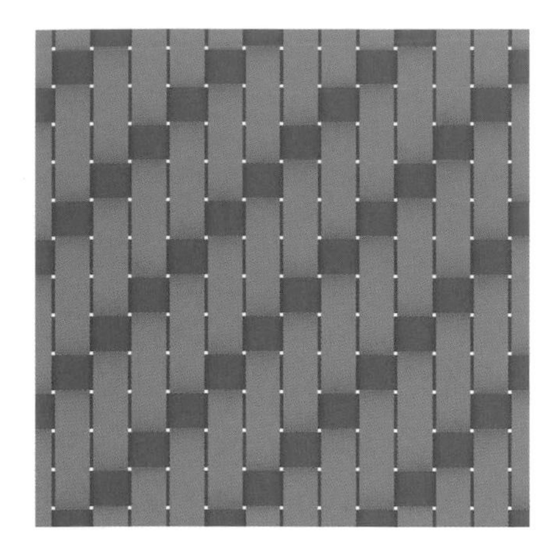

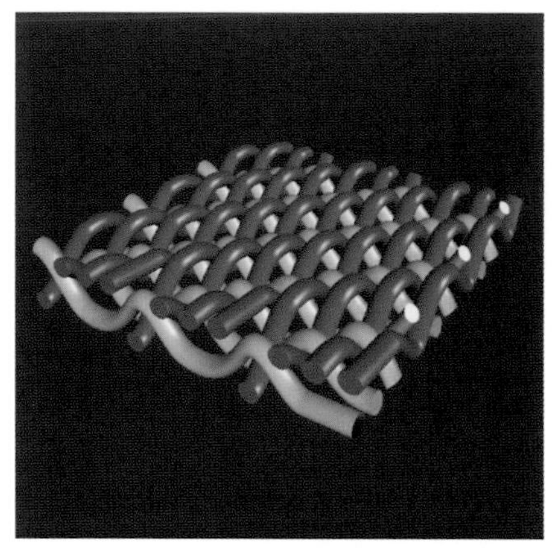

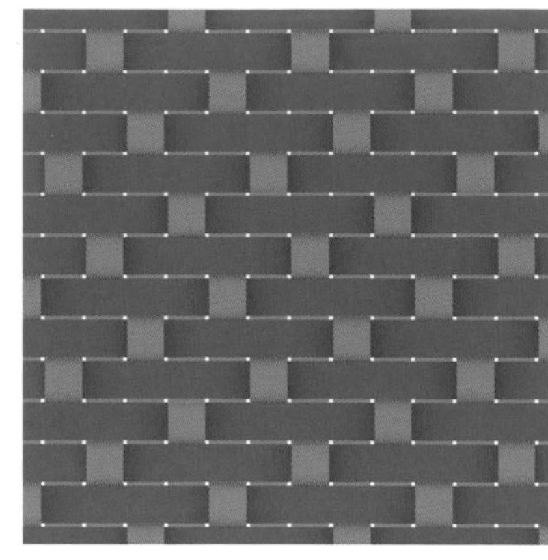

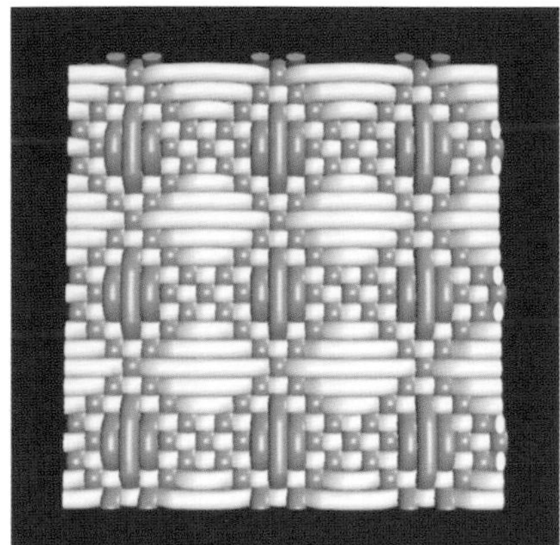

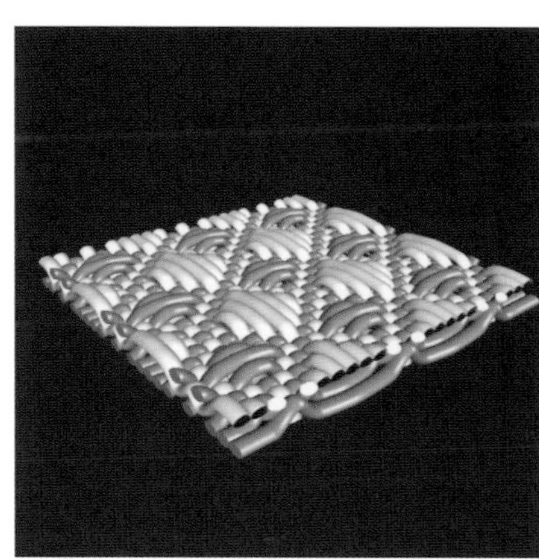

Above, left
Twill weave. This is used for denim from which jeans, the world's most ubiquitous clothing item, are made.

Above, centre
3-D technical digital illustration of twill weave, side view (produced in ScotWeave).

Above, right
Satin weave.

Far left
3-D technical illustration of honeycomb weave, top view (produced in ScotWeave).

Left
3-D technical digital illustration of honeycomb weave, side view (produced in ScotWeave).

Twill weave

Twill weave is characterized by diagonal lines in the cloth. In its simplest form each weft thread is set one warp thread to the right of the preceding weft thread. This may be repeated over three or more ends and picks. Because more weight and a better **drape** can be achieved with twills due to their diagonal structure, they are particularly popular in the fashion industry. A variety of recognized twill structures, including **herringbone**, **braided** and **undulating**, can be woven in addition to the regular twill.

Satin and sateen weaves

Satin weaves are predominantly warp-faced weave effects, whereas sateen weaves are predominantly weft-faced weave effects; one is in reality the reverse side of the other. Silk or rayon yarns are traditionally used for satin weaves and cotton for sateen ones. The interlacing between the warp and weft threads is not as tight as it is in plain and twill weaves. A nearly unbroken warp makes up the surface of a satin weave whereas the opposite is the case for a sateen one: the fabric is woven with a nearly unbroken weft. Satin has a smooth and often lustrous surface, and has always been considered a luxury fabric. Both weaves are frequently combined in jacquard weaving to create dynamic patterns.

There are many other weave structures of varying degrees of complexity. **Waffle**, **double**, **pile**, **leno** and jacquard are a few examples. The extensive range of weaves provides designers with opportunities to experiment creatively within existing structures and explore the potential they offer for new woven-textile designs. **Tweed** is another distinct weave which has a strong Scottish border heritage. It is a thick woollen or blended cloth, which can have irregular **slubs** or knots. Twill or herringbone are common weave structures used to make tweed cloth.

Weave finishes

Once a fabric has been woven it is finished with treatments that enhance its aesthetic and/or functional characteristics. Wool fabrics are normally scoured after weaving to remove natural fats, waxes, dirt and impurities. This can be in addition to scouring the yarns before weaving. Finishing achieves a variety of different effects, a number of which can be created by calendaring.
In this process the fabric is passed between heated steel rollers that apply extreme pressure to create a smooth, even lustre on the surface of the cloth. To achieve **embossed**, **moire** and **watermarking** effects, just one steel roller is used and the others are covered with fibre; the design is engraved on the steel roller.

Fabrics can be treated with chemicals to improve their resistance to water, fire and even moths. Other finishing processes include printing, which can utilize a variety of methods, such as devoré. **Piece dyeing** involves dyeing the whole cloth after weaving. The effectiveness of a finish depends on the type of yarn in the fabric.

Fulling has become popularly known as **felting**. It is a permanent finish used on wool fabrics involving a carefully controlled scouring and laundering process that induces shrinkage to create a smoother, more compact cloth; the yarns are more tightly embedded than in an unfulled fabric. Fulling is used in the production of blanket cloth: it makes the weave indistinct before the blanket is given a final raised finish. It is also used to create fabrics such as **beaver** and **doeskin** cloths, to simulate the characteristics of these animals. The process is also applied to make **velour**, a plush woven fabric similar to velvet that is used mainly for soft furnishings and hats. **Melton** is a heavy woollen cloth with a close-cut nap achieved through fulling, and is used for overcoats and jackets. Fulling has also been used to create the loden cloth that was developed to deal with the Alpine climate in Austria and Germany.

Maharam and Kvadrat: woven textile manufacturers

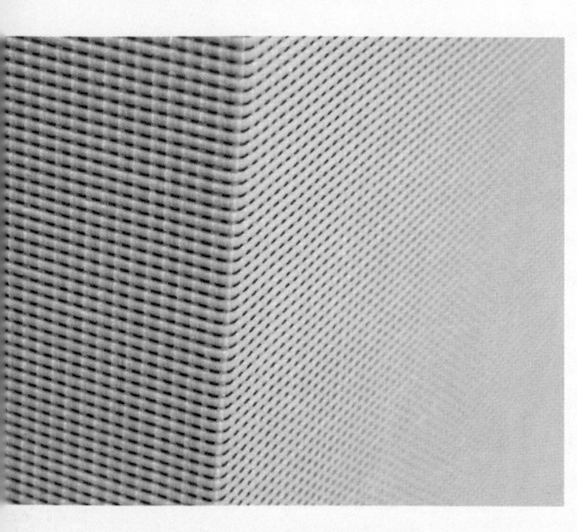

Louis Maharam triggered the Maharam textile phenomenon when he opened his shop on Lower Broadway, Manhattan, in 1902. By the 1920s, a second generation had established the Maharam reputation by providing flame-resistant fabrics that improved the acoustics in movie houses and theatres, and following this success the family extended the business nationwide. The third generation pursued the concept of contract textiles that had specific functional attributes. While performance continues to be a key characteristic in the development of Maharam's woven textiles, the current generation also focuses on cultural traditions, innovative design and new technology to create textiles through the exploration of pattern, material and technique.

The progressive design studio at Maharam is responsible for developing the company's extensive textile collection and also prepares enduring designs from the twentieth century's most notable textile designers – Anni Albers, Alexander Girard, Ray and Charles Eames and Verner Panton, among others, for reissue. Its inspirational in-house woven textile designs include the Inox structure weaves, which are constructed with a semi-transparent polyethylene tape yarn. The studio also cultivates working with avant-garde artists and designers who have no connection with the textile industry, so as to introduce fresh perspectives into woven interior textiles. The collaboration between Maharam and Maira Kalman, a New York-based illustrator known for her kinetic illustrations, absurdist humour and eccentric appreciation of the mundane, is a case in point, and developed when Maharam, seeking to explore figurative and narrative themes, enlisted her. Kalman's range of designs titled The Story of My Life displays hieroglyphic arrangements of people, places and objects. Luisa Cevese and Hella Jongerius are two of a number of designers who have recently worked with Maharam to produce outstanding woven textiles.

Maharam's partnership with Denmark-based Kvadrat, Europe's leading contract textile resource, formed in 2001, produced a dynamic alliance that is global in outlook. The companies share philosophies on design innovation and service excellence, and Maharam represent Kvadrat in North America while Kvadrat represent Maharam in Europe.

Left
Inox by Maharam (2007) is an inspirational woven textile that was developed in-house. Constructed with semi-transparent polyethylene tape yarn, it possesses a modern technical aesthetic and its performance as a woven wall covering is excellent.

Below, left
Detail of a design from The Story of My Life range, a collaboration between Maharam and New York illustrator Maira Kalman (2005). The designs display hieroglyphic arrangements of people, places and objects.

Below, right
Design 9297 by Josef Hoffman (1913) was originally created in 1913 as a tapestry sample and not manufactured. Maharam has produced it in a satin weave (2007), which creates a sheen and purity of colour, emphasizing the modern and graphic design.

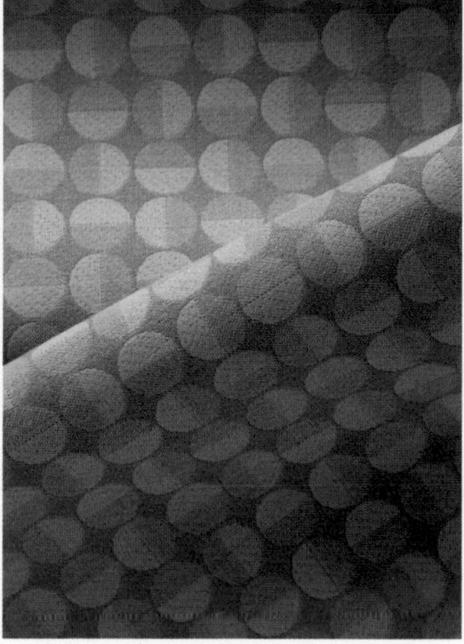

Established in 1968, Kvadrat is owned and managed by the Rasmussen and Byriel families, now in their second generations. The company creates quality modern textiles and textile-related products for both public spaces and private homes. Kvadrat is highly attuned to the appearance and function of textiles, and how they create impressions and generate atmospheres that influence perceptions of furniture and space, to the extent that many of their textiles participate in and inform contemporary design cultures. Its ambition is to extend the boundaries of textiles and contemporary design by aesthetic, technological or artistic means. Echoing Maharam's approach, they achieve this by producing innovative collections that develop through close collaboration with a range of independent designers who often find their inspiration in different design disciplines, such as furniture, jewellery, graphic design and architecture. They include the internationally renowned architect Jean Nouvel, whose architectural expression is poetic and often takes advantage of untraditional materials and technical solutions. Woven designs by Fans Dijkmeijer follow a tradition of almost mathematical and logical simplicity, despite their extreme technical complexity, and encapsulate Kvadrat's commitment to colour and simplicity. Other recent high-profile collaborators are the designers Tord Boontje, and Ronan and Erwan Bouroullec. This experimental and innovative outlook has enabled the company's weaves to be integrated with some of the world's most spectacular architecture and visionary furniture design, an achievement that it recognizes as being both an opportunity and a responsibility that requires it to play an active role in contemporary design cultures.

Kvadrat also has a twentieth-century designer collection that mirrors Maharam's. It includes work by Arne Jacobsen, an architectural and industrial design icon, who is perhaps most appreciated for his furniture designs. Less well known are his stunningly bold woven-textile designs, which the company has reissued.

Since 2006 Kvadrat has collaborated with international designers and architects in the design of its showrooms, reinforcing its commitment to active engagement in contemporary design. It takes the view that it is more important to show how different designers and architects express themselves rather than to have uniform showrooms. Its Stockholm showroom was designed by Ronan and Erwan Bouroullec, who applied their North Tiles system, and the showroom in Milan is the work of the Agentinian, Swiss-based designer Alfredo Haberli. In the showrooms the designers emphasize and play with the functionality of textiles.

Kvadrat's art projects extend the field of textiles and its uses: an artist or designer is given total freedom to create whatever they want; the one requirement is that their work involves textiles and investigates how they can be used. Collaborations with artists like Rosemarie Trockel and Thomas Demand, and working with artist Olafur Eliasson and architect Kjetil Thorsen on the Serpentine Gallery Pavilion in London in 2007, have produced striking results. In the case of the pavilion Eliasson and Thorsen wanted to add a separate tactile element and chose to work with Kvadrat's Tempo form weave because of its versatility. It was used as a curtain in the entrance, for cushions inside the pavilion and as upholstery on the specially produced inflatable furniture.

Above, left
Nectar designed by Tord Boontje for Kvadrat (2005) is one of three designs that form a floral series for curtains and blinds. It captures the essence of Boontje's decoration-as-design outlook. Nectar was developed on the computer and then constructed as a burn-out sheer (devoré). The design consists of pixellated botanical motifs trimmed in red.

Above, centre
Spot and chevron design (2002) from an original 1960s printed textile design by the 20th-century design icon Arne Jacobsen.

Above, right, top
The Kvadrat showroom in Stockholm was designed by Ronan and Erwan Bouroullec in 2006, using their innovative North Tiles system which creates textile walls constructed with individual foam-fabric tiles that yield infinite design permutations. The system provides a new way of dividing space and incorporates good soundproofing properties.

Above, right, bottom
Because of its versatile qualities, artist Olafur Eliasson and architect Kjetil Thorsen used Kvadrat's Tempo as a seating fabric in their design for the 2007 Serpentine Gallery Pavilion in London.

Digital jacquard weaving

A mathematical machine that is recognized as being a precursor to computers, the jacquard loom lends itself to the contemporary world of computer-driven technology. Computer systems enhance design opportunities because of the increased weave complexities that digital can provide.

While working with the upholstery manufacturer Maharam, in Chicago, Hella Jongerius, a contemporary designer with an individual outlook on pattern, utilized the company's jacquard fabric archive to create innovative textile designs. Repeat Dot incorporated a repeat pattern that was out of scale with the office furniture for which it was intended. The outcome was that individual pieces of furniture were created because of the infrequency of the repeat pattern. The oversized repeat remained in similar fabrics, but what was novel was that the jacquard weave was overprinted with codes from jacquard punchcards and hand-written pattern codes.

American design guru Karim Rashid has a multidisciplinary approach towards design and recognizes the opportunities provided by ornamentation, embellishment and decoration. In one project this led to the development of a range of digital jacquard-woven textiles for Edra Spa in Italy.

Left
Repeat Classic, from the Repeat collection designed by Hella Jongerius for Maharam, is a ribbon of classic jacquard motifs. A distinctive feature is the infrequency of the repeat, which means the fabric can be used innovatively on the kind of custom-made office furniture for which it was originally conceived in 2002.

Left, below
Product designer Karim Rashid's eclectic outlook on design is clearly evident here, where he sits among a range of new digital jacquard weaves (2003).

Opposite
Also from Hella Jongerius's Repeat collection for Maharam, Repeat Classic Print (2002) goes one step further than Repeat Classic by enhancing the weave with a white overprint. The overprinted motifs refer to technical data used in weaving such as the codes for colours, the number of the warp and the abbreviation used for 'cotton'.

UI 1315
CO 4017
CO 4273
CO 4030
UI 2600

Chuck Close and the Magnolia Tapestry Project

The Magnolia Tapestry Project, developed by Magnolia Editions, a fine art print studio in Oakland, USA, in the 1990s has led to the creation of innovative tapestry pieces by fine artists such as Chuck Close, John Nava and Nancy Spero. Magnolia Editions collaborate closely with a weave mill in Belgium where Joseph Jacquard pioneered the development of the first mechanized loom. With the exceptional technology at the Belgium mill it has been possible to capture the details within painting and photography.

The innovative American portrait artist Chuck Close collaborated with Magnolia Editions in the design of a series of limited-edition woven textiles based on his daguerreotype portraits. The gilded, silver-coated plates were scanned at high resolution and converted into digital weave files. The black-and-white daguerreotypes required the accurate assembly of 500 shades of woven whites, greys and blacks, and a digital sphere spectrometer (an alien technology to most weavers) determined which optically blended colours would emerge when the colours were combined. The closest analogy might be to that of a painter mixing 500 unique and precise hues via a lengthy process of measurement, calculation and experimentation – and leaves out variables like differing weave structures and issues such as the optical interaction of adjacent colour combinations. Close had control over each pixel of the weave file, ensuring complete fidelity to what might anachronistically be referred to as the artist's hand. A series of proofs was woven for each edition, and Close supervised revisions to palettes and weave files until every thread of each edition reflected his artistic intent.

The weave files were woven at Flanders Tapestries in Belgium on a 2-metre (7-foot) wide, double-headed electronic jacquard loom, that utilized 17,800 warp threads of repeating groups of eight colours.

Kate by Chuck Close (2006), 261.6 x 200.7 cm (103 x 79 in). Jacquard tapestry, based on a photograph by the artist of Kate Moss. (Magnolia Tapestry Project, exhibited at the White Cube gallery in London.)

Design and production

Three integrated pieces of equipment enable the realization of the digital jacquard weave. The first is the dedicated computer software that creates and prepares a finished design for weaving. The second is the **jacquard controller**, which receives a design, stores and edits it, and transmits its data to the third piece of equipment: the electronic jacquard loom that weaves the design into cloth.

Dedicated CAD software is available from a number of specialist textile-design software companies. It can create a design from scratch, or adapt and refine one that has been hand-rendered and scanned in; and can then prepare the finished design for weaving on the electronic jacquard loom.

Below, left
Computer monitor displaying a design produced in the weave software ScotWeave.

Below, right
Electronic jacquard loom and computer in operation, 2009.

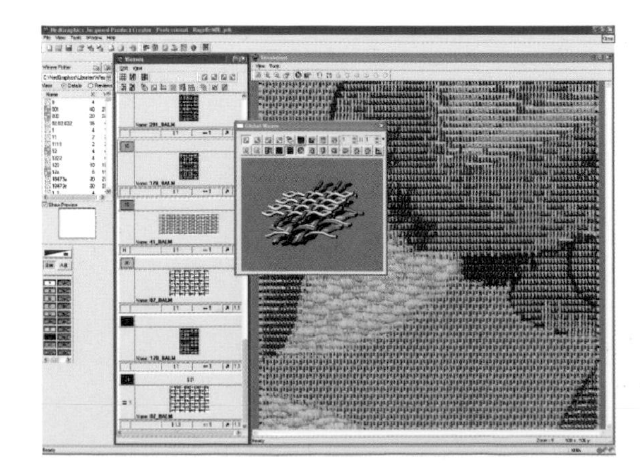

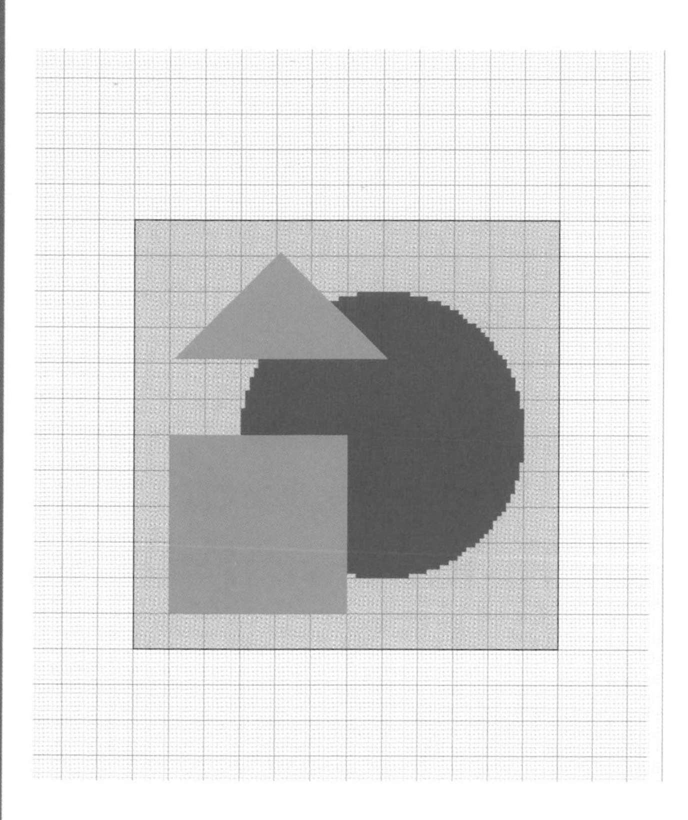

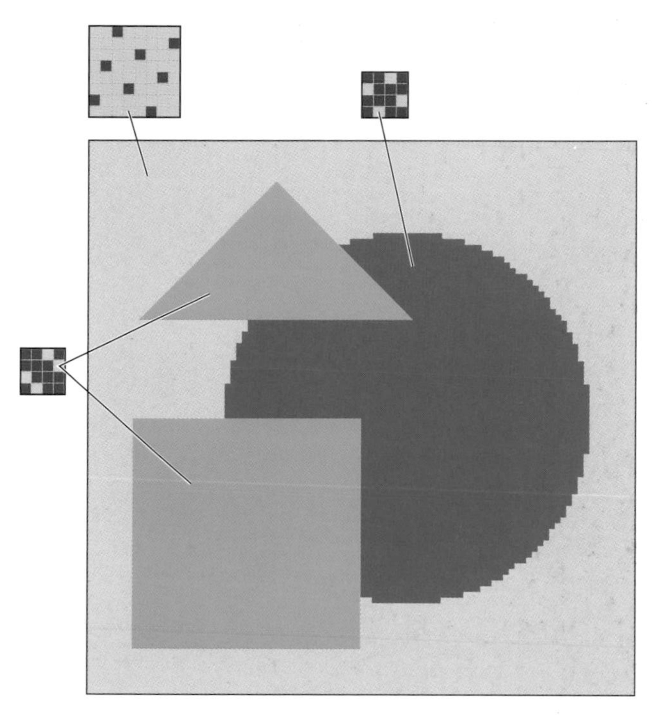

For the weaving to be effective, it is crucial that the design is accurately planned out in advance. The following is a brief general description of how a design is prepared for weaving that uses dedicated computer software. However, it must be noted that ultimately there is no single definitive way to do this.

Planning a design involves considering its overall size on the loom (in terms of both centimetres and inches, and the number of weaving ends and picks used), the type of weave structure, and the size of repeat motifs in the design. Consideration must also be given to the warp- and weft-thread patterns and the possible weave effects that are available.

Once the design has been planned out the designer should know the size and type of base weaves required. The base weave structures, which define the motifs or pattern elements in a design, are created by the designer or may exist in a weave library within the computer software. It is important to remember that each motif that is initially shown as a colour in a design for a jacquard weave will be reinterpreted into a base weave structure, using the computer software.

Simple jacquard designs consist of fewer than ten colours/weave structures. Although there is no definitive rule regarding the number of colours in a design, it follows that the more colours there are, the more weave structures will subsequently be required. And more weave structures, in turn, will require more editing of joins between weave structures in the final jacquard design.

A **yarn palette** is a working area for yarns that can be used in the design, which are sourced from a library of yarn files in the software. Yarns from the

Above, left
1. CAD (ScotWeave) illustration of a design for weave, with each motif in the design represented in a different colour.

Above, right
2. CAD (ScotWeave) illustration of a design showing the weave structure for each coloured motif.

Ismini Samanidou: bespoke digital jacquard weaves

The Greek-born and British-based weaver Ismini Samanidou's use of a digital jacquard loom to produce one-off pieces and bespoke textiles for interior spaces enables her to produce large-scale complex work unachievable in hand weaving. She starts by taking photographs, then imports. selected images into the weave software and develops them into designs by applying weave structures to the patterns. Yarns are selected according to her response to the photographs and are used as a palette when she weaves. They tend to be a combination of synthetic yarns, such as metallic yarns, and natural ones, like linen, paper and silk. She operates the loom herself, which enables her to design during the process of weaving like a traditional hand weaver.

In Feather Grass Scape, which was commissioned for international law firm Allen & Overy's meeting room at the top of a newly designed Norman Foster building near Liverpool Street, London, Samanidou wanted to keep the project site specific and drew inspiration from the building's tenth floor roof garden as she thought it would be a good idea to bring the outside inside. She took photographs of feather grass in the garden responding to the abstract qualities of the plants. However, Samanidou makes it clear that the design is not about recreating a photograph on woven fabric. Rather, it is about trying to show what she saw from different vantage points, looking from here, from there, looking upwards and from above. Red silk-thread stitching in the fabric refers to her personal affinities with traditional Greek weavers: women used to sew their dowries with red silk thread to protect them from the evil eye. So, as Samanidou liked this story, she sewed different areas of red thread into the woven panels to protect the lawyers.

Above, right
Ismini Samanidou's visual research for Feather Grass Scape. She took the photograph of feather grass on one of the roof terraces at the international legal practice Allen & Overy's Bishops Square office, a Norman Foster building in Spitalfields, London.

Right
Feather Grass Scape (2007), a textile wall piece by Ismini Samanidou, commissioned by Allen & Overy for their Bishops Square office, where she also found her inspiration for the piece. Woven on a digital jacquard loom using cotton, linen, silk and metallic threads.

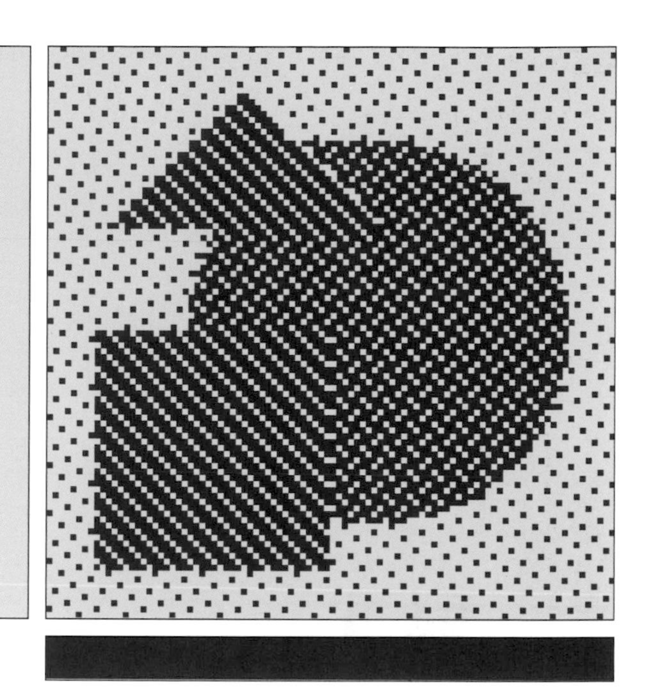

palette are used to create warp and weft patterns for the jacquard design. The warp patterns denote yarns used in the warp of the fabric and the weft patterns denote those used in the weft. They can be simple or complex depending on the designer's intentions.

After the warp and weft patterns have been set up the weave structures are added; these can be viewed on screen to see, overall, how the initial coloured design has translated to woven structures. It is possible to make additional adjustments to the warp and weft patterns at this stage.

Once the warp and weft colours and base weaves are in the design it should be reviewed by the designer for warp and weft floats. The computer can highlight these and automatically break them where necessary. The weave structures of the design can be displayed in accurate warp/weft colourings, or in high-contrast guidance colours for clarity. Once the weave structures have been edited to ensure there are no unnecessary floats the design can be stored in preparation for weaving.

At present it is common practice to convert a design to a format suitable for driving an electronic jacquard loom by creating a floppy diskette. This is inserted in the jacquard loom controller, which interfaces with the loom to convert the computer data into woven fabric.

In jacquard weaving the repeating series of multicoloured warp and weft threads can be used to create colours that are optically blended: the human eye interprets multicolour or tonal values in a combination of threads as a single colour, as in Chuck Close's designs for the Magnolia Tapestry Project.

This method is similar to pointillism, a painting technique in which small tonal or colour dots are painted in close proximity to achieve a similar effect. Pointillism originated in discoveries made in the tapestry medium.

Above, left
3. CAD (ScotWeave) illustration of the design with weave structures applied to the graphics image to give a total weave structure.

Above, right
4. CAD (ScotWeave) illustration of the design with warp and weft patterns applied to the weave structure to create the jacquard design.

Nomad is a hand-drawn design (2007) inspired by the African Bakuba cloth and translated into a digital jacquard weave by Makeba Lewis.

Weave designer Makeba Lewis produces digitally designed textiles for production on the digital jacquard loom. The weaves in her Nomad collection reflect her research into Bakuba cloth, a traditional African textile made by the Bakuba tribe of the Bushoong kingdom in Zaire. The cloth is hand-woven and is either embroidered or appliquéd using patchwork techniques. The blending of traditional motifs with new technology in Lewis's weaves is an intriguing reinterpretation of this African textile.

New technologies

In recent years there have been many developments in the creative blending of woven textiles with technology, and in particular with science, an interface that presents designers with a wealth of dynamic opportunities. Sarah Taylor is pushing the boundaries of weave by investigating new technology. Her woven textiles employ pioneering lighting effects that blend fibre optics with traditional weaving methods. They develop from research into different types of fibre optics and their ability to effectively withstand the mechanical processes of weaving. Taylor has experimented on dobby looms with transparent monofilaments as the warp and fine optical fibres as the weft threads to create innovative woven textiles. Her recent work Inner Light, a culmination of new research, incorporates programmable, light-emitting, woven paper which utilizes laser cutting, LED (light emitting diode) and DMX (Digital Multiplex Protocol – a digital lighting control system) technology. The time-based artwork promotes new aesthetics and material concepts, and is designed to create diverse colour and lighting moods.

At the end of the twentieth century a group of sophisticated textiles made from conductive fabrics started to emerge. The intention was to design interactive textiles that had an electrically conductive network integrated into the fabric structure. The network was designed to work in concert with the

Inner Light by Sarah Taylor (2007) is a paper weave which uses LED technology. This innovative artwork challenges the perceptions of weave by extending the traditional design and technology boundaries of woven textiles.

environment, soft switches and microcomputers, to be multifunctional and active, and to be able to sense, respond and adjust to stimuli such as pressure, temperature or an electrical charge. These new fabrics are called **smart textiles** and incorporate nanotechnologies. Both the textiles and nanotechnology are still being researched and developed.

Another major breakthrough in intelligent textiles is **actuation** – technology that enables textiles to move in response to stimuli, adapting their structures or properties to suit particular environments. Fibres will be able to lengthen or shorten, making the fabric structure looser or tighter: a water-absorbent fabric could become water repellent when it rains.

For the textile technologist, there are many new challenges in weaving such fabrics. It is often necessary to cut or weld the yarns within the electrical network, a process that is currently achieved manually, which slows down the loom's running time although conductive yarns can be in ribbon form, which although an improvement, need to be fed by hand into the weaving process to avoid twisting. Weaving fabrics with an electrical network is a significant shift from traditional manufacturing. As the technology still requires refinement, smart textiles are produced in short runs as precision and quality are of paramount importance.

New applications

Smart textiles and nanotechnology possess great potential to enhance efficiency and performance in military and sporting situations. In the military context, concepts where weave nanotechnology and other advanced technologies are woven into battledress fabrics have been devised to enhance the performance of soldiers on the battlefield. They focus on a number of areas, including improving protection against enemy fire, reducing the weight of equipment, optimizing camouflage and amplifying a soldier's physical strength. Also under development is the idea of weaving batteries into garments, in order to power night-vision goggles and other equipment such as advanced radios. In sport, added comfort, protection and performance in clothing is being achieved with woven multilayer composite materials that protect athletes against overwarming or rapid cooling.

Architecture draws on woven textile structures to generate new architectural forms and is the area where new applications for woven textile design have become visually prominent. In his unrealized concept piece for the Astor Place Hotel in Manhattan Frank Gehry was inspired by felt.

Ove Arup was a major twentieth-century structural designer whose most significant achievement was to establish Arup, a company that employs the best engineers in the world. This innovative and visionary institution has a liberal philosophy that is clearly evident at the Arup Advanced Geometry Unit where research into, and development of, methods for making woven and other textiles are producing new visual perceptions in relation to structures for buildings. This can be seen in the surface-mapping technique developed

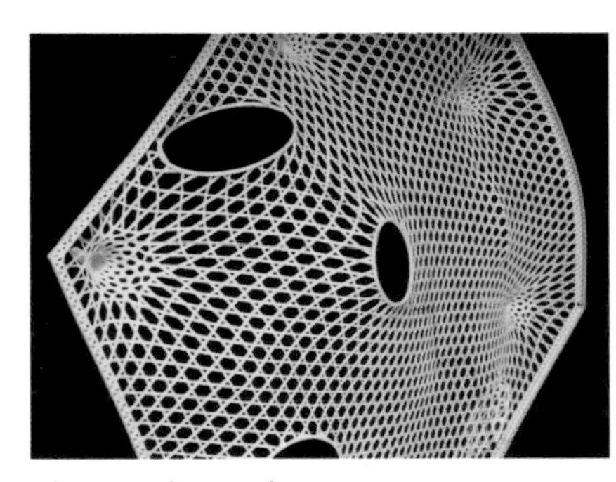

Above and opposite, top
Digital simulations of the roof design (2005) for the Pompidou Centre in Metz, France. The design was inspired by a Chinese woven bamboo hat and is the result of a collaboration between architect Shigeru Ban and Arup AGU (Advanced Geometry Unit).

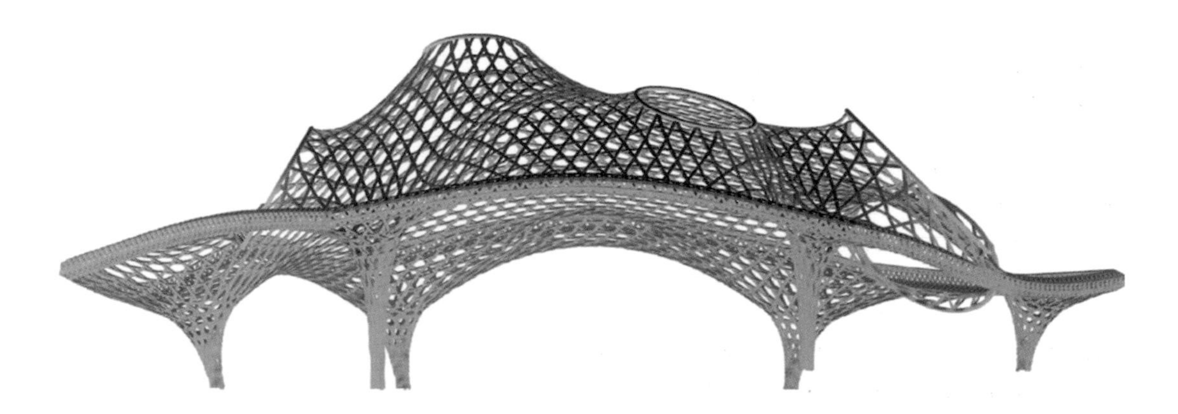

during the concept design of the roof of the Pompidou Centre in Metz, France, which was inspired by basket weaving.

Another innovative solution produced by the unit was for the Weave Bridge project at Pennsylvania University. The project involved conceptual experiments with the weave elements for the bridge to models illustrating the structural elements of the Weave Bridge. In this bridge, designed by Cecil Balmond, the span doubles as the support. Balmond, a structural engineer, has produced in the Weave Bridge his first solo architectural project which embodies a simple philosophy in which he sees structure and design as one and the same; a philosophy akin to that of many a weaver.

Above, left
Night-time visualization of the woven roof structure from within the interior of the Pompidou Centre, Metz, France, by architect Shigeru Ban and engineers Arup AGU (2005).

Above, right
Virtual visualization of the woven roof structure from within the interior of the Pompidou Centre, Metz, France, by architect Shigeru Ban and engineers Arup AGU (2005).

Far left
Preparatory virtual rendering of the structure of the Weave Bridge, University of Pennsylvania, by Cecil Balmond and Arup AGU (2007).

Left
Virtual visualization of the Weave Bridge, University of Pennsylvania, by Cecil Balmond and Arup AGU (2007).

It will be interesting to see if more close collaborations will develop between weavers and architects in the future. When such collaborations occur between design disciplines the result is often a lively design discussion, which in turn can lead to new innovative cross-disciplinary design solutions for a specific product or location. The sculptural piece for the interior of the Issey Miyake Tribecca store, New York, by Frank Gehry featured in chapter 6 is one example (see page 193).

Ozwald Boateng works closely with textile mills to achieve unique woven fabrics and finishes for his garments. He gives careful attention to yarns, colours and weaving techniques to ensure the highest possible creative and functional standards are attained in every collection. 2008 spring/ summer collection.

Summary

Woven textiles are used in a wide range of contexts and have aesthetic and functional qualities that are appreciated by people throughout the world. At the top end of the market are exclusively designed and woven textiles that utilize carefully sourced yarns and thoughtfully combined warp and weft colours. The use of individually designed cloth is apparent in suits designed and crafted by tailors, such as Ozwald Boateng, in London's Savile Row; and is equally notable in haute couture, in particular in the garments by Yohji Yamamoto.

A number of companies are involved in the design and manufacturing of high-quality woven textiles for interior and fashion contexts. The Italian Antonio Ratti is an example: his enterprising outlook led to an international portfolio of textile-manufacturing facilities. Perhaps more significantly, the Antonio Ratti Textile Center at the Metropolitan Museum of Art in New York City holds 36,000 textiles from 3000 BC to the present.

As important as the high-quality textiles, and arguably more universally beneficial, arc the practical, utilitarian applications of basic woven-textile design. An example is the basic weave used to make some low-cost synthetic mosquito netting, a prerequisite in regions of the world where malaria is endemic. The creative and functional flexibility of woven textiles ensures they will continue to travel alongside mankind into the future. It also seems likely that woven textiles will flourish, and interlace with as yet untapped potential, making them one of the keys to perpetuating and enhancing the aesthetic and living experiences of the human race.

4.

Mixed media textile design

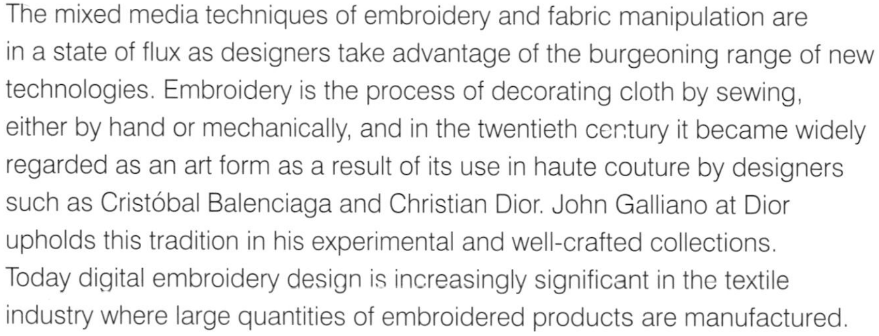

The mixed media techniques of embroidery and fabric manipulation are in a state of flux as designers take advantage of the burgeoning range of new technologies. Embroidery is the process of decorating cloth by sewing, either by hand or mechanically, and in the twentieth century it became widely regarded as an art form as a result of its use in haute couture by designers such as Cristóbal Balenciaga and Christian Dior. John Galliano at Dior upholds this tradition in his experimental and well-crafted collections. Today digital embroidery design is increasingly significant in the textile industry where large quantities of embroidered products are manufactured.

Fabric manipulation enables flat cloth to be transformed, to varying degrees, into structural and sculptural forms, and embraces a broad spectrum of creative and technical possibilities including **pleating**, **appliqué** and **quilting** as well as **laser cutting** – a new technology that brings into focus how the technique continues to evolve to achieve creative design solutions. It is a field in which Japanese fashion designers are particularly prolific experimenters, and the innovative inflatable garments developed by Michiko Koshino in the 1990s illustrate its creative possibilities. In London Tord Boontje is one of a number of designers who have utilized laser cutting imaginatively. His interior textile piece Little Flowers Falling demonstrates its potential.

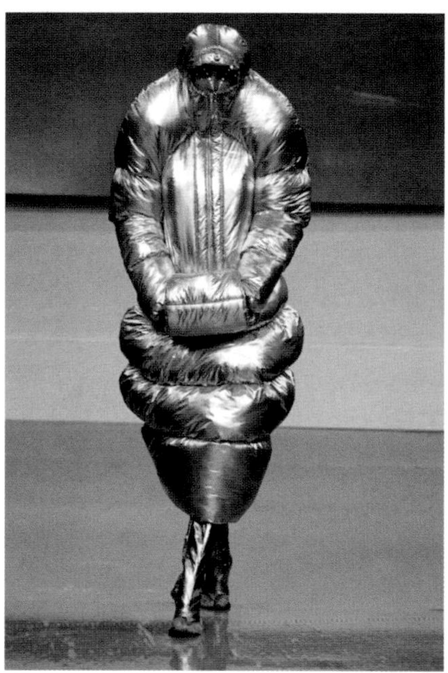

Top right
In John Galliano's sculpted, brilliantly coloured dress with striking embellished details there is a hint of inspiration from Japan and Gustav Klimt. Dior, 2008 spring collection, haute couture.

Above
Japanese-born and London-based fashion designer Michiko Koshino designed this innovative inflatable rain jacket in the 1980s. It is based on the thickly quilted B-boy 'goose' jackets that were popular with clubbers at the time.

Opposite page, far left
Little Flowers Falling, Moroso (2005), design by Studio Tord Boontje. Curtain/screen; microfibre, laser-cut. This delicate length of repeating laser-cut floral motifs shows the scope of laser cutting for both interior and fashion fabrics.

Left
Automatic Orgasm (2001) by Tracey Emin. Appliqué blanket, 263 x 214 cm (103 9/16 x 84 1/4 in). Using appliqué and embroidery, Emin blends talk-show television, tell-all newspaper exclusives and mass-media strategy with a folklore style of storytelling to reveal and edit her autobiography, in which she is both subject and therapist.

Although embroidery and fabric manipulation are predominantly used by textile designers to create designs for the interior and fashion markets, fine artists have begun to recognize their potential to communicate concepts. A case in point is the British artist Tracey Emin, who has used embroidery and appliqué techniques in the realization of a number of her installation pieces.

While textile design and fine art applications are visually prominent in many aspects of contemporary Western society, there are other regions in the world where embroidered and manipulated fabrics maintain rich cultural traditions and play an important role in local economies and community lifestyles; this is true of the embroidery work produced by local women's groups in the Eastern Cape region of South Africa. Traditional cultural textiles remain an area of fascination and a source of inspiration for many contemporary Western designers. This chapter explores the creative possibilities mixed media techniques offer to textile designers and also to fine artists.

Historical background

Needles with eyes, the main tool of the embroiderer, have existed since mankind began to develop early tools. Early needles with basic thread would have been used to sew together animal hides to make simple items of clothing. Embroidery from the Bronze Age (about 4500–1100 BC) has been found in Siberia and in the Middle East its history stretches back some 4000 years to the Babylonian, Phoenician and Hebrew cultures. In China embroidery dates to the Zhou dynasty (1100–256 BC). Embroidery is thought to have been inspired by tattooing, and there is evidence to support this: in Bulgaria and Tunisia tattoos have been translated into embroidery patterns and **Kuba cloth** from the Congo is inspired by traditional tattoos.

Although industrial embroidery is now the predominant commercial production method, hand embroidery has persisted. The French fabric manufacturer House of Lesage has played a pivotal role in this, through the twentieth century and into the twenty-first, by providing unique hand embroidery for its haute couture clients.

Quilting has a rich history in the Middle and Far East, and was brought to Europe by Crusaders who used the technique to make protective doublets which they wore under their chain mail or plate armour: unspun wool or cotton

Top
Detail from the 14th-century Tristan quilt. It is thought to have originated in Sicily, and the stuffed quilting technique was used to make it. It illustrates the legend of Tristan and the oppression of Cornwall by Languis of Ireland and his champion Morold.

Above
François Lesage works tirelessly to create innovative embroidered and beaded textiles for haute couture fashion houses.

was sandwiched between two pieces of linen, and vertical or diagonal cross-hatch stitching held the layers together. In his 2007 autumn/winter collection the fashion designer Alexander McQueen used contemporary interpretations of the technique for a number of his coats.

The fourteenth-century Guicciardini quilt, commonly known as the Tristan quilt, is an example of stuffed quilting. Here, cotton wool was introduced at the back of the work after the decorative stitching had been completed. The **ground fabric** between the motifs was sewn with close rows of running stitches in white linen thread, while the outlines of figures, ships and buildings were in backstitch, in a brownish thread.

The technique of pleating has a long history; the invention of the folding fan in Japan is just one early example. In the early twentieth century the fashion designer Mariano Fortuny pioneered the tight pleating of satin silk, a technique that is still not completely understood today. Contemporary fashion designer Issey Miyake continues this now established tradition of pleating in fashion design.

Embroidered textile design

The embroidery industry is international and extensive, ranging from haute couture to lingerie, the largest market sector for the technique. Embroidered textiles offer an array of creative possibilities for designers once they have acquired the basic techniques and knowledge of tools and materials.

Hand embroidery

In Victorian England girls were taught to embroider on samplers that depicted family events, such as births, deaths and weddings, among many other themes. Since then, even though traditional **stitch** techniques persist, hand embroidery has evolved in vision and creativity – a result of designers and artists seeing that its potential is virtually limitless. The contemporary British artist Grayson Perry has created his own interpretation of the traditional sampler in his Recipe for Humanity.

Design and production

The basic items needed to produce hand embroidery are needle, thread and a ground cloth to work into. An **embroidery hoop** or **frame** creates a stable, tensile fabric surface. A metal or plastic thimble protects the sewer's finger and can be used to push the needle into the cloth.

Needles, threads and fabrics

There are a number of different types of needle, each of which is designed for a specific sewing activity. Embroidery needles are similar to sewing ones, but have a bigger eye so that thicker threads can be inserted more easily. A large needle with a sharp point is a **glover**, and is used for sewing on leather. A shorter needle is used for hand stitching quilts, to enable the

Top
Bronze duchesse silk quilted coat by Alexander McQueen. 2007 autumn/winter collection. In memory of Elizabeth Howe, Salem, 1692.

Above
Recipe for Humanity (2005) by Grayson Perry. Embroidery, 48.5 x 36.5 cm (19 x 14 3/8 in). Edition of 250 plus 10 artist's proofs. From The Charms of Lincolnshire exhibition, 2006.

embroiderer to work through the fabric layers more easily. A very fine, long needle is used for **beadwork** and for sewing sequins on to fabric. A milliner uses specialist needles.

Threads for embroidery come in a variety of types, from natural fibres such as wool and silk to synthetic ones like polyester and rayon. Metal threads, **raffia** string, plastic and leather, as well as plain and fancy yarns, can also be used. The fabric options are extensive, ranging from transparent materials like silk georgette to heavier woollen cloths, and the type of cloth influences the overall aesthetic of a design. A number of companies, of which Zweigart is one of the most well known, produce specialist embroidery fabrics. One novel group of fabrics used for embroidery is dissolvable; when the embroidery, which can be created mechanically as well as by hand, is complete, heat is applied to the fabric using an iron or hot water, which then dissolves leaving only the embroidery. Cold water will also dissolve some types of this specialist fabric.

A design can be achieved by working freehand on the fabric and referring to the original design, or it can be drawn on tracing paper and then transferred to the cloth. Its lines are pricked with a fine needle to perforate the paper and the tracing is placed over the cloth and made secure. Chalk powder mixed with crushed **gum arabic** and methylated spirit is applied to the paper and filters through the fine holes so that the design is marked on the cloth. Where a design is complex, this type of planning ahead applies to machine as well as hand embroidery.

Stitch types

The movement of the needle from the back of the cloth to the front and back again is called a stitch, as is the visible thread that appears on the front of the cloth. In the context of embroidery, a stitch is one or more stitches that are produced in the same way to achieve a recognizable style. The stitch is the smallest motif in embroidery.

Straight stitch

Straight stitches pass through the cloth ground in a basic up and down movement. Running, whipped running and simple satin stitch are examples of this technique.

Backstitch

In a basic backstitch the needle comes up from the back of the cloth, makes a stitch to the right and then goes down to the back of the cloth. The needle then passes behind the first stitch and comes up to the front of the cloth to the left of the first stitch. The needle goes down to the back of the cloth through the hole the stitch first came up from. It repeats the action to the left of the stitches and continues. Stem stitch is an example of this technique.

Chain stitch

A chain stitch catches a loop of the thread on the surface of the cloth. In basic

Opposite page
A hand-stitched sampler showing a variety of stitch types.

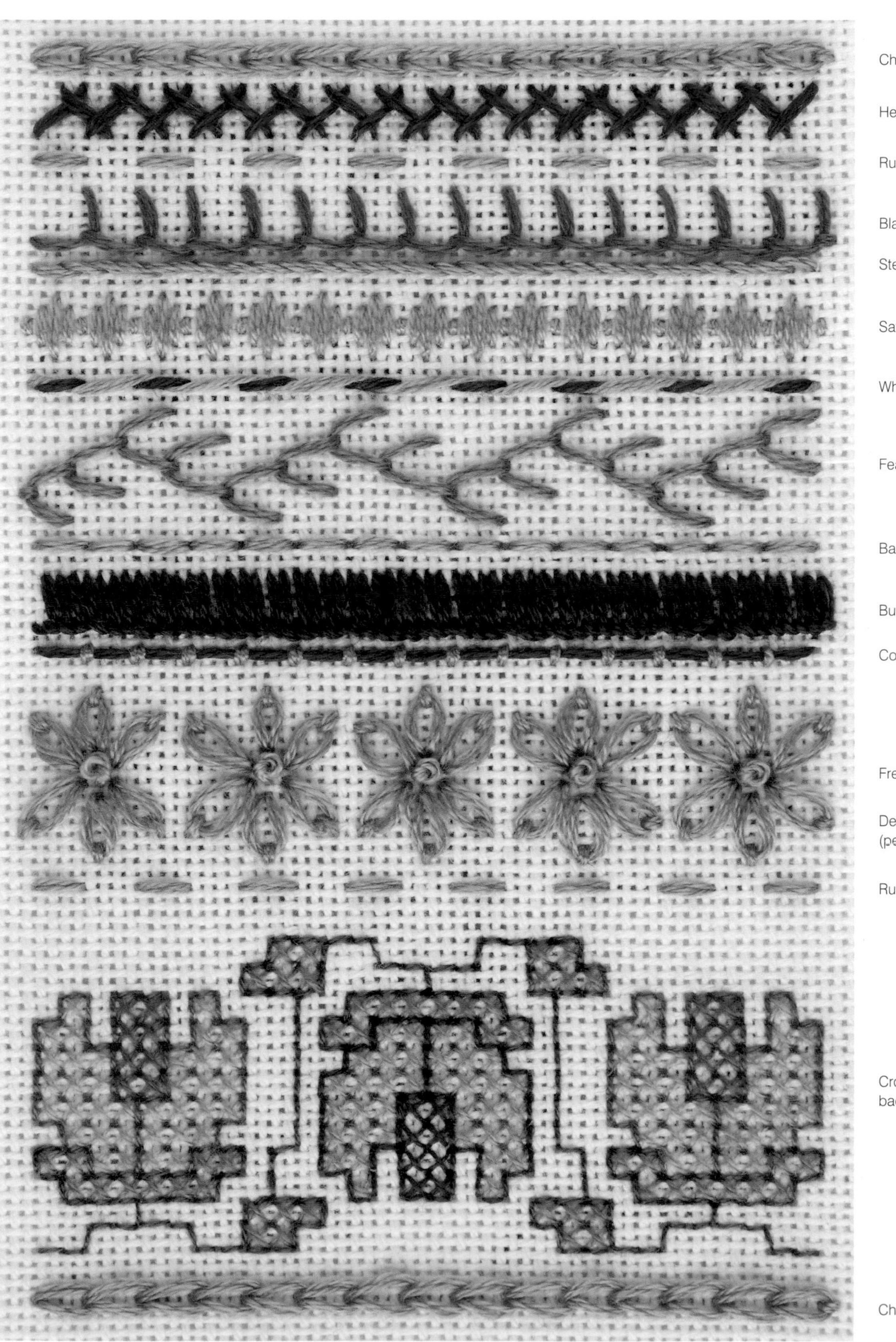
Chain stitch
Herringbone stitch
Running stitch
Blanket stitch
Stem stitch
Satin stitch
Whipped running stitch
Feather stitch
Backstitch
Buttonhole stitch
Couching
French knot (in middle)
Detached chain stitch (petals)
Running stitch
Cross stitch (with backstitch outline)
Chain stitch

chain stitch the needle comes up from the back of the cloth and then returns into the hole it came out of, pulling the loop of thread almost completely through to the back; before the loop disappears, the needle comes back and passes through the loop to prevent all of it being pulled to the back of the cloth. The needle then goes down to the back of the cloth and then up through the fabric again to create a second hole to begin the next stitch.

Blanket stitch

A blanket stitch is not unlike a chain stitch as it catches a loop of the thread on the surface of the cloth. The difference is that the needle does not return to the original hole to go to the back of the cloth; instead, it returns to the back of the fabric at a right angle to the hole. The original function of blanket stitch was to finish blanket edges but it is also the basis for forms of needle lace.

Feather stitch

A feather stitch also catches a loop thread on the surface of the fabric. It differs from blanket stitch in that the needle is not returned to the back of the fabric at a right angle to the original hole. It produces an effect that lends itself to plant forms.

Cross stitch

A cross stitch is created by producing a diagonal stitch, or line of stitches, in one direction and then crossing the diagonal stitch, or the line of stitches, in the other direction. The herringbone stitch is an example of this technique.

Knotted stitch

A knotted stitch is created by wrapping the thread around the needle before passing it to the back of the cloth. The number of times it is wrapped determines the type of effect that is produced. French and Chinese knots are examples of this technique.

Couching

Couching requires two threads; one is 'laid' on the surface of the fabric while the other binds the laid thread to the fabric. The laid thread may be heavier than the attaching thread, or it may be a thread with which it is not possible to embroider – threads made of metal are an example. Any type of stitch, such as cross stitch or straight stitch can be used to bind the laid thread to the fabric. Pendant, oriental and battlement are other types of couching techniques.

This selection is a small but representative cross section of a vast pool of stitch types, and embroidery becomes increasingly interesting when a designer uses this resource inventively. Karen Nicol has produced work for many leading fashion designers and has branched out into interior and art projects, illustrating the scope for embroidery in the visual arts.

Experimental embroidery pieces by the designer Karen Nicol (2008), who explores the creative and technical boundaries of embroidery through inventive applications to a variety of contexts ranging from fashion to interiors and art exhibitions.

Machine embroidery

A variety of machines can be used to create embroidered textiles and artworks and the type used influences the technical and aesthetic characteristics of the finished piece. Artists Satoru Aoyama and Carol Shinn use machine embroidery to create photorealist works that vividly demonstrate how it can be manipulated to realize contemporary and refreshingly creative ideas. In the case of Aoyama, he begins by taking a photograph of the subject he wants to embroider and traces its contours on to polyester **organza**. He then works with polyester thread, using an old industrial sewing machine to create his photorealistic embroidery.

Easeful City by Satoru Aoyama (2005) combines photography and embroidery on polyester with super realist results. 56 x 40.2 cm (22 x 15 13/16 in), photograph by Keizo Kioku.

Design and production

Sewing machines are designed to be used manually but increasingly, whether domestic or industrial, they contain digital elements. Typically, hand-operated machines are used in domestic contexts, and for sampling and high-end or small-scale production. However, in large-scale manufacturing of low- to medium-cost products, such as embroidered T-shirts and cap badges, the fast turnaround required by customers demands effective technology, and 12-needle multihead digital embroidery machines are normally used. These have a number of advantages; for example, over 40 designs can be stored to memory and they are supported by dedicated embroidery design and manufacture software. This type of technology is capable of producing 1500 stitches per minute.

Specialist embroidery machines provide additional creative options. The Cornelly is used for free surface decoration and specializes in chain stitch. There is no needle, so a hook pulls the thread up through the cloth from under the machine. The Cornelly is controlled by a crank handle underneath the machine that can turn in a full 360-degree circle enabling flowing curves or circles to be designed. The Irish is also used for free surface decoration and specializes in zigzag satin stitch.

Feeding a fabric through a machine is done either mechanically or manually, depending on the type of fabric, technique and machine. Mechanically, the **feed dog** mechanism which consists of metal teeth lifts up and down and moves the fabric forward on an embroidery machine. The **needle plate** works in conjunction with the feed dog to ensure the effective movement of fabric through the stitching process. The manual feed method is used primarily in freehand embroidery – and also in quilting. A hoop or frame is needed to keep the material in tension and help move it around when it is being embroidered. Often mechanical feeding can be altered on a machine to allow for manual feeding by lowering the feed dogs beneath the needle plate.

Just as there are different feed systems, there are differing mechanical configurations. For most household and industrial sewing machines the most common of these is the flatbed, which is self-explanatory: the material is fed across a simple horizontal surface.

Stitch types

Like hand embroidery, machine embroidery has a repertoire of stitch types ranging from straight stitch, chain stitch and zigzag to programmed novelty stitches.

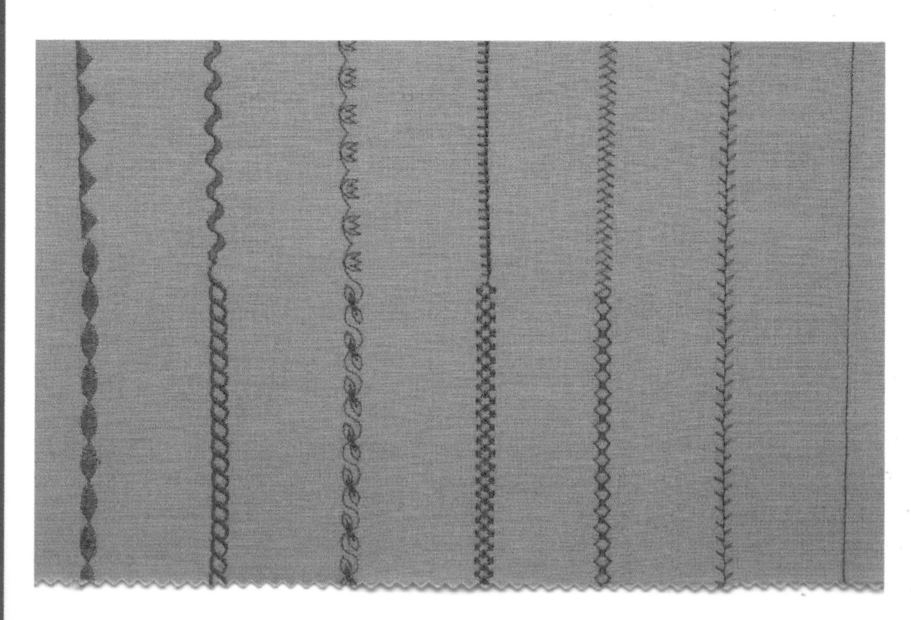

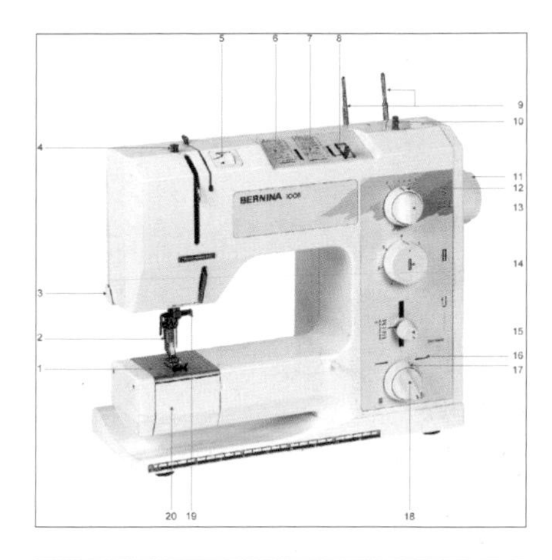

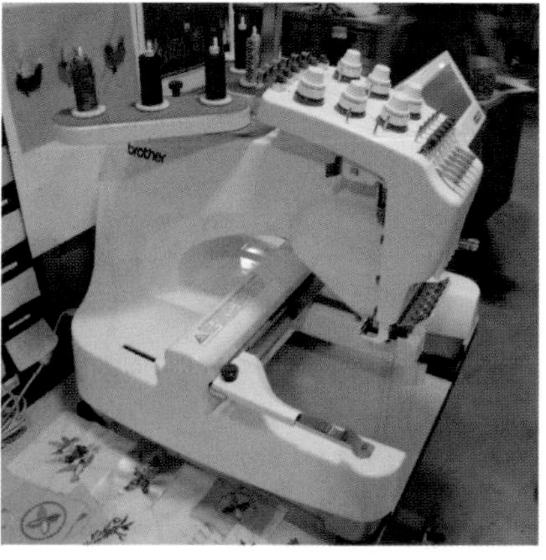

Top
A manually operated Bernina sewing machine.

Above
The 12-needle, 4-head digital embroidery machine with an operation control terminal and supporting CAD consul has become popular commercially as it is quick and efficient. Digital embroidery, like digital jacquard and digital printing, is now being utilized by designers and artists.

Left
Decorative embroidery techniques using a Bernina sewing machine, based on straight stitch, chain stitch, zigzag satin stitch and programmed novelty stitch – just basic examples from a larger range of options.

Beadwork

Many cultures throughout the world produce beadwork that is complex and aesthetically individual, and in the West embroidering cloth with beads, sequins and similar materials is a highly developed and creative area in which the contemporary textile-design companies Jakob Schlaepfer and NUNO have excelled (see pages 130–31). One of the partnerships that utilized beadwork most creatively was that of Cristóbal Balenciaga and François Lesage, who had developed embroidered fabrics for Elsa Schiaparelli. In his designs Balenciaga captured the atmosphere and culture of his native Spain by creatively and generously applying beading and embroidery to garments. He was inspired by the embroidered costumes worn by matadors. Known as suits of light, these are designed to catch the sun with sequins, gems and gold thread used in the embroidery to trap the light. The suits display a variety of recurring motifs which have been assigned names such as vase, wave, Aztec and pine cone.

There is a vast pool of bead and sequin types with which to design. The **peyote stitch** is a hand stitching technique used to create a solid flexible fabric of beads or a solid motif of beads for sewing on to a ground fabric; the Zulu jewellery of South Africa is designed and made using this stitch. **Netting** is similar in that it creates a fabric, in this case a loose one resembling a net, made by sewing strings of beads together. Hand sewing single beads on to a fabric is the simplest beadwork technique.

In **tambour beading** the background fabric is usually transparent and is stretched on an embroidery frame, which is held face down; the working is done from the back of the frame and fabric. A long line of beads is threaded together and held beneath the frame, after which a tambour hook is passed through the fabric from the back and pivoted to catch the thread between two beads. It then pulls the thread back up to form a loop, which is in fact a chain stitch. The hook goes back down through the loop to catch the thread between the next two beads and brings this up in a loop to the surface, catching the previous loop as a stitch on the back of the fabric. It is important to outline the design on the fabric in advance so that there is a clear guide to assist in sewing the beads.

Embroidery is used in many contexts both cultural and commercial. Its use for church vestments and accessories, where it displays symbolic and religious motifs, is culturally significant, while the motifs in military and state contexts signify rank and position. In Britain companies like Hand and Lock have considerable expertise in these markets. Embroidery is also popular in theatre and film, and one of its most extravagant manifestations, where it appears along with beadwork, is in the costumes designed for the Mardi Gras in New Orleans.

Above
This black embroidered garment by Cristóbal Balenciaga (1895–1972) captures the recurring Spanish cultural influence upon his fabrics and fashion designs (early 1930s).

Opposite
The rich use of embroidery materials, techniques and patterns on a matador's jacket graphically illustrate the fine craft of embroidery at its pinnacle. This highly reflective decoration led to matador costumes called 'suits of light'.

Detailed elements from the Keiskamma altarpiece, South Africa (2006/07).

The Keiskamma altarpiece: an African embroidery project

In 2007 Carol Brown, project/curatorial consultant and a former Director of the Durban Art Gallery, brought to the attention of the international community a unique embroidery project from the fishing village of Hamburg in the Eastern Cape Province in South Africa. Instigated by Dr Carol Hofmeyer, a medical doctor and talented artist, the Keiskamma Project aims to empower local women economically and provide self-esteem through art and creativity against the backdrop that many are HIV-positive.

One of the most significant pieces created by the project is the Keiskamma altarpiece, which was inspired by photographs of the sixeenth-century Issenheim altarpiece created when the disease known as St Anthony's fire, which has surprising parallels to the AIDS pandemic, was prevalent in Europe. It took six months to complete with a group of ten women working on each panel. Weekly meetings ensured that styles and colours were consistent, and the companionship of the women who met to stitch the panels was undoubtedly therapeutic as it gave them time to discuss problems in a 'safe space'.

Embroidering the altarpiece was an immense creative act by the women of the Eastern Cape amid illness and death. Opening the panels is a dramatic performance and emphasizes the sacredness of the space, with the interior progressively revealed through the action of the participants.

In another piece called the Keiskamma Tapestry supported by Keiskamma Friends, the design echoes characteristics of the Bayeux Tapestry, but instead represents the history of the San and Xhosa people of the Eastern Cape of South Africa. This monumental 120-metre artwork purchased by The Standard Bank is now on long-term loan to the South African Parliament, where it is displayed.

The Keiskamma altarpiece, in the Eastern Cape Province in South Africa, was the result of an embroidery initiative that set out to empower local women economically, and provide release and therapy in a society where there has been a high incidence of HIV and subsequent deaths from AIDS.

Opposite, top
The closed altarpiece illustrates the crucifixion, using local Xhosa motifs. The traditional biblical characters are replaced by local men and women from the fishing village of Hamburg and surrounding areas of the Eastern Cape.

Opposite, bottom
When the first panels are opened, the altarpiece reveals a vision of hope, redemption and restoration.

Fabric manipulation

Fabric manipulation provides a window into some of the most creative and innovative approaches to textile design and includes techniques such as quilting, appliqué, pleating and laser cutting.

A designer who is widely regarded as an innovator in fashion and art is Hussein Chalayan, whose art project Afterwords, performed in 2000, is widely acclaimed. Fabric manipulation and transformation were fundamental factors in enabling and activating the successful execution of the project. Motivated by events in Kosovo and the plight of refugees during wars, Chalayan connected the refugee theme to the concealment and camouflage of valuable possessions and transporting them to safety. During the performance piece, which was set in a white room containing chairs and a coffee table, models dressed in simple underslips removed the covers from the chairs and wore them as dresses. The chairs themselves folded to become suitcases and the coffee table was turned into a skirt. By the end of the performance the room was devoid of life.

In a slightly different context, but one that is related in some respects, textiles can be manipulated to create mobile transportable dwellings. The tepee of the native North Americans and the yurt in Inner Mongolia are salient examples, and the United Nations has developed tents that can rapidly be deployed in refugee camps and after natural disasters.

Left
A yurt in Inner Mongolia, showing how felt and canvas can be used innovatively to construct portable dwellings.

Opposite, top
In Afterwords, a performance project by Hussein Chalayan (2000), a coffee table transforms into a skirt.

Opposite, bottom
Also in Afterwords, furnishing fabrics on chairs become garments.

Quilting

The main function of the quilt, whether worn as a garment or used in an interior context, has been to protect and to provide warmth: the most commonly designed product has always been the bedding quilt.

The technique of quilting has an established history in many parts of the world, and has produced extraordinarily innovative aesthetics and products,

but perhaps the most intriguing recent phenomenon originated in Gee's Bend on the Alabama River in the United States. Freed plantation slaves founded the purely black community of Gee's Bend which through the twentieth century developed an individual style of quilt-making without the incentives of patronage or commerce. With their generally minimalist geometric form, and the collage-like process used to make them, the quilts became instruments of artistic discourse, a means of talking visually to ancestors, peers, relatives, neighbours, followers and, occasionally, rivals. They were often made with recycled fabrics, and in some circumstances utilized the possessions of deceased spouses, parents, siblings or children, embodying the power, or at least the memory, of departed ancestors and loved ones. Today the quilts are highly valued and are collected by museums.

A totally different perspective on quilting has been pioneered by contemporary product designer Tokujin Yoshioka in his Panna, a chair suitable for mass production, which has a jacket made from the kind of quilted fabric used to protect precision machinery in transit. Yoshioka explains: 'I don't just start looking for materials when I'm asked to design something... I always have materials and ideas on hand. When I get a new offer, I simply pull an idea out of the drawer.' This recent project illustrates his fascination with natural phenomena and his eye for materials. He continues to challenge perceptions of product design methods by carrying out pioneering experiments with materials rather than concentrating on form. 'I like spending a lot of time developing the concept and focusing on the material.' It's a process that allows him to move with ease among disciplines.

The Spanish designer Patricia Urquiola has produced a range of products that utilize a variety of media, techniques and materials. Her design repertoire

Above, left
House Top is a four-block pattern designed and quilted by Mary L. Bennett, a member of the Gee's Bend quilters collective, in about 1965. The quilt is made from cotton and a cotton/polyester blend.

Above, right
House Top variation designed by Mary Lee Bendolph in 1998 and subsequently quilted by Essie Bendolph in 2001. The quilt is made from cotton corduroy, twill and assorted polyesters.

Opposite, top
Panna Chair, a mass-producible prototype by Tokujin Yoshioka (2008).

Opposite page, bottom left
Chair from Patricia Urquiola's Antibodi range for Moroso. Like the chaise longue, its quilted cover is reversible. Whether the petals face upwards or downwards, both options achieve strong aesthetic results.

Opposite page, bottom right
Chaise longue from the Antibodi, 'cellular' genesis range designed for Moroso by Patricia Urquiola (2006). Its quilted cover can be used with the petals facing either upwards or downwards.

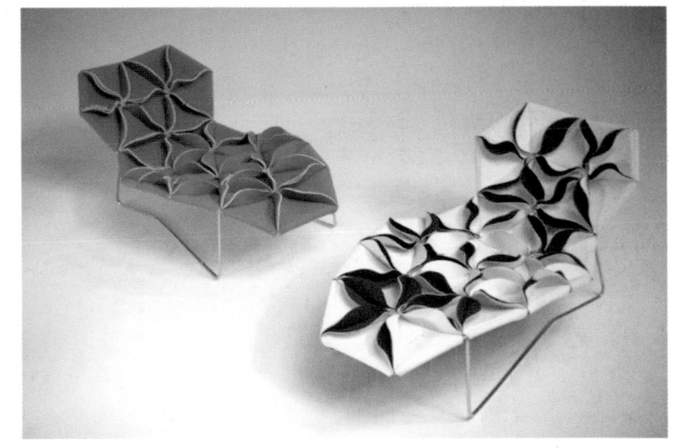

was notable in her exhibition at the Abitare il Tempo trade fair in Verona in 2007. The quilted textile designs for a chaise longue and chair in the Antibodi range were developed from a 'cellular' genesis of lightly padded petals, sewn in triangular shapes to create bold patterns. The petals feature reversible materials: felt and wool fabric, and leather and wool, each paired to create a supporting cover that is fixed to a stainless-steel frame. The cover creates two very different and striking moods. With the petals facing upwards a more unconventional, feminine version is achieved through the felt and wool combination; when they face downwards the wool and leather pairing gives the cover a deliberately severe, quilted appearance.

Design and production

Quilting is a stitching technique that fastens three layers of cloth together: the **top cloth**; the middle cloth known as the **wadding** or **batting**, which can be cotton, wool or polyester; and the bottom layer, called the **lining**. The top and lining materials can be any type of cloth, depending on functional and financial requirements. In patchwork quilts the entire top layer can be made by stitching smaller pieces of fabric together to create a patchwork effect before the three layers are quilted, like the Gee's Bend quilts. Once all three elements have been sewn together the result is a stable textile that is more than the sum of its parts. The stitching indents a design into the malleable layers and can be done either by hand or mechanically. The aesthetic effect and the quality of the padded surface differ depending on which method is used.

While small stitches were traditionally intrinsic to the hand-quilting aesthetic, more inventive contemporary methods have adopted the decorative qualities of embroidery. Although there is no prescribed process, and there is ample opportunity to deconstruct standard patterns, in both hand and machine quilting there is an established tendency towards recurring design themes that are broad in scope. These range from abstract geometric forms to more pictorial commemorative and political quilts like that of an American ninteenth-century Confederate appliqué quilt and more recent American quilts to honour soldiers lost in the conflicts in Afghanistan and Iraq.

In hand quilting, control when pulling the thread through the fabrics is essential as its tension must be correct in order to indent the stitches effectively into the surface of the textile. If the tension is too high the quilted fabric will look distorted. The running stitch is commonly used but the backstitch and **stab stitch** are alternatives. The edge finish for a quilt is important. A method that is often used for this involves binding the edge by turning excess lining fabric to the front of the quilt and neatening its edge by turning it under, before sewing through all the layers.

For machine-guided quilting, a design with straight and slightly curved lines is the easiest to follow; angled and deeply curved lines require constant stops to redirect the stitching. As with all textile design, the key to success is to learn through testing out design ideas and practising techniques.

Cording, which involves stitching a cord into the cloth, is often used in quilting to create elevated linear forms on the surface of the textile and adds weight and firmness. The flexibility of the quilt is affected by the thickness and closeness of the cords and how tightly they are enclosed by the cloth. A stuffed quilt is created by inserting wool or fabric padding between two layers of cloth; this is confined within seamed boundaries that have an effect similar to cording. **Stuffing** creates a high or low **relief** surface which is achieved by developing design motifs that are cut out from the stuffing material and stitched between the quilting fabrics. It adds height and weight but reduces flexibility.

Wade by Anna Keck, appliqué and photogravure (2006), is one piece from a collection of works inspired by old family photographs, and which explores the simplicity of life that the photographs depict.

Appliqué

Appliqué is a versatile technique that can incorporate a number of other mixed media methods. It is applied in a variety of interior and fashion contexts and sits comfortably in the design, art and craft disciplines. This is particularly apparent when considering the fine artist Tracey Emin and her use of appliqué in her work featured at the start of this chapter (see p. 107). The appliqué Asafo flags discussed in a profile in this chapter (see p. 126) graphically illustrate the design and craft skills that can be deployed within this textile technique. A positive quality of appliqué is that it can produce a finished outcome relatively quickly, although this depends on the complexity of the design.

Anna Keck has used the technique to communicate her artistic concepts. The current inspiration for her textile pieces is her desire to step away from the complexities of modern American society, and old family photographs are a direct influence on her work. This nostalgia for lost rural lifestyles is perhaps best captured in Wade, which combines appliqué with **photogravure**.

Design and production

Appliqué involves stitching different fabrics to a background cloth to create a textile piece, either by hand or with a machine. The tools and materials required are the ones normally used in embroidery and quilting.

Asafo flags: appliqué and embroidery

The Asafo flags of the Fante people of southern Ghana are a unique combination of appliqué and embroidery. They originated in the small states along the country's Cape Coast area and date back to at least the eighteenth century. Historically, there were rivalries between states over who traded with European merchants and the flags were made for the competing military companies known as Asafo that emerged as a result. The challenge to a rival state was proclaimed by the imagery on a flag.

The original inspiration for the flags comes from those displayed on European, mostly British, ships – an influence that is notable in early examples, which feature a Union Jack motif in the top left corner of the design. After 1957, when Ghana gained independence, this was replaced by the Black Star, the country's national flag. There is usually a single ground colour in the remaining area of the flag, to which pieces of cloth of contrasting colours are applied. These are cut into the shapes of people, animals, plants, pools of water, atmospheric phenomena, monsters, aeroplanes and other artefacts and are, for the most part, immediately recognizable. The selection and combinations of motifs in a design are narrative-based and depend on a proverb that is appropriate to the circumstances in which a particular flag was made. Flags are intended to challenge, but are also a source of knowledge through the proverbs they communicate pictorially. The textiles used are European, and the shapes are sometimes cut from damask tablecloths, though lightweight cotton is more usual.

This appliqué Asafo flag, made of cotton and designed by A. Achempong (c.1935), shows an elephant grasping a palm tree, a man with a bird on his head and a bystander.

Most appliqué methods require a backing cloth, although this is not essential. Its overall size should be 10 cm (4 in) larger than the finished design to allow for **seams**, hems or **mounting**, depending on what the textile will be used for. An initial stage in creating an appliqué piece involves positioning the design elements on the background fabric. This can be done by eye or, where precision is crucial, by tracing the design on to the cloth. Appliqué generally consists of precise shapes that correspond to shapes in a design originally developed on paper, and paper patterns or templates must be cut from a tracing of the original design. Alternatively, dressmaker's **carbon paper** can be pinned on to the fabric. The design, placed on top, is then traced and transferred on to the fabric, which can then be cut out. If the appliqué design is complex, numbers can be given to the shapes on the original design and each tracing given a corresponding number to indicate the order in which the appliqué fabrics will be applied to the background cloth. How design motifs are marked on the appliqué fabrics or cut out of them depends on personal preference, but some methods work well on some materials and less well on others. For example, it is difficult to make marks on felt, and shapes are therefore most effectively cut out by pinning the paper template to it. However, this is not possible when cutting shapes out of materials like leather or suede as it is difficult to pin paper to them, so the shapes are marked on their reverse sides with a fabric marker. When doing this it is important to remember that each template must be positioned right side down, or the cut shape will be a mirror image not an exact copy.

While shapes that have been cut from a non-fraying fabric can be attached to the background cloth without turning the edges under, **turned-edge appliqué** is usually used with fabrics that **fray** – although it is also possible simply to stitch them into position using a zigzag satin stitch to cover the edges. To prevent fraying in fabrics that are difficult to handle – such as fine silks, synthetics, nylons and polyesters, as well as some cotton fabrics – an iron-on **interfacing** can be applied before the shapes are cut out. An alternative is to use a **fusible web** material, which produces a flatter effect than interfacing when the cut shapes are applied to the ground cloth. As well as being used for fabrics that fray, turned-edge appliqué is suitable for ones that are fine enough to allow a **hem** to be turned under neatly. It is also used where a **blind edge**, without decorative stitching, is required and for padded appliqué to prevent fraying.

The stitching techniques for appliqué are as varied as they are for embroidery, but the ones that are most frequently used are the hidden and appliqué stitch, and the zigzag stitch. Reliefs can be applied in appliqué in the same way that they can in quilting, using stuffing between cut fabrics and background cloth.

Pleating and related manipulations

In simple terms the pleat is a double or multiple folding in a garment or other item made of cloth. Other related techniques include **gathering**, **ruffles** and **smocking** – just a few examples of the many creative options in this field of fabric manipulation.

A number of fashion designers have seized on the creative potential within the traditions of pleating cloth. Junya Watanabe, in his **origami** garments constructed from **honeycomb weaves** that fold and pleat, is a classic example. And at Givenchy the young Italian designer Riccardo Tisci explored folding and pleating in his 2006/07 autumn/winter collection, which balanced precise tailoring with more sculptural forms to unique effect.

Design and production

Traditionally, pleats are measured folds formed at the edge of a piece of fabric where they are secured with stitching. Beyond the stitching, they become loose folds that continue the arrangement set at the edge, where they are either levelled or manipulated to project. They are released in sharply creased order through heating and pressure or are unpressed and modify into softly spreading rolls. Fabric measurements are reduced at the source of the pleats, and the full extent of the fabric becomes apparent where the folds are unconfined. There are many types of pleat, such as flat, partial and double controlled pleats.

Top
This original yellow pleated dress by Junya Watanabe is constructed from honeycomb weaves that fold and pleat as they fit around the human form. 2000 autumn/winter collection.

Above
In this dress by Riccardo Tisci for Givenchy his powers of invention are shown in the creative way he has utilized and contemporised the traditional process of pleating. Givenchy 2006/07 autumn/winter collection, haute couture.

Issey Miyake is perhaps one of the most innovative of the fashion designers who have embraced technology, and pleats set by heat pressure have become synonymous with his label. His classic pleated Minaret dress from 1995 incorporates a plastic hoop and is designed to be suspended from the wearer's shoulders so that with each movement the garment moves like a Japanese lantern swinging in the wind.

Many other folding and pleating methods have been assigned names to distinguish them as specific techniques. Gathering converts the edge of a piece of fabric into mini folds that are bunched together on thread. It reduces the fabric measurement at the stitching line, and beyond the gathered stitching the full extent of the fabric expands into irregular folds. When strips of fabric are gathered on opposite sides, variable folds flow between rigid edges. Both hand and machine stitching achieve the required results.

A ruffle is a strip of fabric that is reduced in length by gathering or pleating, which releases folds that make up a floating edge. Ruffles have been used in the past, and continue to be used, for structural decoration on a garment – for example, on a sleeve or collar. A ruffle can be narrow or wide, and have either one or two floating edges that hang down, stand up or extend sideways. Ruffling is a very flexible technique that can be applied to achieve both basic and complex designs, either singly or in combination, separated or crowded, localized or all over a garment.

Smocking uses hand stitching to secure and adjust the folds of a finely pleated area of cloth. When the stitching is visible it superimposes a decorative design on the surface of the pleats and simultaneously orders and bends the underlying folds into cellular formations. When the stitching is invisible, the pleated folds become the decorative focus. Smocked fabric acquires the same thickness as its pleats and therefore loses flexibility across the pleated area.

As with most techniques, when fabric manipulation is combined with another method the overall creative result can be enhanced, whether the method is from within the discipline of mixed media or from within another textile discipline such as printed textile design.

Laser cutting and engraving

In his laser-cut Little Flowers Falling, Tord Boontje exemplifies the aesthetic possibilities of laser cutting in relation to interior textile design. The technique has also added a creative tool to the armoury of the fashion designer. Since the late 1990s it has increasingly been applied to generate new textiles for use in haute couture and ready-to-wear fashion design. In the adventurous, sports-led 2008 autumn/winter collection for Miu Miu, a more affordable Prada range than its haute couture counterpart, designer Miuccia Prada made imaginative use of the technique, with **neoprene** wetsuit shapes and bold laser-cut patterns that achieved a dramatic and powerful effect on the catwalk.

Top
Issey Miyake transformed the way pleats are used in fashion. This is perhaps most effectively exemplified in his classic Minaret dress, designed in 1995.

Above
Issey Miyake collaborated with James Dyson in 2008, working around the concept of wind in all its forms. He dynamically integrated his methods of pleating and origami folding and pleating to dramatic effect. 2008 spring/summer collection, Pleats Please.

The red smocked theatre curtain designed for the Hackney Empire in London by Petra Blaisse (2005) transcends former perceptions of smocking applications. Her unique vision highlights the inventiveness that is increasingly being applied to established textile techniques.

Jakob Schlaepfer and Welsh/Huddleston: laser-embellished textiles

Jakob Schlaepfer of St Gallen, Switzerland, is famous worldwide for the design and manufacture of innovative textiles for haute couture and ready-to-wear collections. Among the designers who use its fabrics are Karl Lagerfeld at Chanel, Louis Vuitton, Jean Paul Gaultier, Vivenne Westwood and Georges Chakra.

Founded in 1904 as an embroidery business, Schlaepfer has become synonymous with advanced design and manufacture. Since 1960 developments in its production methods have enabled traditional embroidery techniques to be combined with machine-made sequins, crystals and 3-D embellishing and digital printing. Led by Schlaepfer's creative director Martin Leuthold, the in-house design and production team produces textiles in which techniques and materials are often integrated, customized or mixed with those sourced from outside: an approach which enables the design and manufacturing process to be as versatile as possible.

In 1998 Schlaepfer developed and expanded its laser technology, becoming the first textile producer to industrialize the laser cutting of textiles so that they could be used for fashion. The technology interacts with its other production techniques and provides a wide range of possibilities for structural innovations and embellishment.

In 2006 textile designer Cheryl Welsh approached Schlaepfer with a novel laser process for embellishing metallized fabrics, an idea with which she had been experimenting since 2002. Welsh, with a background in jewellery and silversmithing as well as textile design, had discovered the laser process when she was researching embroidery with precious metals, with the intention of reinventing its richness for contemporary applications. She explored fine-gauge metal, goldwork embroidery, and adaptations of metal and stitch techniques, and her research was also inspired by Indian metal filaments and gote, a metal thread decoration used in braids.

In 2002 Welsh won a Great Britain Sasakawa Foundation Award to visit Japan to support her research. There she sourced high-technology metal textiles as substrates to receive experimental stitch and other embellishment treatments. On her return to England she began by applying computer-controlled laser technology designed for hard materials to the fabricated metal textiles sourced in Japan and to her own fabricated metal textiles. The first tests produced a variety of delicate structures. They demonstrated how a laser could be used as a fine tool, capable of interacting with complex new material, to produce new decorative forms. These sample fabrics showed great design potential, meriting industrial production. To move to this stage in an environment that would give the greatest creative scope meant finding a suitable industrial partner. Welsh identified Jakob Schlaepfer as the textile producer potentially capable of moving the research forward from sampling to the highest standards of industrial production.

At the time that Welsh approached Schlaepfer with her samples Leuthold was already looking for new laser possibilities with a view to planning the next stage of the company's development in this area. When he saw the fabrics developed by Welsh he recognized the potential for a collaboration that could lead to using the process industrially.

Developing the process involved researching design and production software, machinery, methods of manufacture and potential substrates. Directed by Leuthold, a project team of designers and engineers worked with Welsh on a design and production system that would provide the greatest creative flexibility together with high-quality production. Other members of the project team were Regula Stuedli, Robert Huddleston and Herwig Peter.

Regula Stuedli studied textile design at the School of Art and Design in Zurich, and developed digital printing for couture and interiors at Schlaepfer. Her CAD expertise enabled the design studio's methods to be integrated into the laser development. Robert Huddleston studied fine art at the Royal College of Art in London and collaborated with Welsh on developing the design possibilities of the laser process from the outset

Above, left
Laser-cut ribbon fabric by Jakob Schlaepfer for fashion designer Georges Chakra. 2008 winter collection.

Above, right
Laser-cut and printed fabric for fashion designer Georges Chakra. 2006 summer collection.

Opposite, top
Stitch, laser-treated aluminium-coated polyester sample (2004). Jakob Schlaepfer and Welsh/Huddleston collaboration.

Opposite, centre
Concentric Circles, laser-treated metallized polyester (2007), Jakob Schlaepfer and Welsh/Huddleston collaboration.

Opposite, bottom
Basel Mesh, laser-treated aluminium-coated polyester sample (2007), 16-spot repeat. Jakob Schlaepfer and Welsh/Huddleston collaboration.

of her research. Currently teaching textile design at the School of Art, University of Southampton, his interest in prints and drawing connects with the linearity of the process. In particular, his research, in 2003, into early Japanese printing, funded by the Arts and Humanities Research Council, provided graphic points of reference that complemented Welsh's focus on shape and materials. Herwig Peter is one of the technical designers at Schlaepfer who are involved from the earliest development stages of a textile and make it physically possible to produce the studio's designs. As a member of the project team, his expertise enabled an understanding of the complexity of possible software and materials interactions, based on the principles of the process.

Leuthold proposed developing a laser machine that would integrate cutting with the laser embellishment process introduced to the company by Welsh. Researching the machine began with the project team visiting two specialist St Gallen textile manufacturers, both of whom had worked with Schlaepfer over a number of years and had used the Schiffli machine for handling fabric to develop integrated laser cutting with embroidery and sequinned fabrics. The machine provided a possible solution for the proposed laser cutting and embellishing machine, as a length of fabric can remain static while the cutting and embellishing applications move across it; this gives maximum flexibility for the scale of designs and the precision required to combine cutting and embellishing.

While Schlaepfer is currently making final plans for using the new process in production, Leuthold and the project team envisage extensive further research and development, including designing special substrates: they recognize that there is immense scope in the sensitivity, precision and versatility of the technology. The high investment and commitment to research and development required to reach the production stage, and the plans that are being made for the future, exemplify how Schlaepfer are maintaining and enhancing their worldwide reputation for innovation and the highest quality standards.

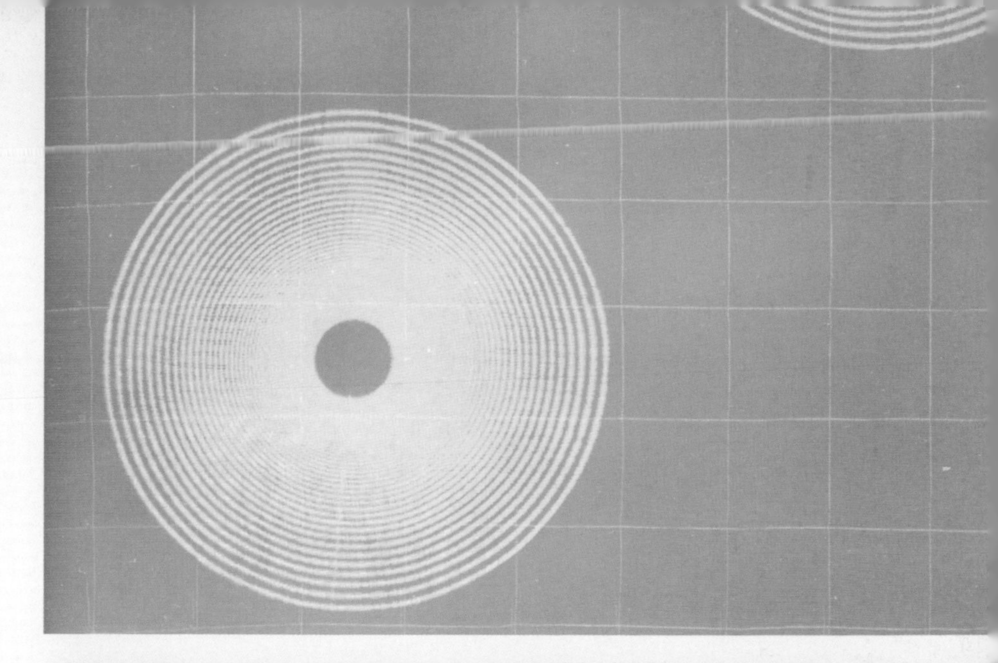

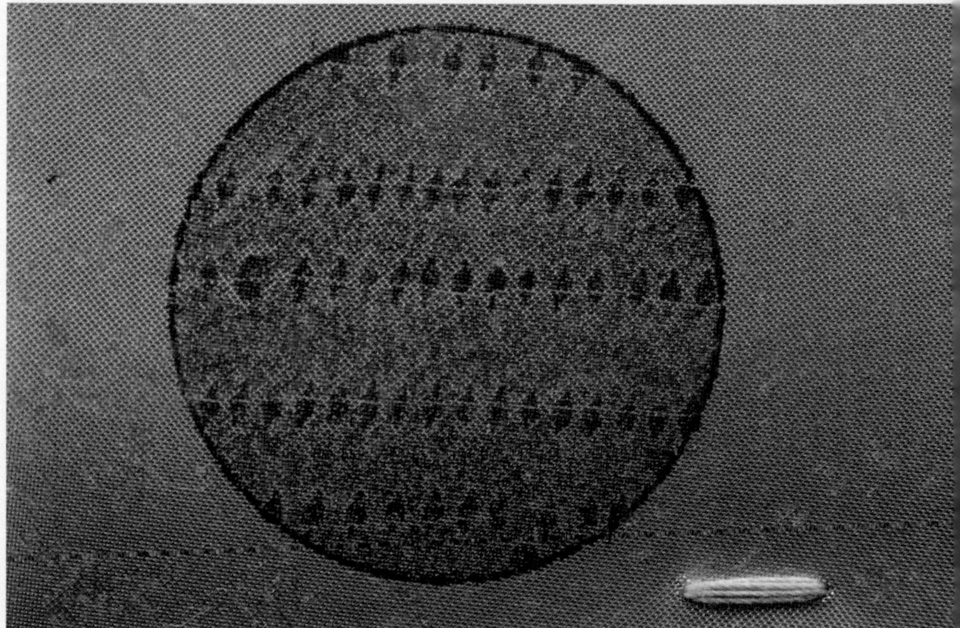

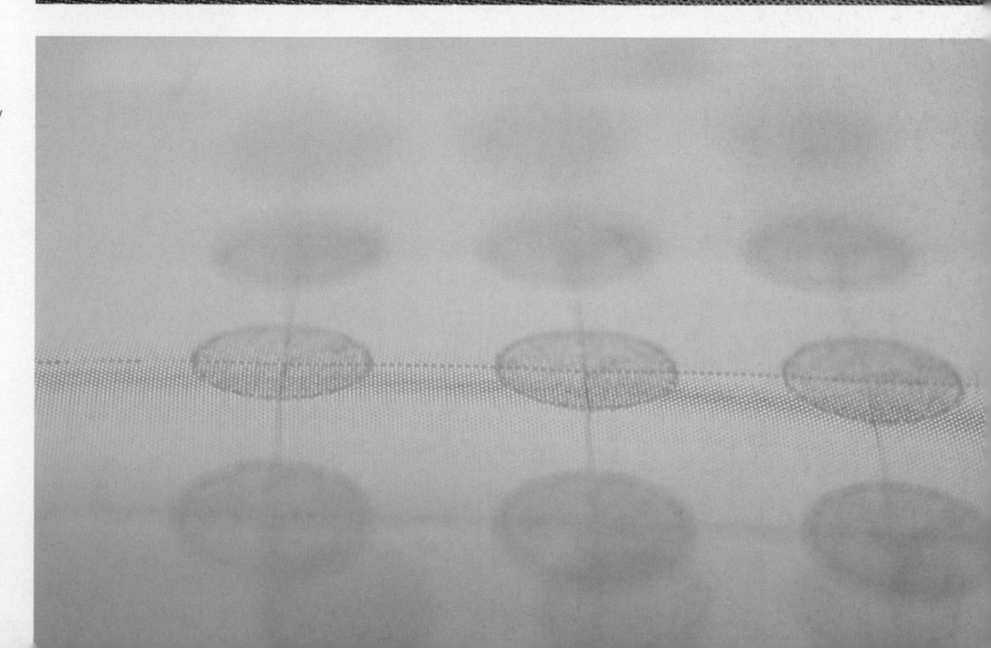

Design and production

Laser cutting is far superior to other cutting methods because it can cut intricate details on a broad variety of fabrics from light nylon and silk to sail fabrics containing **Kevlar**, a synthetic fibre of significant tensile strength. Its other applications include its widespread use in the fashion industry to cut out garment shapes, and it is popular in more niche areas such as balloon and kite design.

Laser cutting cloth involves a number of stages, the first of which is to input the pattern into the laser-cutting computer. The pattern can be generated by hand on paper or with computer-aided design (CAD), and is transferred on to the software in preparation for cutting. The textile fabric is then placed beneath the laser beam. Finally, controlled by the software, the laser beam moves over the material and burns out the pattern shapes.

A fine, clean and accurate depth of cut is achieved by software-controlled adjustments to the cutting speed and the power output of the laser. An air irrigation system attached to the cutting head sends a stream of air to the point of cutting to assist in controlling the cutting process. Fumes are drawn away through an extraction system.

Laser engraving is similar to laser cutting, with the fundamental difference that rather than cutting a hole through the fabric a pattern is engraved on its surface. It can effectively mimic hand processes to create patterned and **distressed** areas with precision and consistency, and is frequently used for this purpose on denim fabric; the laser beam burns away the indigo dye and patterns can be placed on any area of a pair of jeans, such as over the pockets or matched at the seams to create an overall design.

By adjusting the speed and power output of the laser beam different degrees of engraving can be created to generate differing engraved effects. Using the technique on pile fabrics like velvet and corduroy has proved successful: the laser burns away the pile in selected areas leaving a permanent pattern that closely mimics embossing.

Laser-cut garment designed by Miucci Prada. 2008 Miu Miu autumn/winter collection.

Innovation

Innovation in mixed media textile design can be manifested in many formats and combinations. This is apparent in the work of the Swedish artist Ulrika Erdes, whose imagination and creativity have led to an innovative use of embroidery. It seems she was initially inspired by graffiti and street artists such as Banksy in England and Blek le Rat in France. The fundamental difference between her and them is the media used and its relationship to its surface or context. Erdes has invented public embroidery, described as a new form of soft vandalism, which involves stitching that is performed covertly on woven seating on buses and trains. She uses cross stitching to realize her motifs, which currently include storks, birds and hearts as well as her personal signature. Looked at from a positive perspective, this novel idea enriches what is normally practical, public-transport fabric design. This soft vandalism – or radical art – depending on how it is viewed or who views it, is a fledgling

Ulrika Erdes has taken street art into a new realm with her covert cross stitching on public transport seating. This potentially controversial soft vandalism extends the conceptual and aesthetic boundaries of embroidery.

phenomenon. It will be interesting to see whether other artists become involved in soft vandalism, enabling it to spread beyond the Swedish border into other parts of Europe.

Still in the realm of innovation, but emerging from Anish Kapoor's Marsyas – an art installation the sculptor created in collaboration with the engineering company Arup for the Turbine Hall at the Tate Modern in London – fabric manipulation has been pushed further in terms of the concept, scale and form of an artwork, and the materials used to create it. Another equally significant contemporary project that involved fabric manipulation was the aptly named Cosmic Egg Pavilion, a structure with an asymmetric, large floating roof, lighter than air, that was temporarily erected next to the Serpentine Gallery in London in 2006. Architect Rem Koolhaas, and Director of Arup AGU, Cecil Balmond, together with Thomas Demand who created an interior wallpaper frieze, produced this particular phenomenon. The pavilion set a benchmark for future projects of this kind. The roof was a huge, translucent canopy, filled with helium, which rose and fell according to weather conditions. When it was cold and windy, the canopy lay low; on fine days, the cables holding it down were loosened and its bulbous form rose like a balloon, higher than the gallery itself.

The annual pavilion project at the Serpentine Gallery in London has generated innovative architectural solutions. This was the case with the 2006 Cosmic Egg Pavilion by architect Rem Koolhaas and Cecil Balmond of Arup. They designed a giant, helium-filled, translucent canopy for the pavilion that rose and fell depending on the weather.

Summary

The three innovations discussed above are representative of a large number of inspired projects that can be associated with mixed media textile design. With digital embroidery, and advances in fabric technology and engineering, this field will play an increasingly visible role in many societies – not only in enhancing aesthetic and functional achievements in the design of fashion and interior textiles, but also in key situations, such as providing shelter for refugees or when there is a natural disaster. In hot climates like North Africa and the Middle East architects recognize the functional potential of fabric manipulation, specifically its tensile manipulation, to create roofing structures. The Sharm el Sheikh airport incorporates this technology in its roof.

Throughout the world, textile manufacturers are significant employers. To remain competitive, many companies have relocated to regions, principally in developing countries, where labour costs are low. Embroidery is no exception to this geographical shift away from textile manufacturing in the West. Mequila, an innovative video by the Mexican artist Ana de la Cueva, is an alarming and illuminating piece that explores ethical and labour issues through embroidery. It shows a digital embroidery machine stitching a white-on-white outline of the contours of the United States and Mexico. A bright red thread highlights the Mexican border and the planned wall that is intended to

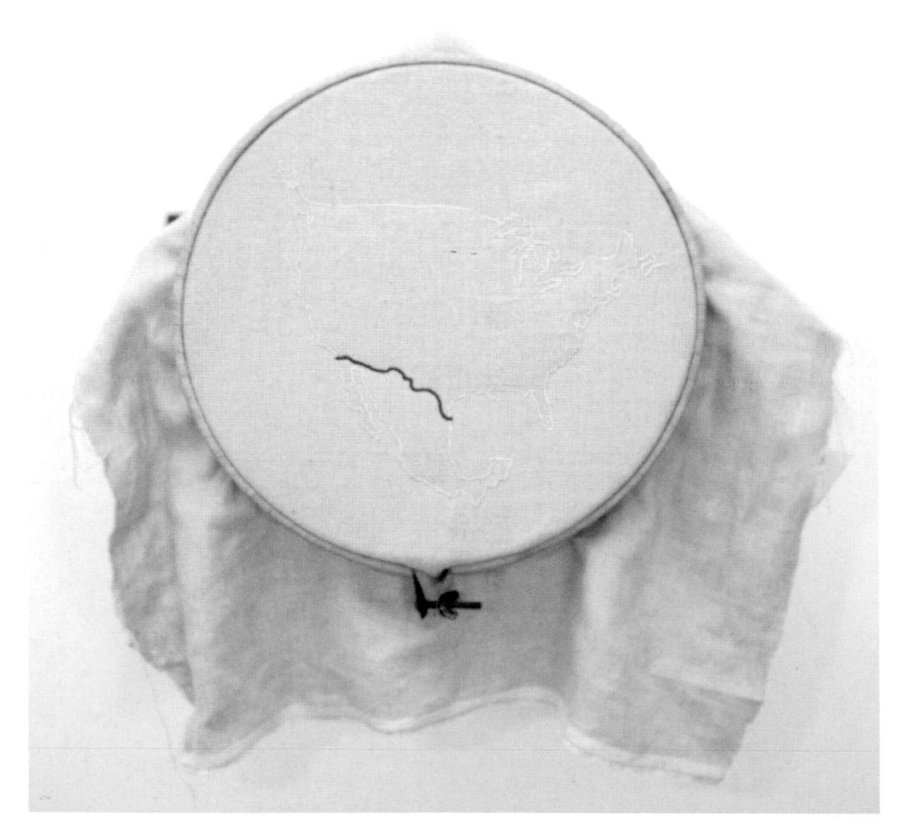

Left
Mequila by Ana de la Cueva (2007) is a video piece which incorporates digital embroidery. The resulting sample, shown here, is a stitched outline in raw linen and thread that defines the contours of the USA and Mexico. A bright red stitched area highlights the Mexican border where a wall may be built in the future to keep out illegal immigrants. The piece alludes to the American embroidery manufacturers scattered along the border who use cheap Mexican labour.

Opposite page
Bleigessen by Thomas Heatherwick is a sculpture made of glass diachronic beads, created for the Wellcome Trust, London. Heatherwick first made a 5-cm- (2-in) long blob by pouring molten metal into water. The form was digitized with a 3-D face scanner borrowed from a hospital near his studio. The scanner's modelling program assigned coordinates to every pixel, each of which was made into a glass bead 4 cm (1.6 in) in diameter. The beads are supported by 26,732 stainless-steel wires and small springs at the base of each wire keep the 30.5-m (100-ft) high sculpture taut and in place. Heatherwick's bead and construction ideas may have been informed by knowledge acquired from his mother, who was a bead designer.

Left
Wrapped Trees, Fondation Beyeler and Berower Park, Riehen, Switzerland, 1997–98, created by Christo and Jeanne-Claude, shows the large-scale potential of fabric manipulation.

Left, below
Christo and Jeanne-Claude's The Pont Neuf Wrapped, Paris, 1975–85, shows the creative vision that can be applied to fabric manipulation – in this instance in the context of a temporary large-scale environmental work.

keep illegal immigrants out of America. Mequila also refers to American manufacturers using embroidery shops, scattered along the border, that employ cheap labour. This is a concern in many developing countries, where there is the dichotomy that the exploitation of a surplus of labour brings a degree of personal and regional economic growth to places that may have been experiencing low levels of economic growth and high levels of unemployment.

5.

Design principles

Textile design is generated by the ways in which designers react to and apply a range of key design methods and principles: the tools they use and the relationship between traditional ways of working and computer-aided design (CAD), concepts – the source of inspiration for a textile collection – and **trend forecasts** which, while they are conceptual, indicate the way the textile market is likely to develop in the future. Colour can evoke atmosphere and emotion, and is a key aesthetic consideration.

Drawing, image generation and pattern have the potential to evoke a variety of artistic and design responses; and the ability to visualize how a textile will look and function within a specific context – fashion or furnishing – is key to creating a successful design.

This chapter discusses these themes and describes how the differing ideas and perspectives they generate enable designers to perform both efficiently and with imagination. It also emphasizes the digital **contextualization** of a textile design, as this provides both the designer and customer with the opportunity to see how it will function before committing to sampling and product manufacture.

Design tools

The selection of a particular tool and a specific material naturally affects the aesthetic style of a design. Simultaneously, designers impose their personality and will on the tools and materials they choose to use. It is this combination that can lead to the generation of a specific textile-design style.

Design tools in CAD software systems developed from traditional tools, methods and principles used in art and design, result in some consistencies in the two ways of working. However, there are distinct aesthetic differences. Some designers celebrate these and generate their designs from within the digital realm precisely because of the different effects CAD produces. Others are concerned that expression and spontaneity can be reduced through protracted designing in this way, though advances in drawing tablets and digitized pens mean these can emerge, in a new form, in CAD.

Blending traditional design practice with the digital is effectively realized by scanning drawn, painted, collaged and photographed ideas created on paper into the computer. Other media and materials can also be scanned. In the computer, the ideas can be enhanced by minor or major modifications that may involve refining a design that is difficult to achieve by drawing or painting. Equally, working in CAD can enable a designer to develop a repeat pattern or create a series of colourway options that can be visualized in a fraction of the time it would take if this were done by hand – although obtaining the required level of aesthetic finish may be more time consuming.

CAD has transformed the designer's traditional realm to the extent that it has become a ubiquitous design tool, like pencil and paper. It has also enabled many aesthetics originally generated by hand on paper to permeate through to become CAD-generated textile designs which are manufactured

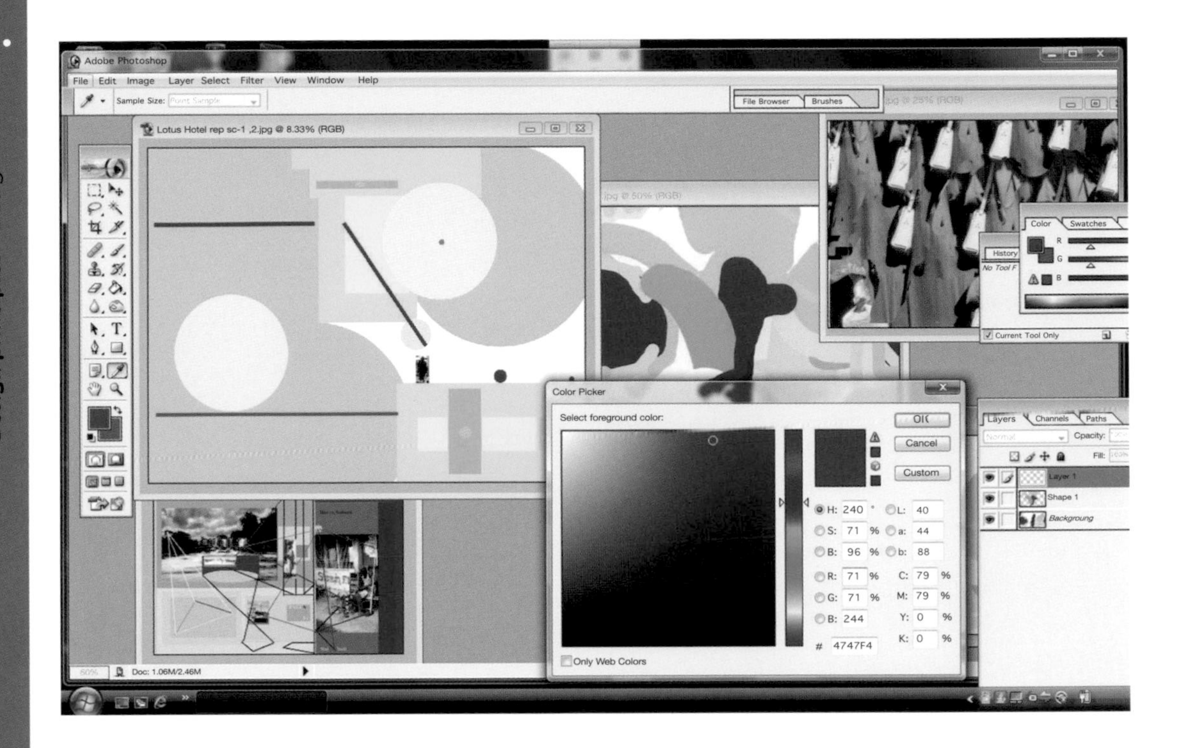

commercially, either mechanically or digitally. There are concerns about digital manufacture, but provided a design is generated to a sufficiently high quality and formatted correctly the desired qualities of colour, line and texture can be maintained.

However, despite the omnipresence of CAD, for now, at least, it seems unlikely that it will become the predominant textile-design tool. There is still a need for designers to possess technical skills that involve the creative handling and use of traditional tools and media, such as paint and brush, pencils, pens, pastels and paper. This is driven by the desire of the designer, customer and consumer for variety, choice and change. On a seasonal basis, the fashion industry has the capacity to accommodate a broad range of design outputs, including the manufacture of designs developed purely from traditional design tools. While CAD does bring a plethora of design opportunities for new aesthetics, and the potential for the fusion of traditional tools with the digital tools to create new aesthetics, it is unable, at least for the moment, to dominate as there is still an innate digital aesthetic in its design. This aesthetic, while appealing to many, is not appealing to all, and that goes for designer, customer and consumer. CAD's inability to truly capture the essence of a hand-drawn pencil line or painted brushstroke on paper will ensure traditional tools will persist.

Computer-aided design (CAD) software has revolutionized the design process for textile designers, enabling them to develop ideas more swiftly than by traditional hand-drawing and painting methods. While this technology provides many new aesthetic directions, its commercial future, in the shorter term at least, lies in working in tandem with traditional design approaches, with designs generated by hand, then refined and put into repeat patterns in CAD. In this Photoshop screengrab showing a work in progress by Simon Clarke (2009), photography and virtually generated design ideas are blended together.

Concepts and trends

Cultural, historical and contemporary art and design, new media, material culture and the natural world all provide the visual impetus that feeds the design process. While there is a wealth of inspiration, the ability to recognize and act upon a concept, and developments in trend forecasting, enable designers to produce designs that reflect and fit in with the colours, motifs or fabrics that are required for a particular market and forthcoming season.

What is a concept?

A concept is defined as an abstract idea, a plan or intention. In philosophy an idea or thought is conceptual, a notion that is applicable to textile design where the concept is the trigger that stimulates the development of a new collection.

The scope of the sources from which inspiration for a concept can be drawn is truly extensive, and a variety of visual elements can be fused to create hybrid textile designs. How a concept is researched, interpreted and translated into a design is informed by the individual designer or studio team, who have to evaluate the initial visual material and then make the necessary adjustments during the design process to enable the concept and the visual elements to be developed into a textile for a specific context and market area. Whether a designer or design studio is a trend leader or a trend follower impacts on the design aesthetic and product outcomes. A trend leader in fashion, for example, may produce a distinct original printed textile-based collection that follows no existing trend forecast, such as the experimental spring/summer 2009 collection Inertia by Hussein Chalayan (see page 214 and also pages 120–21). Trend followers, on the other hand, which are often larger companies, tend not to be able to take such large risks when introducing a new product.

Trend forecasting

Designers draw on their own research and on research by trend-forecasting agencies, the results of which are published in specialist magazines. In addition, the agencies produce books that often focus on specific aspects of textile design; for example, one book may be concerned with colour whereas another might deal with pattern. Fabrics and yarns are another key aspect, and textiles for the fashion and furnishings industries are also shown. To suggest trends, the books contain a diverse range of materials, such as photographs, fabric swatches, yarns, threads, newspaper clippings, fetishes and gadgets. The format always varies in style and content, depending on the trend agency, some of whom produce truly innovative prediction presentations. For example, *Bloom: A Horti-Cultural View*, is a visionary forecasting publication pioneered by the Dutch visionary, Lidewiji Edelkoort, forecasting trends in plants and flowers, and linking them with key social, political, fashion and textile design trends. Trend books like this display a remarkable balance between freedom of expression and realistic research. Forecasts are also displayed at trend forums at international textile trade fairs.

Trend forecasts are valuable indicators of creative developments in the textiles market. While many companies use them to develop collections, totally or in part, others acknowledge and reflect on the trends, then navigate around them to produce their own unique fabrics. Yet others ignore forecasts and deliberately go their own way to generate difference.

Well-regarded international trend-forecasting agencies for fashion, interiors and industrial products include Promostyl, Peclers and Trend Union,

Fashion fabric directions, winter 2009/10, Peclers trend-forecasting agency.

Domestic life
Domestic life

Blottie chez soi, tout est permis, s'amuser avec la lingerie coup de cœur, oser l'été en hiver, s'offrir une cure anti-morosité.
Satins caressants, coton frais et soieries frémissantes, toute la féminité de matières sensuelles, légères et fines.
Se lover dans un petit cocon duveteux, souple et dodu, tout en molleton, éponge et velours, doux en matières comme en couleurs.
Coton doux et nylon coquin, maillot de corps et petite culotte, la lingerie baby-doll se consomme comme une gourmandise sucrée acidulée.

Cocooned at home, anything goes. Have fun with irresistible lingerie, dare to wear summer in winter,
Caressing satins, cool cottons and quivering silky fabrics, sensuous, light and fine materials with total femininity.
Curl up in a downy, supple and plump little cocoon, all in fleece, terry and velour, in soft materials and colors.
Soft cotton and flirty nylon, undershirt and little panty, baby-doll lingerie is consumed like sweet and sour candy.

City rock
City rock

Bousculer le formalisme, électriser les codes... quand le strict devient fun.
Pied-de-poule, tartan, rayure tennis... tous les classiques lainage s'invitent sur de nouveaux supports, plus modernes et plus cool, avec de nouvelles colorations.
Entre costume et jean, la confusion se poursuit : aspect vintage et supports clean, rajeunir le chic rétro des faux-unis sur des bases coton.
Secouer la chemise : griffures, splash ou trait de fluo, casser la rigidité des tissés-teints avec des matières plus floues où les dessins se brouillent.
Exagérer les échelles, augmenter les titrages, épais, hirsutes, les draps classiques prennent une autre dimension.

Disrupt formality, electrify codes... strict becomes fun.
Large houndstooth check, tartan, pinstripe... all the woolen classics can be found on more modern and cooler new grounds, with new colorings.
Suit-cum-jeans, the confusion continues: vintage look and clean grounds, update the retro chic of faux solids on cotton fabrics.
Shake up the shirt: scratches, splashes or day-glo strokes, break up the strictness of yarn-dyeds with more flowing materials with blurred patterns.
Exaggerate scales, increase counts, thick, shaggy, classic broadcloths take on a new dimension.

Nature sublimée
Enhanced nature

Par les textures, les couleurs et les dessins, une envie de s'engloutir et se sentir tout petit dans une nature vue à la loupe.
Reliefs d'écorce, surfaces moussues, des tissus touffus, embrouillés, épais et profonds, pour s'enfoncer au cœur de la matière vivante.
Reflets dans les flaques, couleurs de boue et d'humus, aspects mouillés, les techniques moirés se fondent dans un camouflage marécage.
Comme des ailes de papillon, les motifs tremblés, tachistes, nervurés vibrent sur des matières légères et mouvantes.

Using textures, colors and patterns, the desire to be engulfed and feel really small in nature seen through a magnifying glass.
Sink into the heart of living material, with bark textures, mossy surfaces, bushy, entangled, thick and deep fabrics.
Reflections in puddles, mud and humus colors, wet looks, moiré technicals blend in with marshy camouflage.
Like butterfly wings, quivering, splashy, veined motifs flutter on light and shifting materials.

Héros, héroïnes
Heroes, heroines

Sous influence des années 80, les armes de séduction d'une combattante sexy.
Prêts à sortir leurs griffes, ouvrir leurs écailles ou replier leurs allerons : le double jeu des tissus complexes où l'envers surgit par intermittence sur l'endroit.
Loin de tout romantisme, les nouvelles dentelles, tantôt laquées, tantôt laineuses, plongent dans le mystère intriguant des réseaux enchevêtrés, entrelacs complexes et fausses transparences.
Maintien ferme et confort stretch, les jerseys jumpsuit, texturés et serrés, moulent la silhouette du haut en bas.
Nerveuses, fines et claquantes, des matières ailes de chauve-souris qui lancent de sombres éclairs aux reflets scarabée.

Under the 80's influence, the seductive weapons of a sexy fighter.
Ready to show their claws, open their scales or fold up their fins, complex fabrics play a double game where the back sporadically emerges onto the face.
Far from any romanticism, sometimes lacquered, sometimes woolen, new lace plunges into the intriguing mystery of entangled neworks, complex interlacing and faux transparency.
Firm control and stretch comfort, tight and texturized jumpsuit jerseys hug the body from top to toe.
Springy, fine and crisp, batwing materials sparkle darkly with beetle glints.

Pages from trendbooks by Promostyl, International Trend Research and Design Agency, summer 2010.

Clockwise from top left

Influences (top two images); *Femme; Ultimes.*

all with headquarters in Paris, as well as online agencies like WGSN, Trendstop.com and Stylesight. Pantone Inc. specialize in forecasting colour trends. Trend Union is an association of designers and stylists who work in different sectors of the fashion and interiors industries. Like other agencies it prepares its forecasts for future seasons 18 to 24 months in advance. When its members first meet to decide on a seasonal trend they discuss what has inspired them: their personal reflections and views, fabrics and even objets d'art. It is from this gathering of designers and stylists that Trend Union forecasts are defined.

Colour

Colour can transform and enhance a textile design, and knowledge and experience in how to mix, match and control it is crucial for designers, who often have to work within certain colour ranges or palettes depending on the trend, season or client. Exploring and experimenting with colour therefore leads to a confident approach to design.

Colour theory

Sir Isaac Newton's research into optics and Johannes Wolfgang von Goethe's perceptive theories on colour contributed significantly to our understanding of the subject. Newton showed that it can be analyzed structurally to gain objective knowledge, while Goethe's perceptive and intuitive approach yielded a subjective evaluation of colour.

Johannes Itten was a twentieth-century guru in the area of colour in art and design. A master at the Bauhaus in Germany from 1919 to 1923, after leaving the school he continued to develop his career as an artist while teaching art and design. He was a director of the Krefeld School of Textile Design (1932–38) and director of the School of Textiles in Zurich (1938–54), where he taught industrial textile design.

In his *The Art of Colour*, published in 1961, he outlined basic approaches and principles for colour which can be invaluable for textile design students as, properly assimilated, they will ensure competence in its use. Rudimentary knowledge of colour comes through the colour wheel, which is universally recognized as an informative starting point in understanding the subject. The wheel is based on the three **primary colours** – red, yellow and blue – from which all colours are mixed.

Itten advocated a 12-**hue** colour wheel, where hue describes the different characteristics of colour from red to yellow to blue. Initially these are placed in an equilateral triangle with yellow at the top, red at the lower right and blue at the lower left. A circle drawn around the triangle enables a regular hexagon to be drawn. Three mixed colours are located in the isosceles triangles subsequently formed between adjacent sides of the hexagon, each of which is a **secondary colour** composed of two primaries: yellow is combined with red to produce orange; yellow with blue to make green; and red with blue to create violet. Another circle is drawn at an appropriate radius outside the first one, creating a ring that is divided into 12 equal sections. The primary and secondary colours are sited in this ring, leaving a blank sector between every two colours into which **tertiary colours** – each of which is the result of mixing a primary with a secondary colour, as below – are sited.

Yellow and orange = yellow-orange
Red and violet = red-violet
Blue and green = blue-green
Red and orange = red-orange
Blue and violet = blue-violet
Yellow and green = yellow-green

The result of this process is the colour wheel, which illustrates the possible colours that can emerge from the three primaries.

Colour and contrast

Colour and contrast can generate myriad design effects when they are applied to textiles. Contrast is the clear difference that can be perceived between colours, and intensifies or weakens them. There are a number of different types of contrast.

Hue contrast

This contrast is straightforward because it is illustrated by undiluted colours at their most intense luminosity. Yellow/red/blue is the extreme contrast of hue; others, such as blue/yellow/violet and yellow/green/violet/red are less extreme.

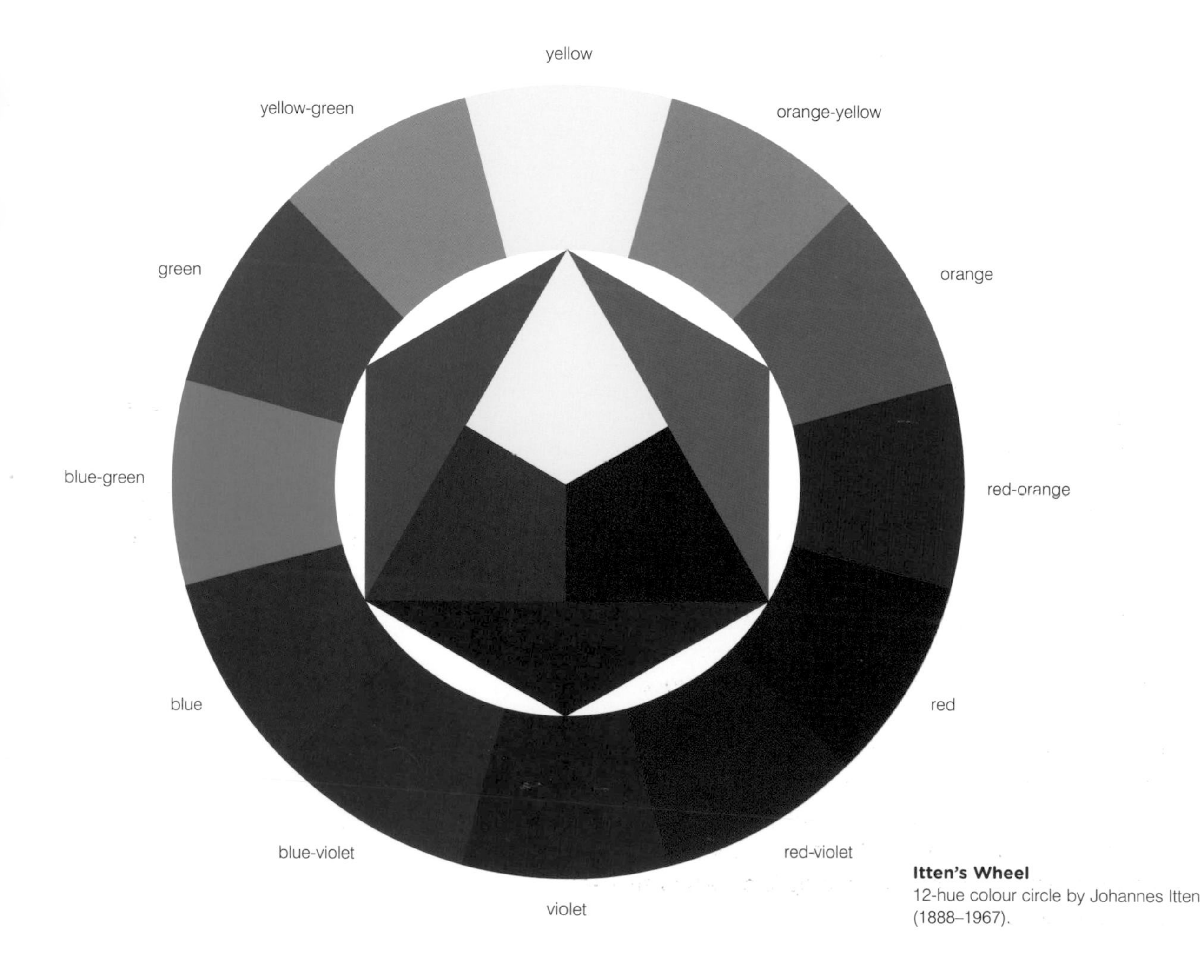

Itten's Wheel
12-hue colour circle by Johannes Itten (1888–1967).

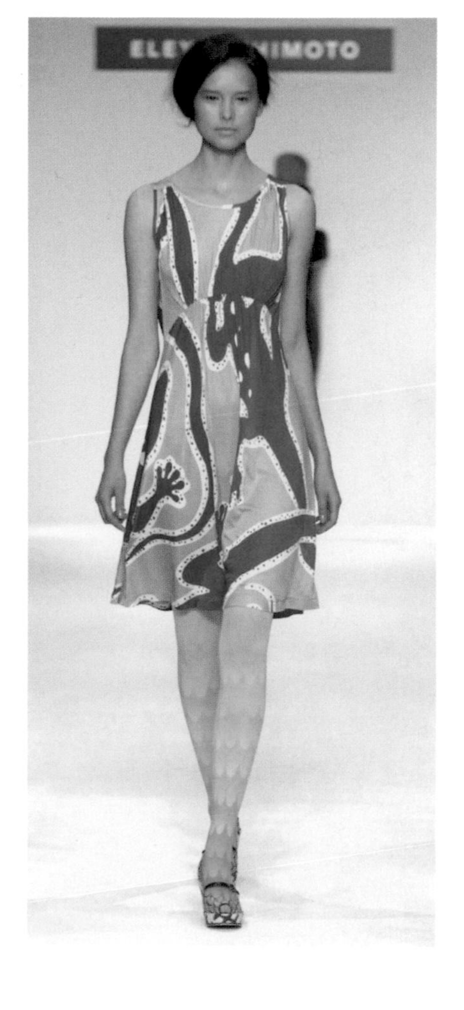

Above, left
These 12 hues in 12 equidistant gradations echo Johannes Itten's black to white gradations.

Above, right
Eley Kishimoto's Mega Lizard Aphrodite printed dress from the Little Devils collection evokes a summery atmosphere through its balance of warm colours. 2009 spring/summer collection.

Black and white contrast

Black and white represent the extreme of light and dark contrast. To get a clear sense of the gradations of transition from black to white, it is useful to define 12 equidistant stages from white to black. This can be repeated for each of the 12 hues of the colour wheel.

Cold to warm contrast

Cold to warm contrasts refer to the 'temperature' created by the visual impact of a colour. An awareness of this effect is important in textile design as it is one of the reasons why a number of colourways are created for a design: each one evokes a different sensation of temperature. For instance, a design that is predominantly blue and green suggests coolness, whereas one that is mainly red and orange evokes warmth. For interior textiles, consideration needs to be given to such contrasts in order to complement a room's functional requirements and create a specific environment. In textiles for fashion, they are important in ensuring that appropriate colours are used to evoke seasonal atmospheres.

Left
Each of these six pure colour squares (yellow, orange, red, green, blue and purple) contains a small neutral grey square of the same brilliance as the background colour. Each grey square appears to be edged with the complementary of the background. This simultaneous effect becomes intensified the longer the principal colour of a square is viewed. From *The Art of Colour* by Johannes Itten.

Bottom
Untitled (1970) by Blinky Palermo (1943–77) is from a series of pictures (fabric paintings – dyed cotton on muslin) made from lengths of intensely dyed textiles. The pictures depict Palermo's compositional concerns with the relative proportions of two or three horizontal bands (in this case tones) of colour suggesting an interest in how the extent to which a colour is used affects the way it contrasts with other colours.

Opposite, left
Wedgewood Blue (1979) is an example of photographer William Eggleston's subjective responses, and interpretation of, a particular colour – in this instance sky blue.
15 chromogenic coupler prints; edition of 20.

Opposite, right
Prima Facie (Fifth State): Enigmatic / Sounds of Nature / Hot Lips / Dream I Can Fly / Golden Glimmer / Fruity Cocktail by John Baldessari (2005). Archival pigment print on ultra-smooth fine art paper mounted on museum board, 339.1 x 90.2 cm (133 1/2 x 35 1/2 in.). The work explores the conceptual, perceptual and subjective aspects of colour. Large fields of colour are accompanied by enigmatic phrases originally chosen by a house-paint manufacturer, each of which is next to the colour it describes.

Complementary contrast

Complementary contrast refers to the use of two colours whose pigments, mixed together, produce a neutral grey to black. Every colour has a complementary one, and within the colour wheel they are diametrically opposite each other. Examples of these pairs include: yellow and violet, orange and blue, red and green (see the colour wheel on page 144).

Simultaneous contrast

Simultaneous contrast is caused by the fact that when looking at a colour the eye needs its complementary one, and creates it spontaneously if it is not already present.

Saturation contrast

Contrast of saturation is related to the amount of pure pigment within a colour: it is the contrast between intense, unmixed colours and dull, diluted ones.

Extension contrast

Contrast of extension involves the relative sizes of two or more areas of colour – for example, between large and smaller ones in a composition.

Subjective colour

Textile designers need to bear in mind the subjective aspect of colour identified by Goethe – intuitive responses to colours, whether these are seen in paintings or at an exhibition of cultural artefacts in a museum, can reflect their impact at particular times, and therefore may well inspire the colours for a new textile collection. How an artist responds to colour can also help designers to conceptualize about it in new ways and this, too, may inform the colour palette for a textile design. For instance, William Eggleston's sky

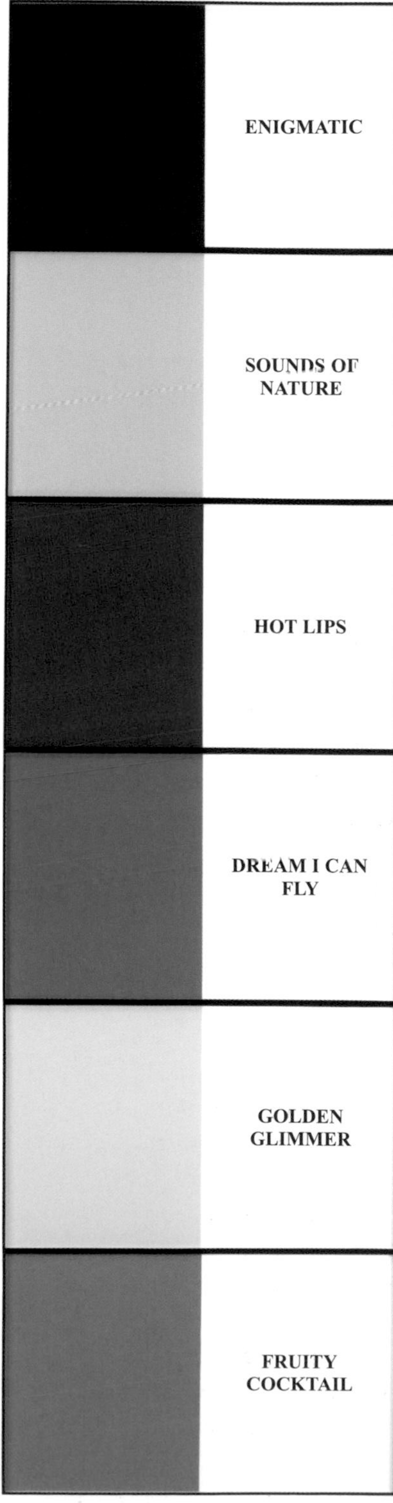

photography series, Wedgwood Blue, is grounded in the ordinary and mundane. However, the photographs question our colour perception, triggered by the remarkable similarity between the sky and the classic blue pottery. Artist John Baldessari explored colour perception by questioning the difference between the house painter and the artist, the paint chip and the work of art. In 2006 he presented Prima Facie, a series of paintings conceived but not executed by him, which features large fields of colour accompanied by enigmatic phrases chosen by a manufacturer of house paints. Each one corresponds with a house-paint colour. Facile phrases such as Happily Ever After and Green with Envy illustrate a marketing approach rooted in colour perception and psychology. Eggleston and Baldessari show the individual, subjective responses towards colour that Goethe described.

Matching colour

There are three strands to matching colour: using traditional design tools, such as pigments, at the manufacturing stage; using traditional tools to create a design that is then scanned into a computer to form a repeat; and matching colour that is produced directly on a computer with the digital or traditionally manufactured output. The last two involve understanding the difference between additive colour, used on the screen, and subtractive colour, used in printing.

There are two types of primary colours in CAD: RGB and CMYK. RGB describes the additive primary colours – red, green and blue – used in coloured light applications. Colours on a computer monitor, for example, are made by combining coloured light. Digital output, like the printed version of a digital document, consists of subtractive primary colours: red, yellow and blue. In printing inks these are CMY – cyan (blue), magenta (red) and yellow. In inkjet printing, whether on paper or cloth, colours are overlapped

Colour forecasts

A number of international agencies provide textile designers and manufacturers with significant and valuable information about colour. One of the most influential is Pantone Inc., whose Pantone Fashion + Home Colour System is a vital tool for selecting and specifying the colours used in textiles. It comprises 1925 colours represented in cotton or paper, that come in varying size swatch and chart formats catering for a range of customer needs. The swatch and chart packages are ideal for assembling creative palettes and conceptual colour schemes, and for enabling designers and textile companies to communicate about colours, and control their use in the manufacturing process. In the case of the cotton swatch sets, Pantone ensure the colours on the samples are compatible with dyes used within the textile industry to aid consistency and efficiency in manufacturing.

Effective **colour-matching** systems increase the speed at which a textile product gets to market. The Pantone View – Colour Planner is a biannual trend-forecasting tool that provides information about seasonal colours 24 months in advance for multiple usages, including menswear, womenswear, active wear, cosmetics and industrial design. Introduced in 2004, Pantone View – Home is a comprehensive forecasting tool for the home furnishings industry. In addition to these and other colour products, the Pantone Colour Institute provides colour information and expertise for a variety of industries including fashion and interiors. It also undertakes research into how colour influences human thought processes, emotions and physical reactions, enabling designers and manufacturers to understand it and learn how to use it more effectively. Leatrice Eiseman, perhaps America's leading colour expert, is the institute's executive director. Pantone Inc. is not alone in this field. The Society of Dyers and Colourists (SDC), for example, is a professional society based in the United Kingdom, which, together with the American Association of Textile Chemists and Colorists, publishes the Colour Index International, which is used globally to identify the pigments and dyes used to manufacture inks, paints, textiles, plastics and other materials.

and mixed optically. Intermixing the subtractive primary colours produces a dark muddy-brown rather than a true black. Therefore, in printing, K (black) is added. This addition also increases tonal possibilities.

Of real importance is the ability to match the colours in a design, whether it has been created on paper or on screen, to the pigment inks and dyes used in textile manufacturing. Colour-matching systems are co-ordinated colour charts. There are, for example, paint or CAD colour charts that correspond to the range of colours a designer uses in a textile design. The colours on the charts are matched with a colour chart for pigment inks or dyes on fabric. By cross-referencing the colours from one chart to the other it is possible to provide accurate information about how the colours in a design will look on fabric, before dyeing or printing. This ensures that colours are interpreted accurately when large quantities of cloth are processed.

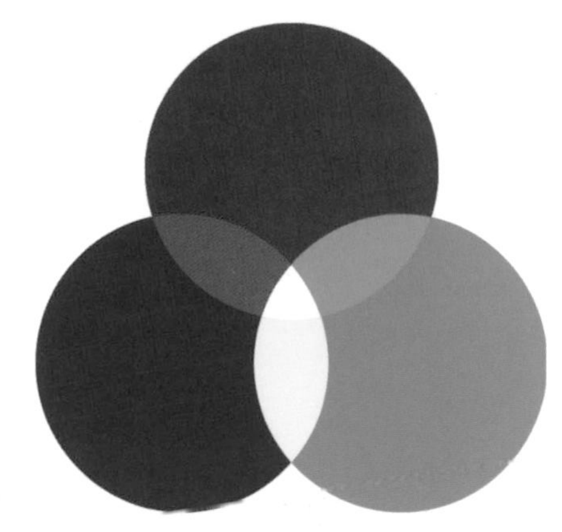

Overlapping the additive primary colours – red, green and blue (RGB) – produces a white light.

Drawing and imagery

Drawing can be traced back to the rock and cave art produced by people like the San of the Kalahari Desert in southern Africa and the Aboriginal people of Australia, and the drawn mark and painted imagery are the primary means through which many visual cultures have evolved. Leonardo da Vinci's cartoons in the Renaissance and the twentieth-century paintings of Pablo Picasso are two very different examples of this evolution. The vast resource of images, in many different media and numerous styles, represents a high proportion of mankind's creative endeavours and achievements. Textile designers can draw on this resource to create new imagery and inform their individual styles.

The many different approaches to drawing range from the expressive to the analytical and, more often than not, can be applied to the development of a textile design. For example, analytical drawings of plants and flowers achieve an aesthetic that lends itself to representational floral textile designs. Interior textile companies like Sanderson, Zoffany and Sandberg perpetuate this long-standing tradition. Analytical drawing is an equally powerful drawing vehicle when applied to subjects such as wildlife and the human form, both of which have been used in textile design. **Primary visual research**, drawing cultural artefacts in museums like the Victoria & Albert in London and the Metropolitan Museum of Art in New York, and in galleries and archives, is a fruitful source of visual inspiration. For some textile designers, research and drawing trips abroad are not uncommon; although potentially costly, they can lead to designs that have real authority and atmosphere.

Secondary visual research involves identifying imagery, motifs and other design information in specialist publications. This is a widely used approach and can be complementary to primary research, or a substitute for it when specific visual material cannot be accessed. Illustrated books provide valuable insights into historical, cultural and contemporary textile styles, and give designers the opportunity to assimilate design imagery that may be

Botanical illustration of *Banksii coccinea* by Ferdinand Bauer (1760–1826). From *Illustrationes Florae Novae Hollandaise* (1813).

reinterpreted in new media and drawing styles. The internet is an increasingly valuable source of visual information, but before using an image it is crucial to find out whether it is copyrighted.

Popular art and culture consistently present textile designers with sources of visual inspiration that can inform how they draw and select images, and extend the traditional textile-design norms. An example from the 1950s is the printed textile designs by the artist Eduardo Paolozzi; and today the street artist Banksy has become an iconic figure in contemporary popular culture. He and other artists and designers who have media profiles can stimulate and motivate debate on the range of aesthetics and methods that are available to generate new textiles. Similarly, art can be popularized through textile design, as in the collaboration between the artist Damien Hirst and Levi Jeans. Hirst's iconic skull, butterfly and spot motifs were used in the design of printed jeans and T-shirts for the 2008 spring collection of the Warhol Factory X Levi range; the artist's aim was to create art that can be worn. The use of creative methods employed in other art and design disciplines enriches textile design. Architecture is another example. Architects including Zaha Hadid and Peter Cook have produced architectural drawings (and paintings) that are genuinely innovative, and there is no reason why the aesthetic ideals they reflect cannot be assimilated into textile design.

New drawing tools and software packages in CAD have enabled innovative and exciting textile designs like those of Hettie Nettheim, discussed in chapter 6, to be created. Nettheim drew upon 3D CAD software and model-making to develop a distinctly individual collection of digitally and hand-printed textiles. And as mentioned in chapter 2, the designs of Jonathon Fuller, Ed Forster and Sheona Quenby demonstrate how CAD tools can be used to create very individual approaches towards printed textile design.

Opposite
B.A.S.H., a fine art print on paper by Eduardo Paolozzi (1924–2005) was published in 1971 to mark Paolozzi's retrospective at the Tate Gallery in London. It blends a variety of iconic motifs with a strong illustrative style and vibrant sense of colour that today could readily be applied to cloth through digital inkjet printing.

Below
Zollhoff 3 Media Park, Dusseldorf (unbuilt 1989–93) by innovative architect Zaha Hadid. This CAD drawing shows the visual and creative opportunities textile designers can harvest through gaining knowledge and skills from other design disciplines.

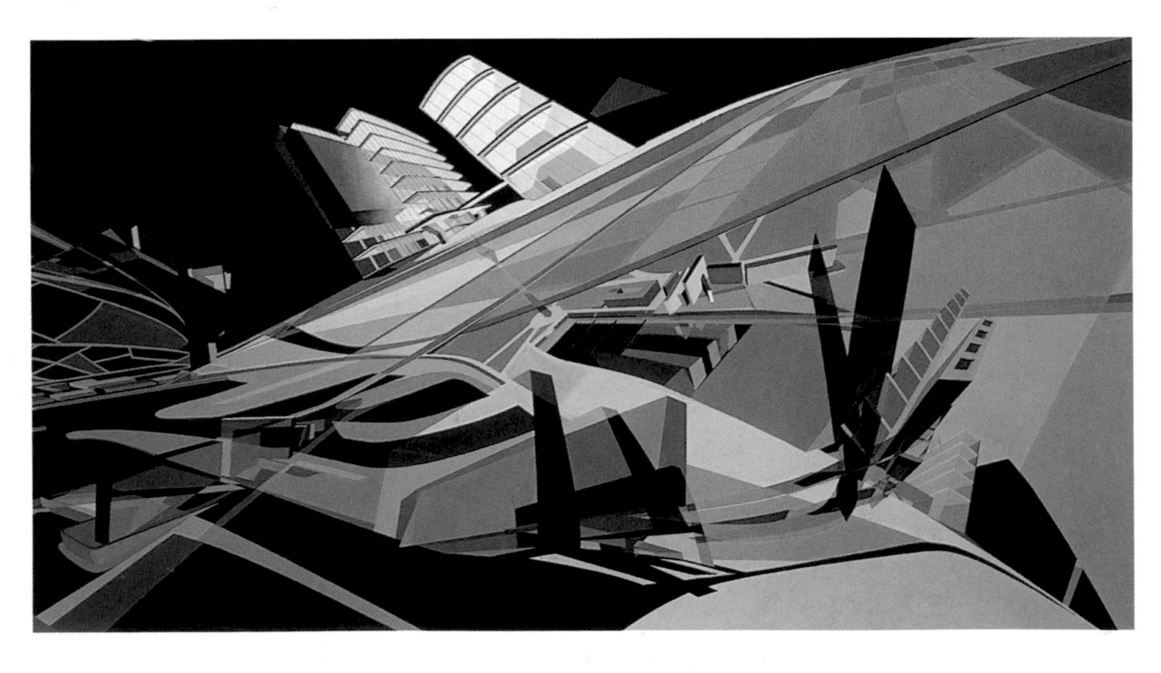

top
FIVE designed by CRAVEN
Fully shrunk Wash or dry clean
Hand Printed by HULL TRADERS Ltd.
A TIME PRESENT FABRIC

Individual styles and print designs

Distinctly individual styles are not uncommon in printed textiles, and are often instigated by the unique personality of the artist or designer. The sculptor Henry Moore used his drawing style, often associated with preparatory sketches for his sculpture, to create striking and provocative designs. This is equally true of artists Barbara Hepworth and Ben Nicolson. From the 1960s the designs of artist William Scott and textile designer Shirley Craven gained widespread acclaim because of their individual qualities. Examples of their highly innovative printed textile designs are discussed here in relation to drawing, image-making and the circumstances in which they were created.

A particularly interesting textile design by Craven, one of many designs she developed during her career, is Five, produced for Hull Traders in 1966. In it Craven shows the powerful effect of drawing: stormy clouds are rendered in a painterly manner in the artist's hand, and the finished design graphically captures the use of 'crayons' and 'soft' pencils. Five was innovative in that it moved away from the abstract movement that had become popular in the 1960s. For this piece Craven won the 1968 Design Centre Award, which was run by the Council for Industrial Design.

In 1961 the painter William Scott, commissioned and supported by Edinburgh Weavers, developed the interior textile design Whithorn to complement his mural of the same name for the Altnagelvin Hospital, in Londonderry, Northern Ireland. The translation of the pattern to the cloth distinctly shows Scott's individual abstract Expressionist painting style. Alistair Morton, founder of Edinburgh Weavers, spent many hours studying designs and paintings before deciding on the right printing technique. He had previously been successful with artist fabrics, and realized that Scott's work had the potential to be transferred to cloth. Whithorn was marketed through *Design* magazine from 1962 onwards. This example of an artist translating his work into a commercially successful fabric indicates the creative scope of drawing and painting in textile design.

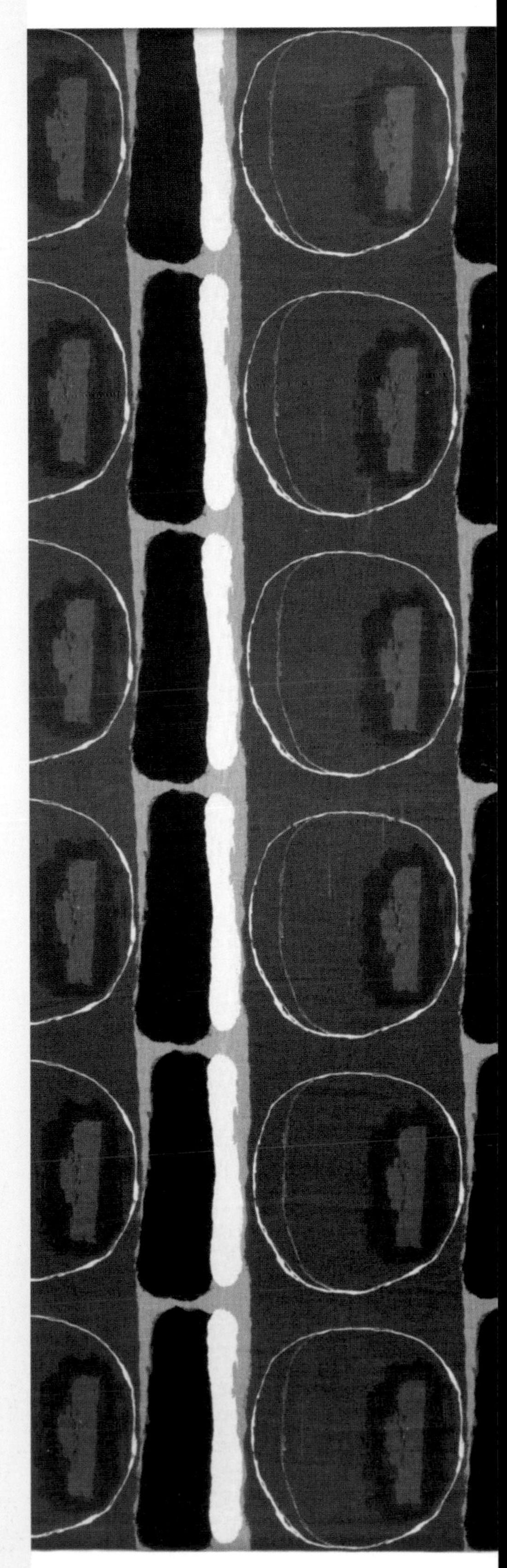

Right
Whithorn (1961, © William Scott Foundation 2010), a printed textile design by the artist William Scott (1913–89) captures Scott's individual drawing style. It was developed for Edinburgh Weavers, whose forte was the production of artist-designed textiles. Whithorn had first been produced as a mural for the Altnagelvin Hospital in Londonderry, Northern Ireland. The architect for the project, Eugene Rosenberg of Yorke, Rosenberg and Marsdall, then commissioned Scott to develop a complementary fabric for curtains, which were also needed for the hospital.

Opposite
Five (1967), a hand screen-printed linen union designed by Shirley Craven, produced by Hull Traders (Private Collection. Photo: Ferens Art Gallery, Hull Museums). The image depicts stormy clouds across the width of the cloth, drawn in a painterly style, the quality of the media used (crayon and soft pencil) permeating through to the printing process. Five radically moved away from the popular abstract look of this period and it won Craven the 1968 Design Centre Award.

Pattern

Pattern is all around us and is a distinct visual presence. It can be found within the animal kingdom, for example in the dramatically bold, dark stripes of the tiger. And it can be seen in geology, for instance in the folding rock formations in the Great Rift Valley in eastern Africa. Pattern created by mankind is evident in all societies and civilizations, past and present, and has often acquired cultural significance, as in Tibetan tiger rugs and the complex geometrical designs on Islamic tiles. It is sources like these that inspire textile designers and inform how they design with pattern.

Pattern in art and design

In the twentieth century artists such as Bridget Riley and Jim Lambie made major contributions to the exploration of pattern, and innovations of the kind they generated have been assimilated into commercial textile design with varying degrees of merit and integrity. Riley has produced remarkable paintings from which textile design students can learn about the interrelationships between pattern, colour and **rhythm**. Lambie covers floor surfaces with a variety of coloured tapes in his installations. In some ways he operates like a textile designer because he selects colours, line widths and the outline of the basic floor pattern in advance. However, the difference is that the work makes itself by initially following the edge of a room. This starting point controls the piece, and a powerful rhythm and pattern tend to build naturally from it. The fine arts continue to inspire design and this inspiration is the lifeblood of many of the best contemporary textile patterns.

The radical Italian designer Ettore Sottsass, founder of Sottsass Associatti and mastermind of the design group Memphis in Milan, Italy, founded in the 1980s, explored pattern in a new and dramatic manner in the products he designed. He was inspired by contemporary fine artists, such as the Constructivist Naum Gabo, in the early stages of his career, and later by Pop artists like Roy Lichtenstein and Minimalists such as Sol LeWitt. The Memphis

Opposite, top
Sottsass carpet pattern design Terrazzo (2007) in situ. It is based upon a former design of the same name, and has been toned down in colour. The design was inspired by traditional 'terrazzo' concrete flooring containing chips of stone and marble.

Opposite, bottom
The Royal chaise longue, an iconic item of furniture designed by Nathalie du Pasquier and fellow Memphis group member George Sowden (1983), makes emphatic use of pattern on both cotton fabric and plastic laminate. The patterns were inspired by animal, Art Deco and African textile patterns as well as 1950s kitsch, all of which are a recurring influence on du Pasquier's designs.

Below, left
This painting from Bridget Riley's High Sky 2 series (1992) displays her highly complex sense of pattern and colour.

Below, right
In his installation Zobop Colour (1999, and recreated as seen here for the Tate Triennial, Tate Britain, London, 2003) Jim Lambie covered the floor with coloured vinyl tape. Dimensions variable.

group's attitude towards pattern was questioning and irreverent; it asserted that structure and decoration were one entity rather than two different ones. Nathalie du Pasquier, a prolific designer of printed textiles and laminates, was a major contributor in the design of patterns used on many Memphis products; after finishing her association with Memphis she became a painter while also continuing to work as a designer.

The last pattern designs by Ettore Sottsass were developed in partnership with British designer Christopher Redfern, head of the Sottsass design studio. The innovative designs were realized using the latest print technology developed for floor coverings. The realization of the designs was a result of a close collaboration between Sottsass design studio and Bonar Floors. The designs included adapted former Sottsass designs Bacteria and Terrazzo.

Pattern in textile design

Pattern is ubiquitous in textile design and has the power to attract and excite viewers in the same way that colour triggers an array of emotional responses. Digital patterns, for example, are not just an expression of a new aesthetic; they can capture the atmosphere of the times in which we live.

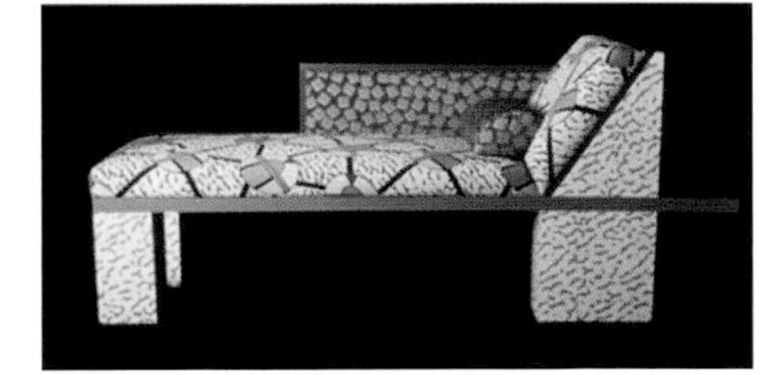

Pattern works physically with cloth in different ways. The structure of a woven fabric yields countless creative interpretations that are very different aesthetically to printed or embroidered patterns, or those on manipulated fabrics. A printed pattern can display a vast array of imagery or motifs, ranging from the pictorial to the abstract, and is principally achieved using either a dye paste or a pigment ink and binder that goes into the cloth or sits on its surface. For embroidered patterns, thread is hand or machine stitched on to the fabric. Patterns created by fabric manipulation may involve pleating or laser cutting the cloth.

Patterns can be simple or complex, symmetrical or asymmetrical, and any identical or similar image or motif that is repeated can become a pattern. The more symmetrical the repetition, the more straightforward it is to recognize it as a pattern. In both furnishing and fashion textiles pattern has undergone many transformations, liberated by digital technology in terms of **scale** and repeat. Where this is most clearly evident is in small batch production runs of digitally printed textile designs where there are no limitations imposed by screen printing frame sizes, enabling pattern to be printed without repeats or with large-scale repeats that could be a metre or more in size. Basso & Brooke and Matthew Williamson are among a number of designers rethinking pattern and engineered design in printed

textiles with remarkable results. The deconstruction of established pattern systems has begun.

Pattern is intrinsically linked with colour, which invariably requires repeated motifs and/or images in order to evoke atmosphere and emotion in a textile design, and when the two are combined they can harmonize to powerful effect. The textile designs of Panton and Pucci, discussed in chapter 1, are striking examples of blending pattern and colour. This can also be realized by using a combination of materials as the fashion designer Ashish Gupta did in his 2005 autumn/winter collection, for which he produced an embroidered coat that incorporated thin intersecting rectangles of woollen fabric in a selection of colours on a ground of black sequins. Minimal pattern in a design can be transformed when it is combined with opulent embellishment; Pierre Cardin did this successfully in the 1960s and was equally imaginative in his use of traditional patterns and scale.

Above
Galaxy (2002), a woven interior textile design from the Cosmos collection for the Dutch company Hybrids + Fusion by weave designer Aleksandra Gaca. Here Gaca achieves a unique three-dimensional repeating pattern inspired by her fascination with innovative weave structures.

Opposite, left
Wool and sequin hand-embroidered coat by fashion designer Ashish Gupta. 2005 autumn/winter collection.

Opposite, top right
Beige and black plaid wool tweed jacket and skirt by Pierre Cardin. 1966 autumn/winter collection. From the Kyoto Costume Museum, Japan.

Opposite, bottom right
The oblique wavy pattern on this A-line minidress is created with embroidery of gold and silver sequins and paillettes. Pierre Cardin, 1966 autumn/winter collection. From the Kyoto Costume Museum, Japan.

Repeat patterns

Although pattern can be used in a variety of ways, established repeat patterns continue to be prominent in designs for fashion and furnishing textiles.

Block repeats

The block repeat where one motif is simply placed alongside another – Andy Warhol's Campbell's soup cans are a good example – is the most basic formula. With imagination, it can be used creatively to generate a variety of responses. **Mirroring** motifs, or **rotating** them, are two options.

Half-drop repeats

The most common repeat in textile design, the half-drop can be manipulated to generate a wide variety of patterns.

Irregular repeats

Irregular repeats are similar to half-drops, but do not follow regular repeat intervals.

Composite repeats

Composite repeats are designed with three or more pattern elements and provide enormous creative scope. Another repeat system, perhaps the half-drop, is used to repeat the composite. Rotations were popular throughout the twentieth century. They can vary in the extent to which they are rotated and are very effective when a grouping of rotations is put into a block or half-drop repeat.

Left
A block repeat.

Opposite, top left
A half-drop repeat.

Opposite, bottom left
A half-drop repeat with a vertical mirror and pillar arrangement. The pillar effect is given by a strong vertical emphasis in a design.

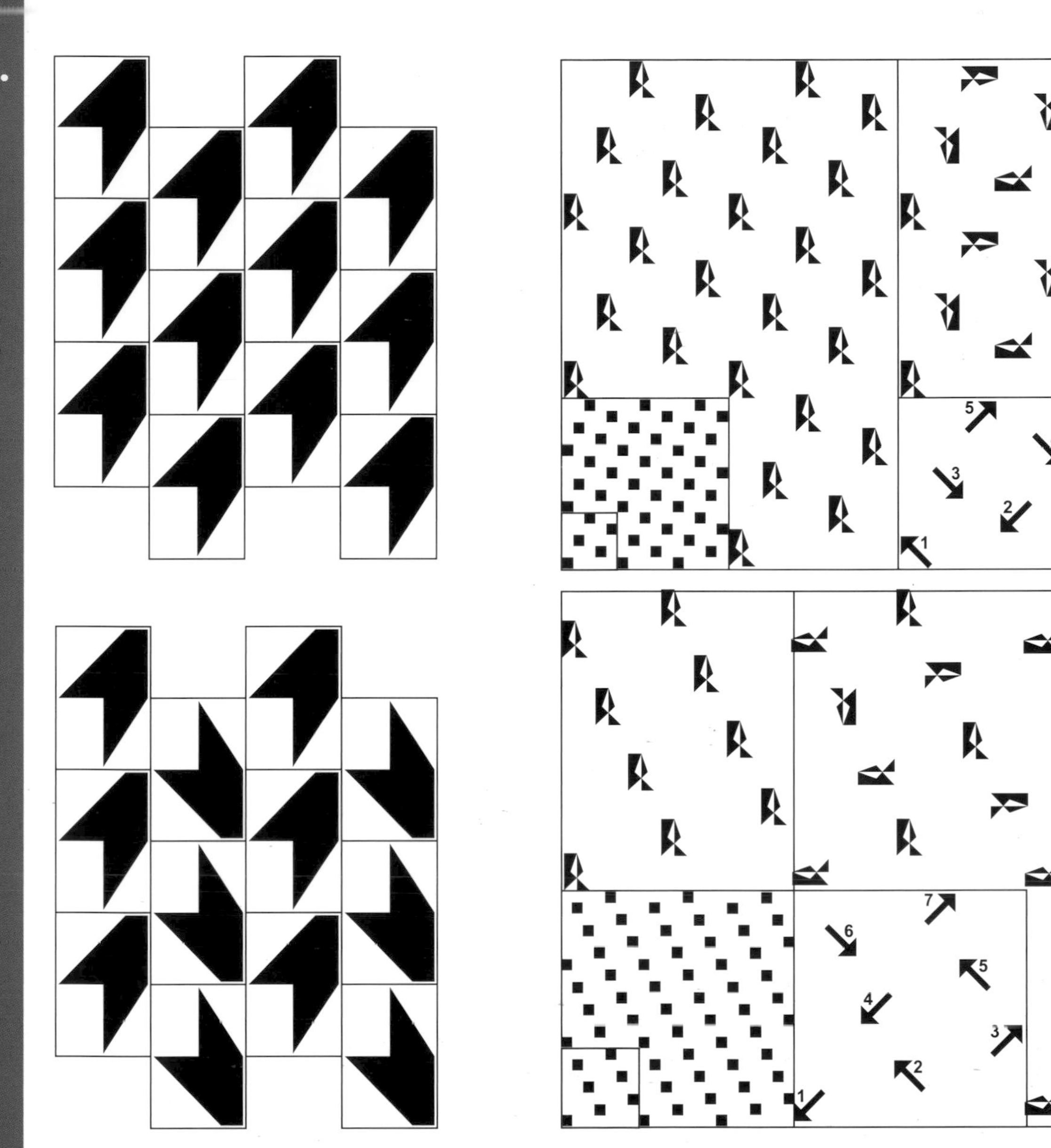

Sateen repeats

Sateen repeats are also known as spot repeats. The motif in a design is angled in a variety of directions and seems to have been scattered at random, which creates a sense of movement in the pattern. Sateen repeats are popular in both the interior and furnishing markets, as the motifs tend to be small and there is therefore little wastage when the fabric is cut.

The wealth of approaches to repeat patterns allows complex designs to emerge through the overlay of different repeat systems. What is always fascinating is the way in which the image or motif imposes on, or dictates, the type of repeat used. For example, a geometric motif generates a very different pattern and rhythm to that generated by an organic or plant motif.

Above right, top and bottom
A sateen repeat, which gives the impression that the motif in the design has been scattered at random, giving the pattern a sense of movement and energy.

Pattern and CAD

Technology, CAD and experimentation in computer programs are creating new approaches to pattern design. Considering the long history of pattern in textile design there is a very strong case to be made for textile designers, as well as artists, architects and scientists, to be pioneers in this field of **pattern generation**.

An unusual method of digital pattern generation has been developed by artist Tom Ray whose experimental approach to computer technologies led to the production of a conceptually and visually powerful piece of work: Tierra. Ray wrote fragments of program code that were designed to reproduce themselves, which he released into the hard drive of a computer. The fragments, which he called parasites, were represented visually as yellow motifs which replaced the original dominant organism, defined visually as red motifs. As the parasites evolved mutations appeared, defined visually as blue motifs, which were immune to the parasites and became the dominant motifs in the visual pattern sequence. Ray called the domain in which the evolving pattern process occured sanctuary. Tierra can be implemented over a computer network of interconnected hard drives, triggering the migration of parasites between computers. Textile designers should at least be aware of developments like these and, at best, could be directly involved in assimilating them and using them to create innovative designs.

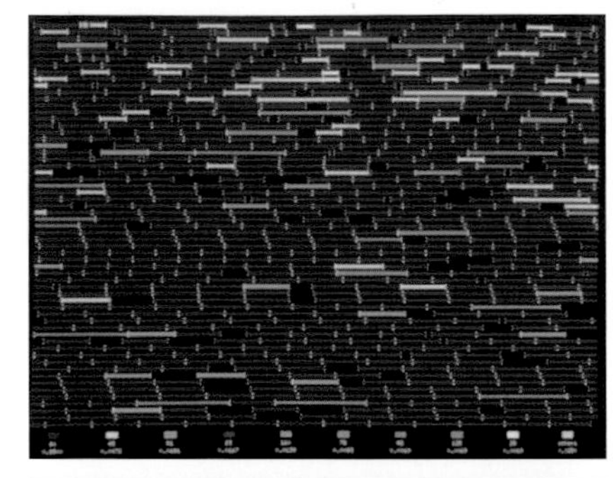

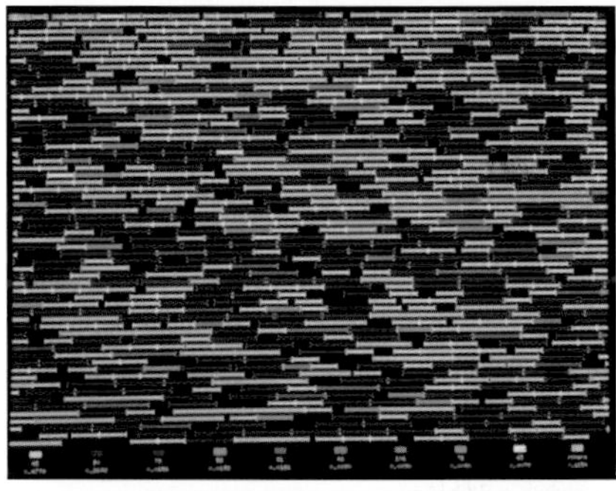

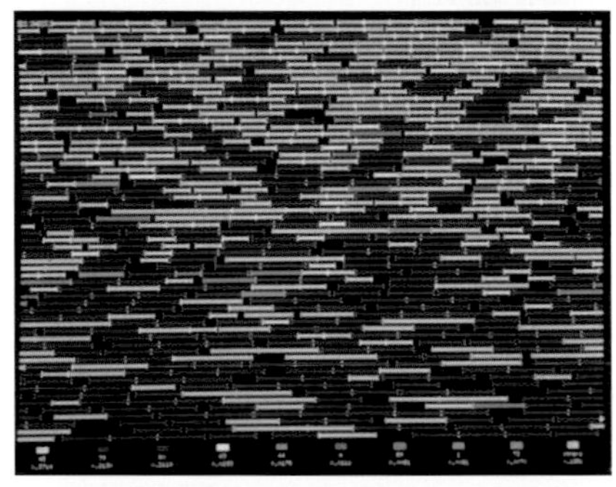

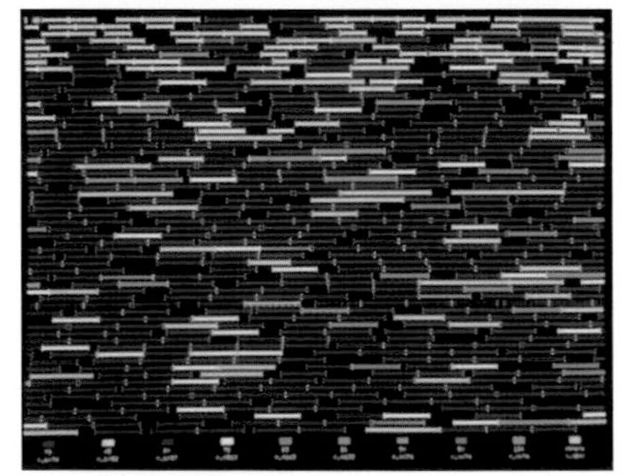

Tierra by Tom Ray (1992) is an example of the new ways of thinking about pattern that continue to evolve through computer technology and programming. This series of four images shows a pattern system evolving through the introduction of a virus. The dominant organisms (red) succumb to parasites (yellow), only to be succeeded by immune hosts (blue).

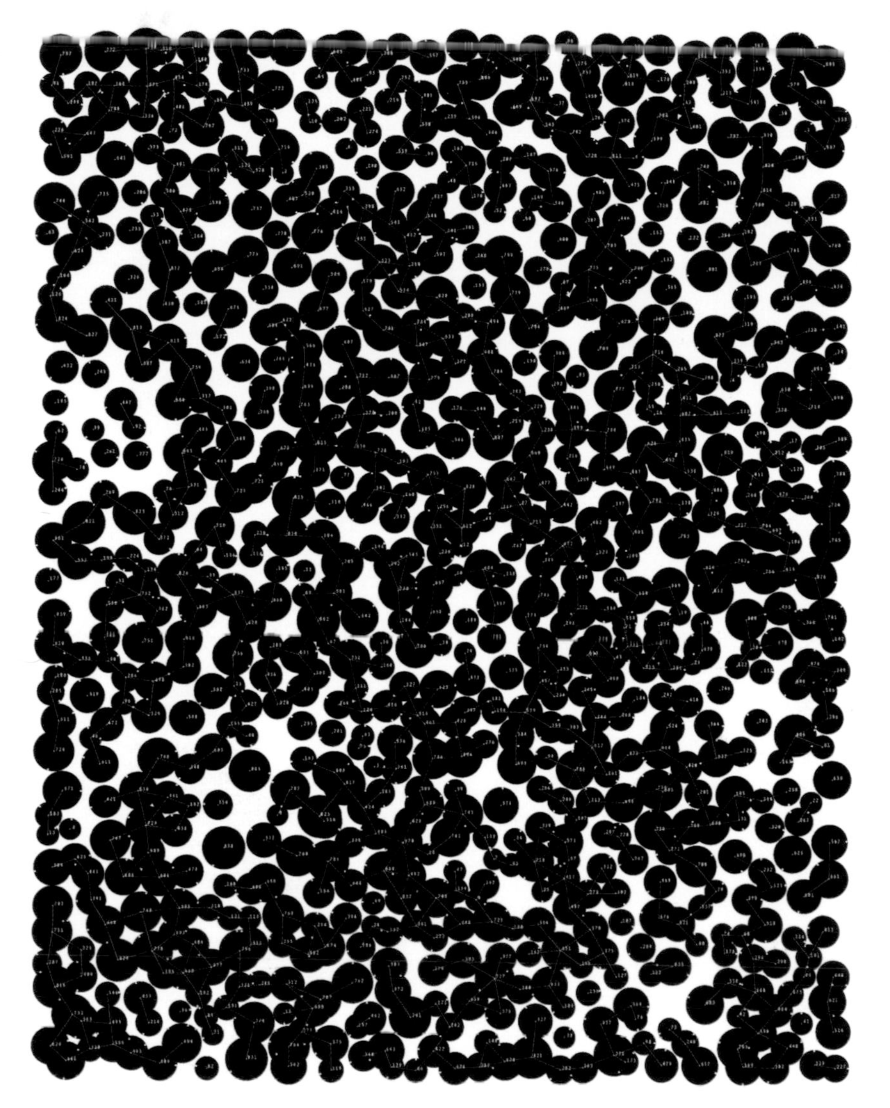

Above
Quasicrystal II by Eric J. Heller (6/1993) looks like a crystal and displays some qualities of crystalline order but there are no repeating patterns. Heller is both a scientist and an artist and works with both science- and design-based software such as Mathematica and Photoshop. His remarkable pattern-based, virtual artworks are subsequently realized on to paper through the digital printing process.

Left
Process 4 (Form 1) (2005), is an inkjet print by Casey Reas who produces unique patterns through his idiosyncratic creative thinking and use of technology. Reas sees his artworks, which are created on specially designed computer programmes, as choreographies. The software arises from short sets of instructions in which processes are described. Static images (patterns) are one form into which the instructions can be translated. Others are languages and machine codes. Each new form makes it possible to view the choreography it describes from another perspective.

The inkjet print Process 4 (Form 1) by Casey Reas is another very individual perspective on pattern generation. Reas creates his artwork with computer programs that are specifically designed for the prints, which are choreographies that aim to influence the viewer intellectually, emotionally and physically. The Harvard chemist and physicist Eric Heller captures the essence of traditional aesthetics in his digital artworks, with **variegated** patterns that hint at Islamic design.

Computer-generated patterns like the ones described above question perceptions of pattern generation and **visualization**. They show how patterns can potentially be created in the twenty-first century using methods and eclectic ways of thinking in CAD that may be developed by new textile designers. Although such developments are perhaps still in the future, there is certainly no reason why the patterns created by Heller or Reas could not be applied in printed textile design, however far removed the original ideas are from this context.

Visualization, styling and design tools

Visualization and styling describe presenting a textile design in the context in which it will be used. This contextualization can be created by a textile designer or through collaboration between a designer, stylist and photographer – which often leads to product marketing and publication in books, journals and magazines, and on websites. Aspects of presentation and display are discussed further in chapter 6. During the design process the visualization of an idea for a textile design in a fashion or interior context, whether drawn, painted, collaged or rendered in CAD, can subsequently inform decisions relating to modifications in pattern, colour and fabric.

When a textile design is presented to a customer a hand-drawn or digital rendering of the design, in context and with a fabric sample, can be persuasive in securing a commission or sale as the relationship between textile and product is explicit. At trade fairs like Première Vision in Paris a sample of the design is sometimes shown in the form of a template garment shape, at actual scale.

When a new collection is being promoted, whether as fabric samples or in a fashion or interior context, it can be styled and photographed in many ways. This provides the designer, stylist and photographer with myriad historical and cultural sources to draw on, ranging from the classical to the avant-garde. Ultimately, the approach is informed by the textile design, and the product, market and budget. Styling and photography can lead to advertising and publicity in international magazines like *Vogue* and *World of Interiors*.

Opposite
Three projects for Futurist suits: morning, afternoon and evening (1914), by Giacomo Balla (1871–1958).

Below
This is one example from a series of styled photographs the Italian textile company Etro displays on its website to market and promote its culturally and historically inspired home furnishing collection (2009). Driven by its founder, Gimmo Etro, the company emphasizes quality in design, materials and techniques to the degree that it has an established international reputation in both the furnishing and the fashion textile markets.

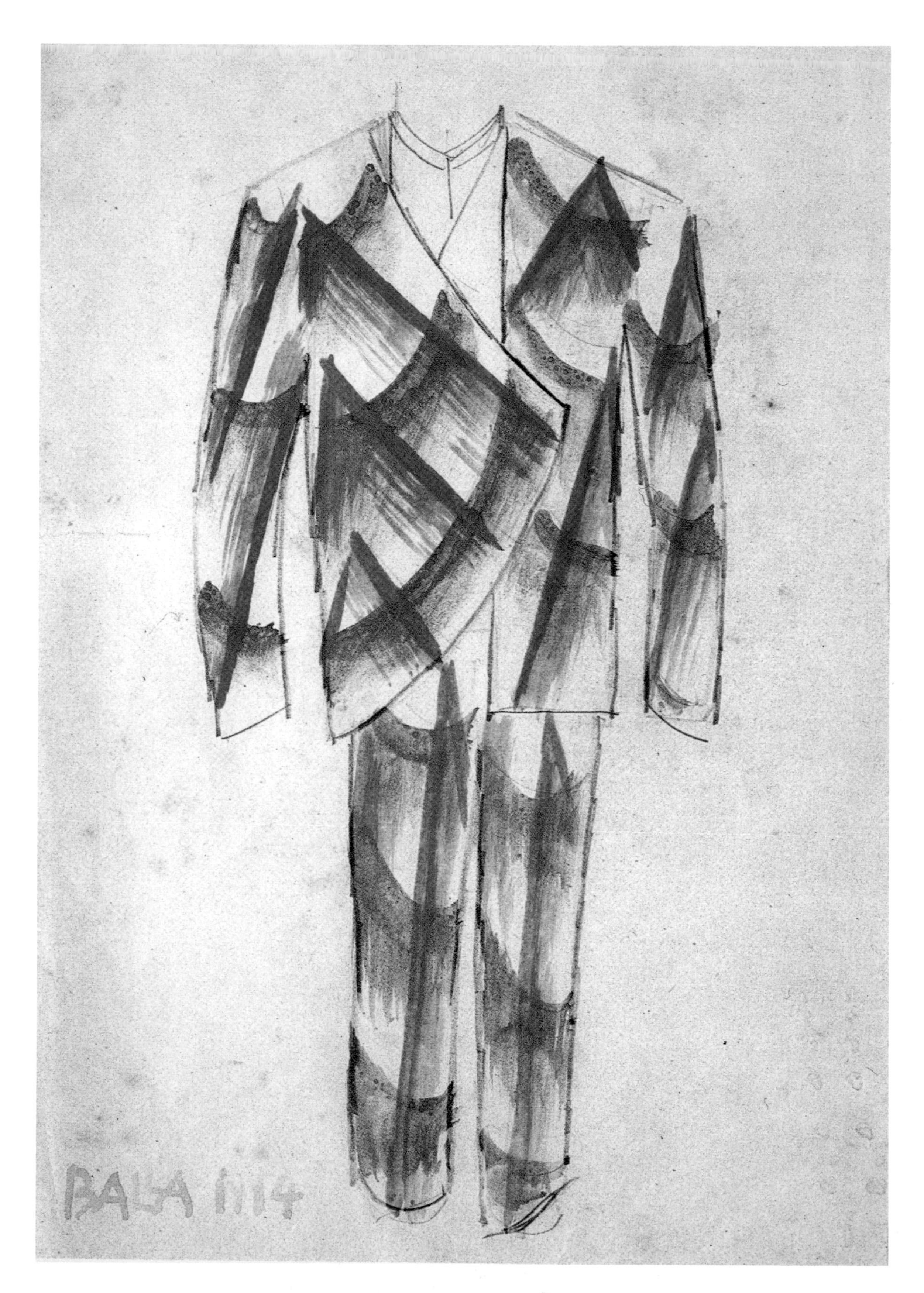
BALA 1114

CAD visualizations

Basic CAD visualizations of textile designs, when a drawn fashion or interior product, or a photograph of a product, is scanned into the computer, are common. Generating a product, and the design, using CAD tools is another option. Applying the textile design to the product involves a process called 3-D digital mapping. Once the design has been applied to the product it can be enhanced with light- and shade-adjustment tools to achieve a greater degree of realism. If a photograph of an actual product is used in the 3-D digital mapping of a textile design it can sometimes be difficult to see the difference between this and a counterpart on location or in a catwalk photograph displaying the same textile design.

Cloth visualizations

Researchers are working on extreme detailing in the virtual visualization of cloth. This involves investigating collisions between cloth and the moving human body, and between different parts of the fabric itself. The effects of other natural phenomena, such as gravity, volume, damp and wind turbulence are now within the virtual domain and are also being studied. This digital progression will significantly advance awareness of how textile-based products function and react in animated situations, such as on a windy day.

It will also enable the designer and manufacturer to judge the functionality and performance of a textile design before committing to sampling, prototyping and production runs.

Innovations by digital animation companies like Pixar, which has a dedicated cloth team, have resulted in remarkable films such as *The Incredibles* that accurately show the details in garment design. Computer software such as Maya cloth simulation and 3D Studio Max are recognized by the fashion and textile industries, and mannequin and runway simulations provide pre-manufacturing information on how a textile will look both in a static state and in movement.

Haptic sensing relates to touch rather than sight, and research and development in this field of virtual textiles requires further technological development. However, in the future it may be possible to perceive, touch and manipulate a virtual fabric as though it were a physical object.

Opposite, top
A virtually generated print design for fashion by Simon Clarke (1998).

Opposite, bottom
CAD-3-D digital mapping enables a textile design to be translated on to a virtual product. This innovative method is commonly used by designers to see how a design will look in a product context.

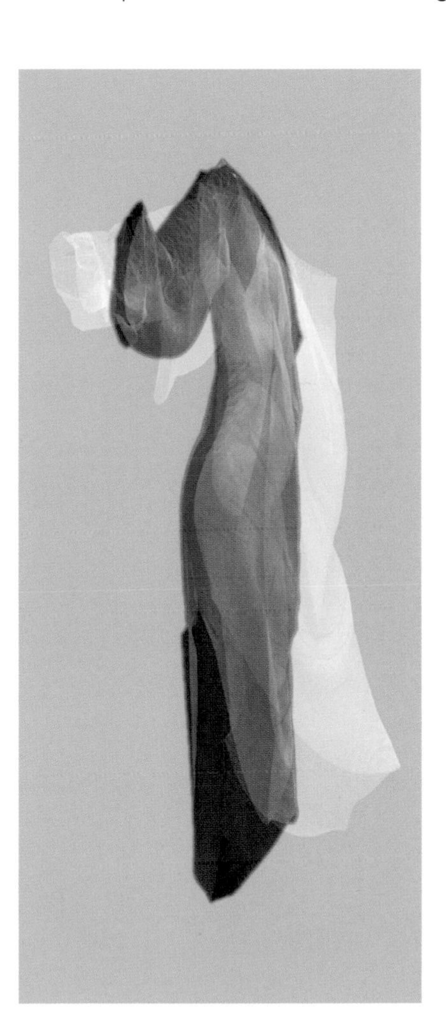

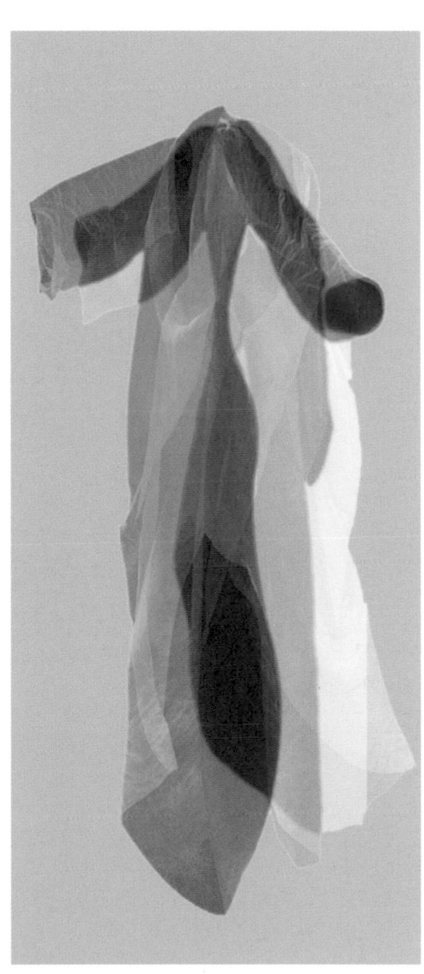

Potential Beauty, a digitally animated cloth by Jane Harris (2003). The realisation of this virtual artwork involved collaborations both with a 3-D computer graphics expert, Mike Dawson, and the performer/choreographer Ruth Gibson, supported by the Arts and Humanities Research Council.

Summary

This chapter aims to provoke reflection, consideration and positive action in developing and applying the basic skills of textile design – not necessarily in a linear or formulaic way, although this may be required, but by considering how flexibly and with what variety they can evolve and be used. The topics discussed are not comprehensive, but are intended to be catalysts for further investigation.

It is, of course, possible for a designer who has the necessary understanding of the basic skills to rebel against these established norms and values. Jason Miller is an example: his home furnishings encapsulate the spirit of experimentation and innovation in design: 'Notes for the upholsterer. It shouldn't take 7 yards of fabric to cover the chair. It's not that big I bought 3 yards. Please make it work. I don't care if the pattern doesn't line up. It's not important if you run out, finish it with some remnants. Mismatch Chairs are chairs upholstered in the wrong way. Patterns don't line up. Prints are upside down. They may even have several different fabrics. Whatever.'

In the design process the balance between creativity and responding to the marketplace is a constant challenge which requires a real understanding of basic design methods and principles. Commercial restraints include client requirements, and the market, season, budget and time. How the designer deals with these demands is discussed in the next chapter.

Mismatch Chair by Jason Miller (2004). The chairs in Miller's Mismatch range are upholstered the wrong way: patterns don't line up, prints can be upside down and several different fabric patterns may be used. This individual approach questions the conventional design process and consequently has intriguing aesthetic results.

6. Creating a collection

The design process requires the designer to think fluidly and structurally: fluid attitudes stimulate intuition and experimentation, while structured ones shape and direct the process. Functional and contextual awareness of the product and its market is a significant element in creating a textile collection, as are the concepts, visual research and aesthetics that define the quality of a design. Ultimately, however, the personality of the designer and how he or she applies their skills defines the creative content of a finished design.

This chapter examines the design process and describes how it leads to a textile collection.

What is design?

Design is an evolutionary process that involves the generation of ideas that lead to the creation of a product. However, although it has been an integral aspect of mankind's development for thousands of years, since the first tools were made, it was only during the eighteenth century, in Europe, that it was acknowledged to be a profession. As the Industrial Revolution gained momentum it was increasingly accepted that a product's functional and aesthetic qualities could be commercially advantageous. Creating these qualities remains a key function of design. Today, the importance of design is recognized globally because of the economic benefits it brings. But this does not overshadow the primary concern of the designer: to produce a product that has functional and aesthetic appeal at the right price for the consumer.

Research and development are core activities in the design process, and vary in emphasis and definition depending on context.

The design process

Essentially, design requires the designer to transform thoughts into realized products, and planning and managing this process is the basis of a

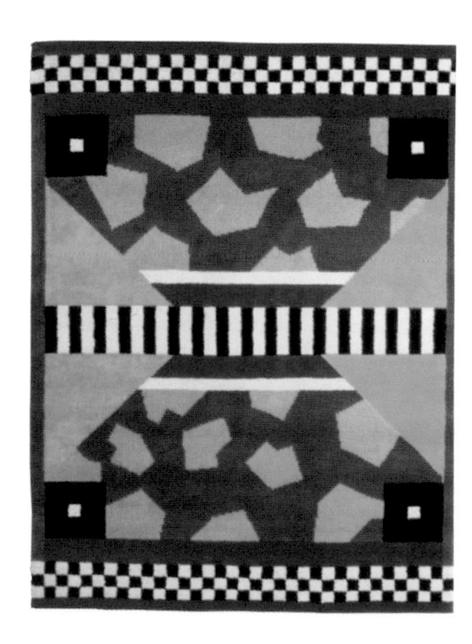

Nathalie du Pasquier's designs – here, the carpets Arizona (1983), **left**, and NDP44 (2005), **right**, provide an interesting insight into how a body of work can develop over a period of time, in this case 20 years. These two designs illustrate how a designer can develop and change their work while retaining innate individual stylistic and aesthetic qualities.

successful project. The scope and limitations of a design project regarding function, aesthetics and market requirements need careful and intelligent negotiation; typically, a designer works towards a design that meets client and consumer needs.

The design process generally begins with the assimilation of information, often provided by the client in the form of a **brief**, followed by an investigation by the designer or design team that leads to possible design solutions, which are then refined. Discussions in-house among designers and externally with the client about how a design is developed and finalized ensure that considered and calculated adjustments are made through consensus. This approach generates the best design results.

It is important that the design process is flexible – it should be seen as a negotiation between problem and solution through analysis, synthesis and evaluation – and allows for return loops between stages in the development of the design.

Developing an idea for a design can lead to many viable solutions, and the designer's central role is to decide which of a multitude of options are the most creative and relevant ideas to develop to a finished state. This decision-making boils down to sound critical judgement, which ensures that the most promising designs are nurtured to their appropriate market conclusion. Time, money and information are important influences and need to be carefully monitored to make sure the design process comes to a successful conclusion and on schedule.

The textile design process

Textile designers operate in a number of arenas and situations. For example, a designer may work in-house for a manufacturer, or in an independent design studio or be self-employed. As in most design processes, the designer's first step when creating a textile collection is to identify and collect research material. This then undergoes a series of developmental transformations using the design tools available within the designer's chosen textile medium, be it print, weave, mixed media or a combination of these. Design ideas are produced to the relevant standard for initial fabric sampling, which is determined by the individual designer or design studio director and depends on the intended textile market. Sampling may highlight the need for minor design modifications, such as pattern and colour adjustments. The designer often oversees the production of the initial fabric samples, which can require discussion with a manufacturer, particularly when large volumes of cloth will subsequently be produced. Finally, designs are presented to clients at outlets like trade fairs and retail establishments.

Research

How a designer identifies a concept and the type of visual research necessary for a textile collection influences all subsequent design process activities.

Far left
Hussein Chalayan opened the show for Airborne, his 2007 autumn/winter collection, with a dress that incorporated LED over 15,000 flickering LED lights. The innovative fashion design reflects the importance of detailed research and design development – without this, the dress would not have been realized as successfully as it was.

Centre and left
Hussein Chalayan's innovative motorized hood, also from his Airborne collection, is designed to offer protection against the wind. Research and development enabled this clever headpiece to be realized.

Both are informed by a number of factors, such as knowledge and experience of the product and its market and whether the designer is traditionalist or innovatory in relation to these. Research should clarify the likely use of the textile design, which is a major consideration in design development.

Different strands of the textile market require different research and development approaches. For instance, creating designs for Hawaiian Aloha shirts in the sportswear market requires a different approach to that required when designing woven textiles for a home furnishings manufacturer in Germany, or developing embroidery for haute couture in France.

Research material can be found in many resources ranging from museums and galleries to botanical gardens. Gathering it may involve **fieldwork** and collecting on location, or finding visual material in libraries and textile archives. All these approaches provide designers with legitimate sources of inspiration. What is fundamentally important is how a designer identifies and engages with their research and how they then extract appropriate designs from it and develop them. In the setting of a design studio team brainstorming sessions at the start of a new project may help to define the directions research and development directions should take.

Concept and trend forecasts, discussed in chapter 5, suggest directions for the future and are consequently valuable guidelines.

Gamodene, a wall painting by Paul Morrison (2006) is typical of the kind of botanical painting that inspired his printed textile designs for Liberty Fabric featured in the case study in chapter 2.

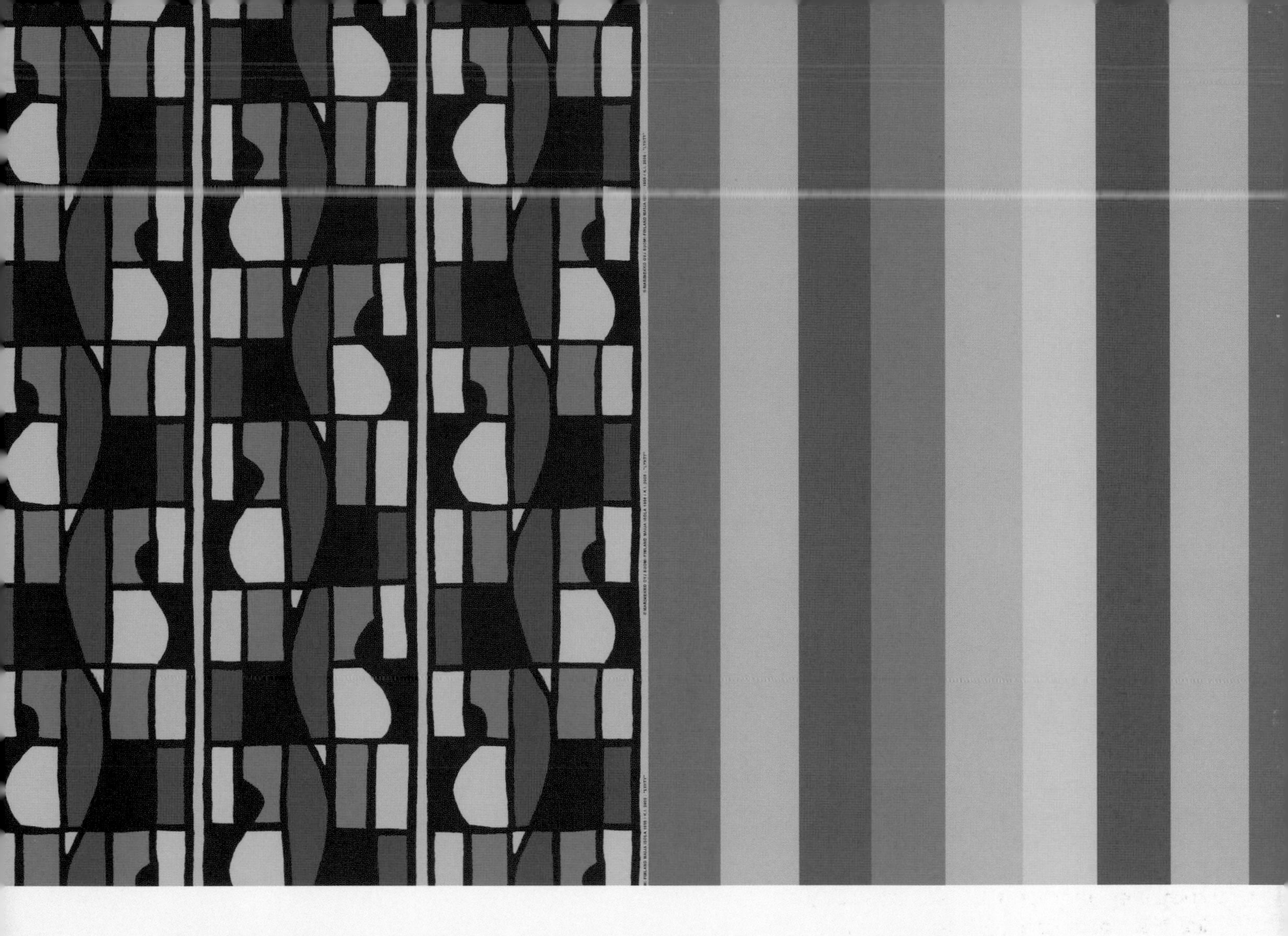

Marimekko: artistic and technical co-operation

The Finnish printed-textile design company Marimekko places artistic and technical skills at the heart of its design ideology, and distinctive and individual designing and functionality at the heart of its design process. A new design is produced in close interaction with production, sales and marketing, and often captures the essence of the enduring Marimekko image.

Marimekko's designers are leading figures in their field, who vary from recognized designers to innovative young designers. The company recognizes the value of collaboration and consequently works closely with design students and young designers. This is a mutually beneficial relationship that provides new designers with a chance to show their skills, while Marimekko benefits from their reactions and the inspirations they draw from contemporary phenomena.

The development of a new design from sketch to printed fabric begins with an exchange of ideas and concepts. The designer and the company's interior textile team discuss the form in which a design idea could function best and have the greatest appeal; the kind of soul it could have and the context to which it could belong. Designers are not given instructions or limitations: they are free to create and to inject their own experiences and views of trends into their designs.

Each new design reflects the imagination, vision and creative drive of the designer. However, it is not until designer and manufacturing professionals have jointly tested how the design idea functions that the design process is complete. The final appearance and character of the fabric emerge through co-operation with those who make the stencils for flatbed screen-printing, work in the colour laboratory and run the flatbed screen-printing equipment.

Above, left
Lyhty, a classic design from 1956, was reissued in autumn 2008.

Above, right
Aino, a classic 1979 design on cotton velvet, by Maija Isola and Kristina Isola, was reissued in autumn 2008.

Mood boards

Formalizing concept and research directions often results in the creation of mood boards that display inspirational images, text and objects as well as textiles. These elements are carefully composed to achieve an impact that motivates the designer or design studio and clarifies the directions their projected design will take. Mood boards are also a valuable point of reference throughout the design process. In a studio they are pinned to the walls so that they are always accessible, and provide an overview of how a design is developing. Fundamentally, a mood board is a visual tool that reflects the overall feel of what a designer is aiming to achieve.

Making a hand-crafted mood board can be slower than creating a digital one, but a board that displays physical objects offers a more complete palette of sensations, and has more impact, than a colour print of one that has been generated digitally.

Above
This mood board was designed by Emma Sheldon for a textile-design brief titled 'Poetic Empire', which was set by the Hand and Lock embroidery company as a competition in 2008.

Opposite
Polly Bell's notebooks illustrate the creative thinking involved in the development of design ideas and their potential applications.

Developing the design

A brief defines a design project's requirements, explaining and clarifying the objectives. It can be set by a client, agent or design studio director; or the design project could be defined by an individual designer for a specific market niche. The designer must be in possession of all the information that is required to achieve a successful design project, so if there are concerns

about what a client requires he or she must take the initiative and ask questions. These can range from aesthetic concerns, such as the type of colour palette for the collection, to questions about the target market and manufacturing opportunities.

The design process starts with a variety of ideas inspired by the research material that has been gathered. Exploring these takes the form of sketches, using traditional pencils, brush and paint or utilizing other creative starting points that may include photography, computer-aided design (CAD), or working directly with textile materials and techniques. All design options are usually nurtured in the early stages of the design process. As ideas progress they undergo an increasingly rigorous regime of selection, development and refinement. Initial sketches are transformed as the direction of a design idea becomes clearer. This process is controlled by the creative management of the designer.

In a studio, designs that are under development are presented to other designers, and the most appropriate directions for developing ideas into finished designs are discussed. A preliminary presentation may also be made to a client or manufacturer. Mood boards are useful in these situations as they provide an overview of the developing design.

Applying aesthetic elements such as motif, pattern, colour and surface treatments, and interpreting the concept intelligently, can produce designs

Hettie Nettheim: the Architectonic project

The inventive Architectonic collection by the textile designer Hettie Nettheim illustrates a design process which, while not typical, is indicative of creativity. The printed textile designs were developed for interior and fashion markets and reflect a passionate interest in architecture. Her design process followed a logical series of inventive and technical developments. The research stage included studying the work of architect Zaha Hadid, after which Nettheim made simple 3-D geometric models out of foam board. From the models she made photographs and drawings which were then manipulated and refined into repeat patterns using CAD. 3-D CAD software techniques, which she specifically learnt for the collection, were used to develop additional, suggestive architectural forms and structures which were also made into repeat patterns.

A selection of Nettheim's designs were initially printed on fabric as test pieces using hand- and digital-printing methods, in preparation for the production of a small number of fabric lengths. Later, the majority of the designs were printed on to an assortment of textiles to form the Architectonic collection of printed-textile design samples. Although quite costly, this enhanced the aesthetic qualities of the designs and gave them context. Printing them on to fabric also gave prospective clients a clear indication of how they would look, feel and potentially function in either interior or fashion contexts.

Important in Nettheim's design process, and for all designers, was the final selection of designs, mounting them on card and sequencing them so that when they were presented to buyers they were in a considered rhythm, suggestive of possible design groupings for perceived contextual settings. The later stages of the design process comprised visualizations that illustrated how the designs could be applied to a variety of furniture and fashion forms. One of the digitally printed photography patterns was upholstered on to a chair to show how a design would work in product form. This contextual work was an intrinsic part of the final collection portfolio and publicity material. A written concept statement outlined the Architectonic project. This is a common practice for designers, and is useful as it can be given to a client in advance of a collection presentation and may also be used for a press release. Nettheim was invited to present Architectonic to the Habitat design studio in London, who subsequently bought her work.

Above, left
Manual screen print and digital print.

Above, centre
Digital repeat print developed from photographs of handmade geometric model structures (2008).

Above, right
Digital repeat print developed from photographs of handmade geometric model structures (2008).

Opposite
Digital print from CAD development (2008).

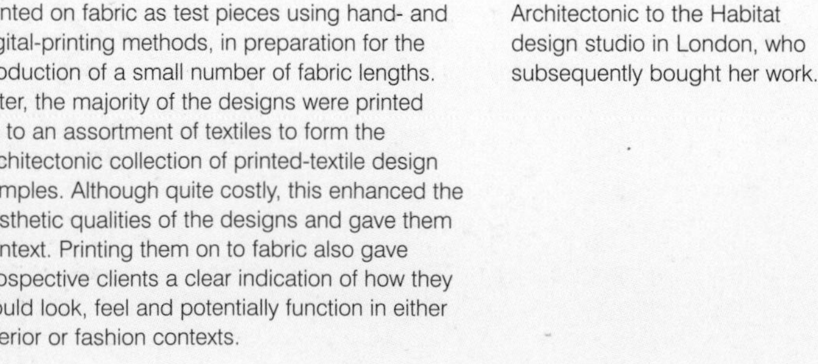

Right
Digital print upholstered on to a chair form (2008).

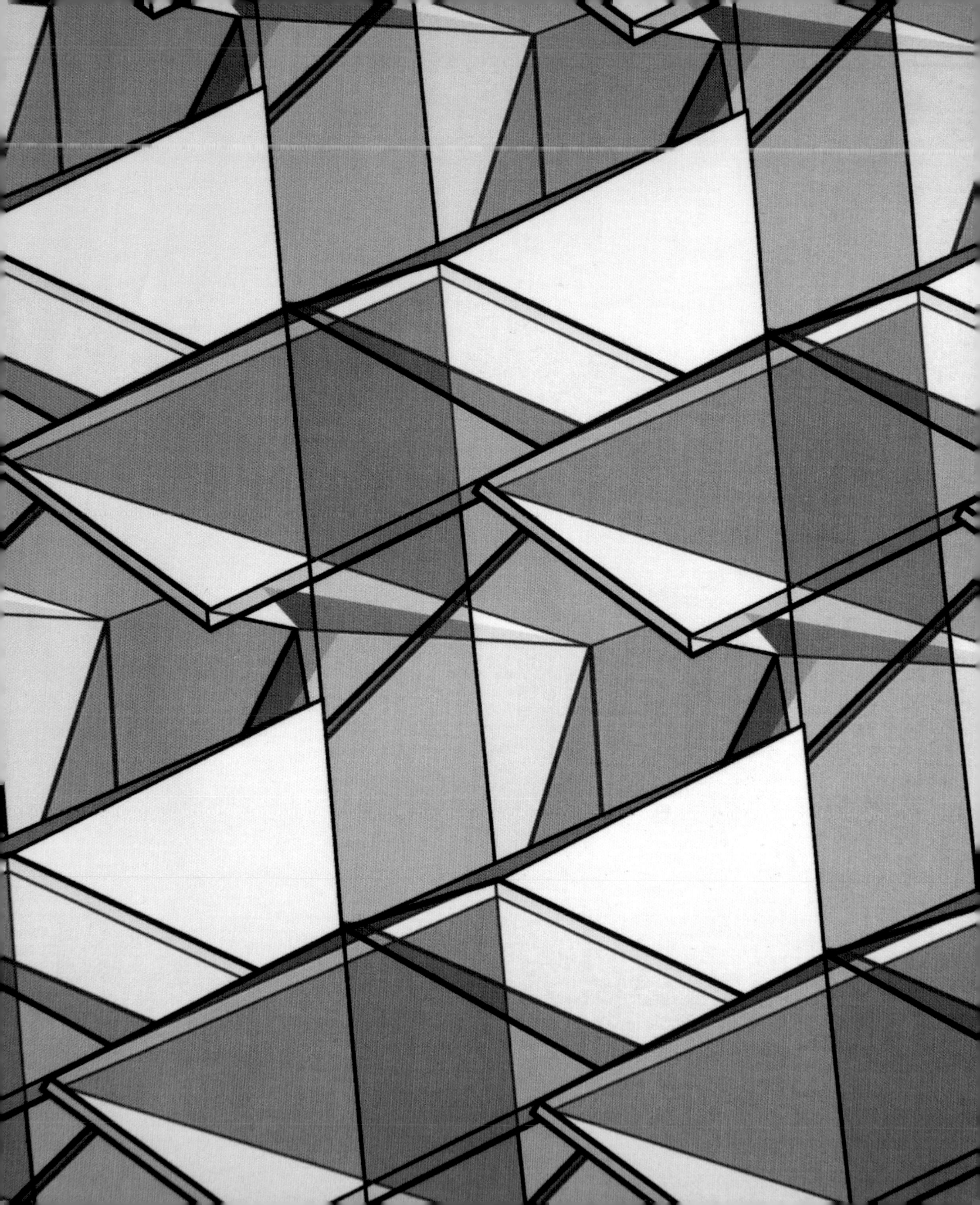

that are different but nevertheless share a common theme. CAD provides new creative potential for this process and is time-efficient once the main software functions have been mastered. This is discussed in chapters 2, 3 and 4.

Fabric sampling

Fabric sampling can take place when the design ideas are finalized, as a test midway through the design process, or at different times depending on the designer or design studio and the textile medium.

The methods used to produce fabric samples for a collection of designs varies depending on the type of textile and who the designer is working for. Practical concerns like cost and the availability of manufacturing facilities can influence whether an independent textile designer presents finished designs on paper or as fabric samples. Or a designer may prefer one method of sampling over another because of the aesthetic qualities it produces. Fabric samples of designs by studios like Marimekko and Liberty Fabrics, which have established outlets, are produced by the manufacturers they work with, and are tested for colour and design quality before the textiles are produced in larger volumes. However, there is no set method; how fabric samples are produced depends on the designer or design studio and the resources available to them.

Textile manufacturers predominantly buy designs as fabric samples from an independent designer or a design studio. If the sample has been digitally designed and made the customer will, in addition, normally receive the design on a disk that contains the aesthetic and technical information required to translate it accurately into larger manufacturing runs.

In the case of a digitally printed fabric the disk contains a design that can be put back into a computer and, depending on the method of manufacture, undergo minor adjustments. For example, if required, a design that will be rotary screen-printed can be adjusted on disk to reduce the number of colours. This might involve bringing 200 colours down to 16, although a prudent designer may well have factored this consideration into the design process. In addition, colour separations for screen printing can be taken from a design on a disk.

It is equally necessary to provide a disk for a digital weave design as it contains the aesthetic and, importantly, technical information required to make the design into cloth. Samples of hand-woven textile designs are predominantly realized through weaving. However, with advances in CAD technology they can be printed on paper, with supporting weave notation instructions, or samples can be displayed virtually. These options may be economic and ecological strategies for the future, but without an actual fabric sample the full aesthetic and textural experience of a woven textile is arguably reduced.

The majority of mixed media textile designs are best realized as fabric samples. This is because of the intricacy of the manufacturing process and the aesthetic 3-D qualities of the design, which can only be appreciated by handling the fabric itself.

The reason why fabric sampling can be expensive is that machinery has to be taken out of larger production runs, and time that is not used to make saleable products on expensive machines is costly. Money caught up in sample stocks is money that cannot be recovered. This is where CAD systems can help to alleviate this kind of concern. They allow many different textile designs to be virtually simulated as fabrics and, if the technology is available, digitally sampled. This is occurring with increased frequency in printed textiles.

Planning

The time frame for creating a new collection is determined by factors such as customer deadlines, trade fairs and seasonal trends, all of which require a collection to be completed and presented at a given time – to coincide with the London, Paris or New York fashion weeks, for example, or with trade fairs like Heimtextil in Frankfurt and Première Vision in Paris. This requires careful organization, to reduce pressure on the designer and ensure that designs are completed on time. Planning is a real necessity if a designer or design studio is dealing with a number of design projects at the same time.

All planning involves deciding how best to interpret and respond to the aims and objectives of a project brief, and then developing a clear strategy to achieve them. A number of methods can be used. Perhaps the simplest is to arrange the elements of the plan in a logical sequence. For instance, working from the brief, the designer determines what is required and decides on a sequence of events that will take the elements involved through the design process to a design solution. Time management simply demands making the best use of the time available.

Textile designers design for the future and need to know about trends in their market. If a designer or studio gets the colour, pattern, fabric or yarn for a particular season wrong, designs can fail to sell and money can be lost. Keeping up to date requires astute judgement and foresight. In addition to being aware of trends, when planning a textile collection it is also necessary to know the types of product for which it will be suitable, and the number of designs and colourways required, along with quality requirements, the client or market area, manufacturing opportunities and capacities, and price points. All of these elements need to be factored into the design plan.

In a design studio the design director often plans a new textile collection in consultation with other members of the team. Discussions with manufacturers and their sales and marketing departments are also important.

Effective planning may take time but it usually yields results as finished designs are presented and marketed on deadline. Lack of planning can result in wasted time, overspending and considerable stress and tension. While design projects do not always go exactly to plan, without a plan it is difficult to monitor progress.

Textile collections

A textile collection is a group of designs that is shown and offered for sale each season, and the main responsibility of a textile designer is to initiate, organize, develop and direct its development. The finished designs are his or her response to a brief. Good design adds value to a product and is the differentiating element when textiles are equal in quality and price.

A collection normally consists of designs for a specific fashion or interior market and season. The classic Hawaiian Aloha designs for men's shirts exemplify creating a particular textile design for a niche market. They evolved from early Chinese and Japanese textile designs and patterns, and Polynesian bark cloth patterns, and were subsequently contemporized utilizing an array of iconic Western motifs – probably as a result of the Hawaiian islands being assimilated into the United States. While Aloha creates new designs, early ones from the 1930s, such as Land of Aloha, persist due to customer demand. Although Hawaii's geographical position means that Aloha designs do not conform to the fashion seasons in Europe and the United States, they are a design classic and never go out of fashion.

Manufacturers who make textiles for the fashion industry generally work one season ahead and launch two main collections each year, for the spring/summer and autumn/winter selling seasons, and some also have mid-season collections. Manufacturers of furnishing fabrics and household textiles produce one main range a year which they showcase at major trade fairs like Heimtextil in Frankfurt.

There may be a predominant theme in the textile designs: for instance, floral motifs that focus on a particular selection of flowers and plants which are sequentially shown in different forms or styles throughout the collection. This can be achieved by using combinations and transformations of drawing style, colour palette and pattern permutations, or in the choice of the medium that is used, whether paint or fabric. Another theme could be more eclectic, with motifs that incorporate abstract and representational elements, but remain unified by the colour palette and drawing style used by the designer.

Collection development

When developing a collection it is essential for the designer or design studio to have clearly defined and well-articulated concepts and themes from the outset, as these inform the choice of image, colours and materials. A well-defined concept is not only fundamental to the design process; it can also be used for publicity and promotional material – in brochures, for example, and for in-store presentations and design stories for magazines and journals. Once the concept is defined the design development begins.

A colour palette is usually decided on at this point to unify developing ideas. Although this does not mean all the different designs in a collection have to be in exactly the same colourways, there should probably be colour relationships between them. Colour trends forecast for the new season are

Opposite
Aloha shirts, series 3 by Paradise Found, made in Hawaii. The classic Hawaiian Aloha designs for men's shirts exemplify the creation of a particular textile design for a niche market.

Cadillac Cruising

Classic Chevy

Marlin

Seaplane

Wooden Boat

Woodie

considered alongside any pre-existing palette for a previous collection. Decisions on whether designs that have previously been successful are carried forward can affect the character of a collection. Although it makes commercial sense to continue to release a design type that sold well, the new season's colour trends mean it will require recolouring.

The designer may sometimes decide to separate image concept and colour inspiration. This might be done to enable the imagery to be more experimental, and have a distinct character, while adhering to future market colour trends. This experimental element can give the collection a distinct character while fitting into its market. When developing a collection one good strategy is to ensure the experimental character of the collection continues to evolve throughout the full range of designs. Perhaps, for example, starting formally with imagery and colour, then becoming eccentric and finally humorous. This kind of approach is sometimes important to consider as it really can capture the imagination of the client and, eventually, the consumer.

Imagery and colour are crucial but are only two of a number of aesthetic elements that contribute to the creation of a design and a collection. Drawing and pattern, discussed in chapter 5, are also important. All these complementary considerations should be explored, in terms of both how they are used and their potential creative impact. Depending on the designer's experience, and judgement of what is required by the market, these elements can be deliberately combined to create either well-balanced or disruptive effects. The type of fabric for which a design is intended also determines its aesthetic qualities, in particular when textile materials are used in its creation. Knowledge of composition – ordering motifs to create balance, harmony and rhythm – is key. And exploring scale relationships to achieve varying degrees of visual impact is another integral element.

While there is a wide range of aesthetic choices in textile design, and emphasis on specific approaches is potentially limiting, the basic considerations described above should be understood, learnt and nurtured. Perhaps one of the most effective ways of doing this is by analyzing historical and cultural fine and decorative arts.

Designs for a collection may be developed in-house, brought in from freelance designers, or a mixture of both. Themes and subthemes, and the number of designs and colourways, are determined by the designer or by the customer's requirements. Establishing an overview of the collection at the development stage is often a good strategy. If fashion fabrics are being designed some may be aimed at menswear and others at womenswear. This requires forward planning to accommodate different design perspectives while at the same time creating an overarching coherent collection.

Once a final design has been chosen, three or four supporting colourways, sometimes more, are often created. Colourways can be balanced, when the colours change but their relationships within the design stay the same, or unbalanced, when there are no easily identifiable relationships between the colours. An example of how this works is a three-colour print design that has

Design collaborations

Design collaborations, like ethical issues, provide the opportunity to create enhanced and imaginative products and there are many design partners in textile design. But working together requires discussion, and design empathy, between the designers involved, who often come from very different disciplines, and the manufacturer. In a design studio relationships are well established, whereas the dynamics in a unique collaboration are often different and potentially energizing. In 1967 two legendary twentieth-century designers, master textile designer Jack Lenor Larsen and Modernist furniture designer Pierre Paulin, worked together to produce innovative results with stretch fabric and the sculptural furniture form. Larsen provided boldly patterned machine-printed stripes on an industrial nylon knit fabric – more commonly used in swimwear at the time – which he called Momentum. Paulin provided the furniture forms, which initially included the Ribbon chair and ABCD sofa. The Dutch furniture company Artifort, for whom Paulin continues to design, enabled the realization of this collaboration. The difference between Artifort and other furniture companies at the time was that they could see the potential in the design, and had the skills to fuse the stretch fabric with the sculptural furniture forms – a revolutionary process in 1967 which may have been overlooked by manufacturers who mass produced textiles and furniture. Larsen believes this three-way collaboration was successful simply because the textile design and furniture form worked together at the right moment. This once revolutionary combination in furniture design is now a design classic, and to celebrate its 40th anniversary Artifort brought the Ribbon chair and ABCD sofa back into production, using the Momentum textile.

In 2005 a project between the innovative product designer Marcel Wanders and the Italian furniture design company Moroso led to the generation of a distinctly individual printed textile for furniture. A comfortable seat and basic form are offset by a fabric with strong colours printed ad hoc on a flat or damasked background of square patterns; the furnitures' power to communicate comes from the blend of apparently simple forms and specially printed fabrics.

Top
This sofa (2005) is the result of a collaboration between Dutch celebrity designer Marcel Wanders and the respected furniture company Moroso of Italy. The decorative printed textile design created by Wanders for the sofa is a bold decorative pattern which challenges the traditional expectations of repeating patterns through its large, singular, decorative motifs. While the design is bold, the attention to aesthetic detail reflects and embodies Wanders' design philosophy of bringing beauty into his designs to enhance the environment and life experience of his customer.

Above and below
In 1967 Jack Lenor Larsen and Pierre Paulin collaborated to blend Paulin's designs for the Ribbon chair and ABCD sofa with Larsen's Momentum stretch fabric. The chair and sofa were manufactured by Artifort, who brought them back into production in 2007.

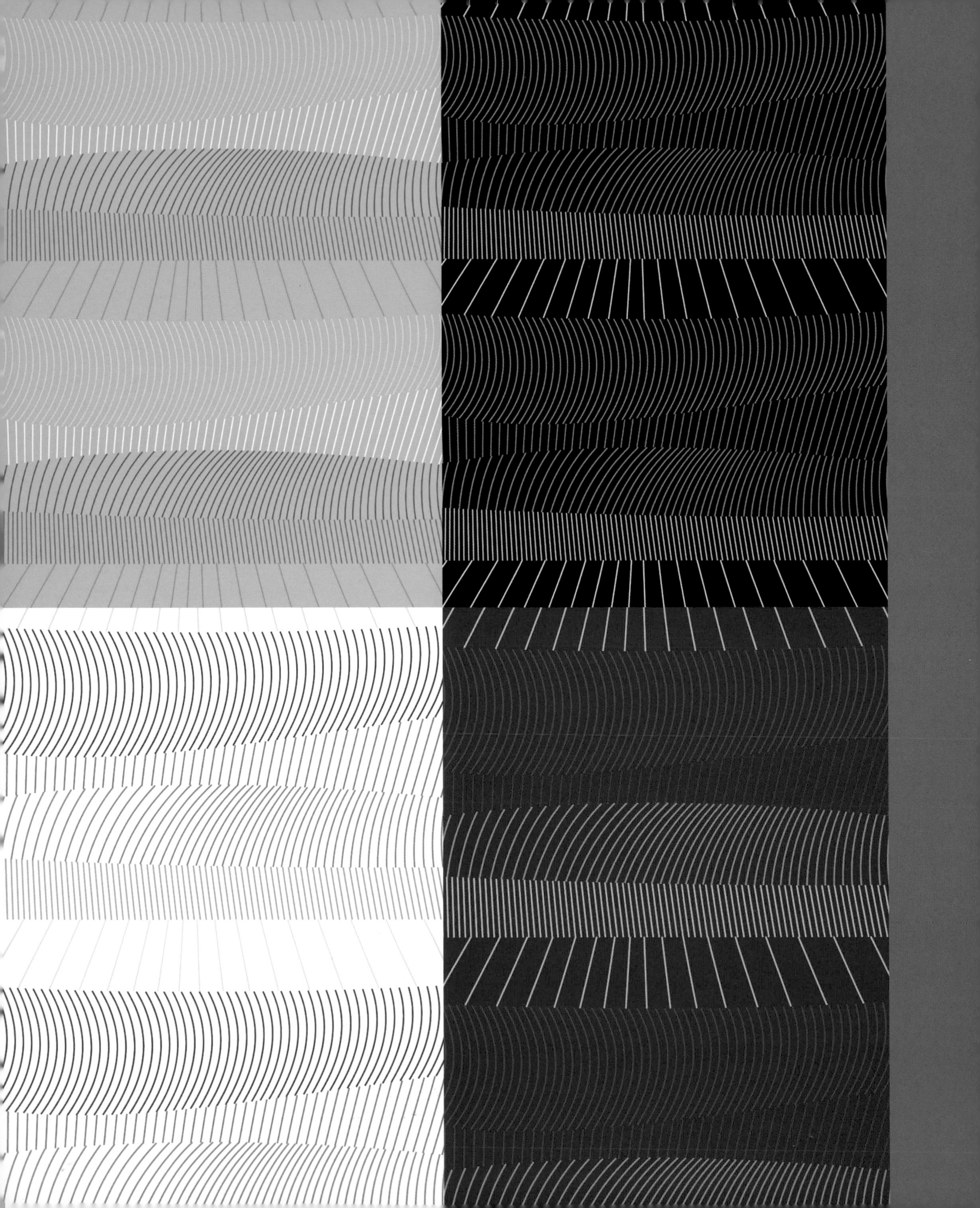

a dark green ground, large circles in mid green and small squares in light green. A balanced colourway would have a dark blue ground, large circles in mid blue and small squares in light blue. An unbalanced one would have a bright yellow ground, large circles in purple and small squares in grey.

Other considerations when developing a collection are whether to include single-coloured fabrics, and how to balance more detailed designs with simpler, supporting co-ordinating ones.

The **brand** of a collection identifies it, so planning and development are important. The image that is created is the image of the designer, design studio and textile company for the next 12 months or until the next collection.

Opposite
These four distinctly different colourways for Vagsvall, a printed textile design by Bjorn Dahlstrom for Marimekko (2007) dramatically or quietly change the design elements, creating differing levels of visual experience from one colourway to another. They also trigger different atmospheres and emotional responses depending on their setting and who is looking at them.

Presentation

Designs can be presented in a number of settings. Clients – for example, a buyer from a textile company that will manufacture large volumes of some of the designs – may visit the designer or design studio, or the designer or a representative of the studio may make an appointment to see a textile manufacturer. And although designers who work in-house for a textile company usually design exclusively for their employer, they may visit other designers and studios and buy their designs to use them as sources of inspiration to develop their own collections. Designs are also shown at trade fairs and fashion shows, where established and prospective clients can see a designer's or studio's new work. Wherever a presentation takes place it requires visual and verbal communication skills.

Visual communication refers to how designs are ordered into a collection and contextualized to engage potential customers, a process that requires the same degree of creativity as developing them: a designer or design studio can invest a significant amount of time and money in creating what can be more than 40 different designs.

Applying intelligent ways to show how a collection evolves while remaining unified is of fundamental importance. Logically, a strong opening series of designs focuses a client's attention and draws them into viewing the full portfolio. A good rhythm and no awkward clashes from one design to another are crucial. Many inventive formats can be used to give a clear sense of how a design or grouping of designs will work in a product context.

In the same way that a collection may have a title, individual designs can be given names. This is useful when they are catalogued and sold. It also creates a narrative and can lead to a discussion about the design, and the collection. The name can be written or typed on to a label and attached to either the fabric design sample or the card to which the sample is attached. The name of the designer or design studio, a number for each design, a date and (when the design uses textile materials) the production method can be included as supporting information. A sample is either flat-mounted on card, usually by applying double-sided tape to the top edge of the design, or attached to a header – a folded-in half-strip of card that sandwiches the top

edge of the sample. This method of presentation makes it easier to handle the fabric.

Contextualization of designs as discussed in the textiles of Nettheim featured in her profile in this chapter is paramount (see p. 174). There are normally drawings and photographs that show how the fabrics in a collection work together, how they work when they are made into or incorporated in products, and how the products work with other related ones. Depending on the standing and finances of the designer or design studio, this may involve applying the fabric to a product and styling it in an interior or fashion setting.

Ultimately, the quality of a presentation reflects the designer's level of professionalism and contributes to the sale of the designs.

It is important for textile designers to be able to talk intelligently and present themselves and their work professionally. A presentation may be made to a specific client who has commissioned the designs; or in a large design studio a new collection may be shown to directors and board members, for their approval, and to sales teams and agents, before being presented to clients. In addition, at various stages of the design process designers are often required to present their ideas to colleagues, managers and directors. Often the most effective presentations are simple and concise: good design requires little verbal explanation.

The experimental printed textile designs and fashion garments in Basso & Brooke's collections succeed because of their visual impact. Nevertheless, there is a conceptual and creative process right through to the presentation of their designs on the catwalk. For the 2009 spring/summer ready-to-wear collection the inspiration was the work of the Japanese artist Hokusai and aesthetics from the film *Blade Runner*. The dramatic results were styled on models who displayed the collection of over 40 garments on the catwalk,

Above
Designers Basso & Brooke at the show for their 2009 spring/summer, ready-to-wear collection.

Top and opposite page
Designs from the Basso & Brooke show illustrate the innovative use of printed textiles in fashion.

to choreographed music. Fundamental details like how these were sequenced for the fashion show, and the impact this would have on the audience, required a tuned design eye to ensure there was connectivity between the variety of designs and garments. This process of preparation generated the distinctive catwalk presentation, which represents the essence of the growing Basso & Brooke design culture.

Marketing, promotion and sales

Marketing, promoting and selling their textiles is central to the success of designers, design studios and manufacturers.

Textile trade fairs

Trade fairs are held throughout the world each year and are vital to the global trade in textile commodities. They cater for both regional and international exhibitors, and participating in them enables designers and companies to showcase new collections and products, maintain existing client relationships and cultivate new ones. They also provide an opportunity to see what competitors are producing and learn about current trends and developments in textiles. In Europe the most established are Première Vision in Paris, which provides a market place for the sale of textiles for the fashion and apparel markets, where fashion can be defined as clothing that changes seasonally, following catwalk trends, and apparel as other less high fashion-dependent clothing, including outerwear. The trade fair Heimtextil in Frankfurt is on a similar footing to Première Vision, the main difference being that it is a market place for the trade in textiles for furnishing and interiors. Pitti Filati in Florence is another significant trade fair event well regarded for its emphasis on yarns and threads.

Above, left
Heimtextil in Frankfurt is the international trade fair for interior textiles.

Above, right
The design studio hall at Heimtextil Frankfurt gives designers and design studios the opportunity to sell their latest textile design collections to the textile industry.

Promotional and trend forecast forums feature at many of the fairs and are presented in a number of different formats. Examples are event-based displays that showcase textile designs for fashion, inspirational films, audio-visual presentations, fashion and colour seminars, catalogues and information about fabrics.

Heimtextil is the biggest international trade fair for home and contract textiles. Held over four days in the middle of January, it is the first fair of the year and has more than 2500 exhibitors from over 65 countries. It is a platform for manufacturers, the trade and designers, and its trend forums, seminars and presentations provide useful insights into what is new on the international scene. Leading interior textile designers, such as Jack Lenor Larsen, have participated in its seminars.

Initial costs for a textile designer or studio exhibiting at a trade fair include payment for the stand, and travel to and from the event, but these are usually offset by selling designs, and showing at a fair can be profitable. However, there are many factors at play which are often influenced by trends in the market. The styling of the exhibition stand is important and should reflect the designer's or studio's aesthetics and the tastes of their target market. This creates a particular ambience and atmosphere that is intrinsic to how collections and products are displayed, and influences how designs are presented to potential buyers. Planning is therefore essential to achieve a professional stand that will attract attention – and subsequent sales.

6. Première Vision: fabrics for fashion

Fabric forum at Première Vision, the international textile trade fair in Paris.

Since Première Vision was formed 30 years ago by a group of Lyon weavers to market and promote their textiles it has developed into the world's leading fabric show for fashion and apparel: it recently accommodated 50,000 visitors from over 110 countries. Its basic aim is to provide a progressive and coherent environment that represents the needs of the textile industry and it is consequently in accord with both the apparel industry and the fashion calendar – it is held in September for the spring/summer collections and in February for the autumn/winter ones. Première Vision's trend forums, which can take the form of small exhibitions, showcase predicted colour and fabric trends 18 months in advance of an actual season.

A number of salons come under the Première Vision umbrella. An enormous variety of new textile design collections, including printed, woven and mixed media ranges, are promoted at Indigo, where fashion and apparel professionals are able to meet exhibiting designers from all over the world. These range from internationally established design studios to recent graduates presenting their collections for the first time. Design schools participate and show innovative perspectives and emergent textile design ideas. Indigo also presents new technology to the fashion world through supporting the representation of companies involved in the development and marketing of the the latest digital software design and sampling methods.

The Expofil salon specializes in textile yarns and fibres and is therefore perhaps not dissimilar to Pitti Filati in Florence. The Mod'Amont provides an international, creative and diversified range of buttons, buckles, metallic and plastic trims, embroidery, lace, braids and cords. Le Cuir, a Paris salon, promotes leather for an array of market contexts.

Creation protection, copyright and intellectual property ownership is a concern for textile designers and manufacturers, and Première Vision was the first trade fair to appoint a group of advisers – attorneys and experts in apparel and textiles – to help exhibitors and buyers to take a strong stand on copyright and the theft of intellectual property. The latter includes stolen patterns and copied designs. Experts in the textile industry are also available to advise exhibitors and visitors and assist in drawing up contracts between designers and professionals.

To participate, exhibitors need to show they have the right credentials, which include quality and creativity, technical expertise, performance and reputation.

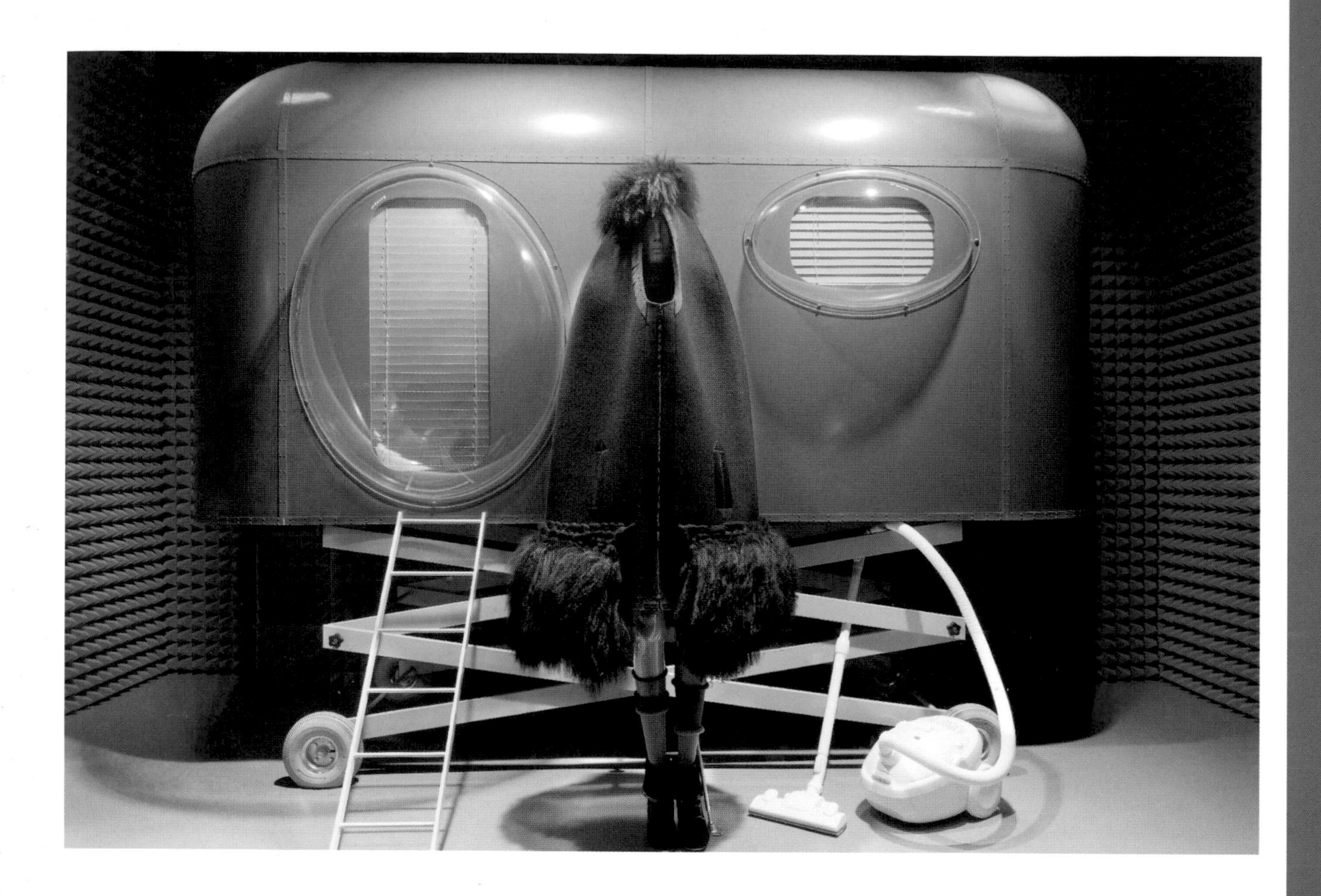

Fashion promotions

Fashion weeks are held throughout the world and give designers the opportunity to display their new collections, with textile design contributing broadly across many haute couture and ready-to-wear collections. Design teams like Basso & Brooke and Eley Kishimoto, who integrate their printed textile designs and garments, promote their collections at these events. The most established and internationally acclaimed fashion weeks are in London, Paris, New York and Milan.

Fashion weeks are held several months in advance of a season to give the press and buyers the opportunity to preview the designs, and retailers the time to buy them or include designers in their retail marketing. Some fashion weeks can be very specific – an example is Miami fashion week, where the focus is upon swimwear.

Fashion designers show their autumn/winter collections from January to March and their spring/summer collections from September to November.

Above and opposite
Two futuristic exhibit details from Selfridges' inspirational window displays in 2009, created to celebrate the store's centenary and titled Future A–Z 2109. The concept was developed by the innovative advertising agency Weiden + Kennedy, and drew on the question 'What's next?' The outcome was window displays that look forward to Selfridges' next centenary in 2109.

The internet

The internet and websites are playing an increasingly significant role in the marketing, promotion and sale of new designs, with dynamic and innovative websites developed by haute couture fashion houses as well as intelligently positioned customer targeted websites developed by high street brands such as Gap. Similarly, in the interior market there are websites for both high-end and more mainstream furnishing-textile designs, many of which give consumers the opportunity to buy textiles online.

The internet is increasingly used by individual designers and small design studios to promote themselves to customers in the textile industry and to the broader design audience, as well to the general public. In the smaller studios digital technology is providing increasing scope for bespoke textile design, and the internet is a prime catalyst for facilitating this in the future.

Below, left
Style.com, the online home of *Vogue*, leads the way in the field of fashion design media. The site provides a comprehensive window on the dynamic world of fashion design and its many characteristics, visions and personalities. The latest fashion shows are made available through the use of video media – a major advantage over traditional media – as well as reviews from the most significant fashion designers in the world, and interviews with designers, critics, models and celebrities.

Below, right
Trend reports on Style.com provide insight into the latest trends in the fashion industry, covering all fashion markets including women's ready-to-wear, haute couture, resort/cruise wear, as well as menswear.

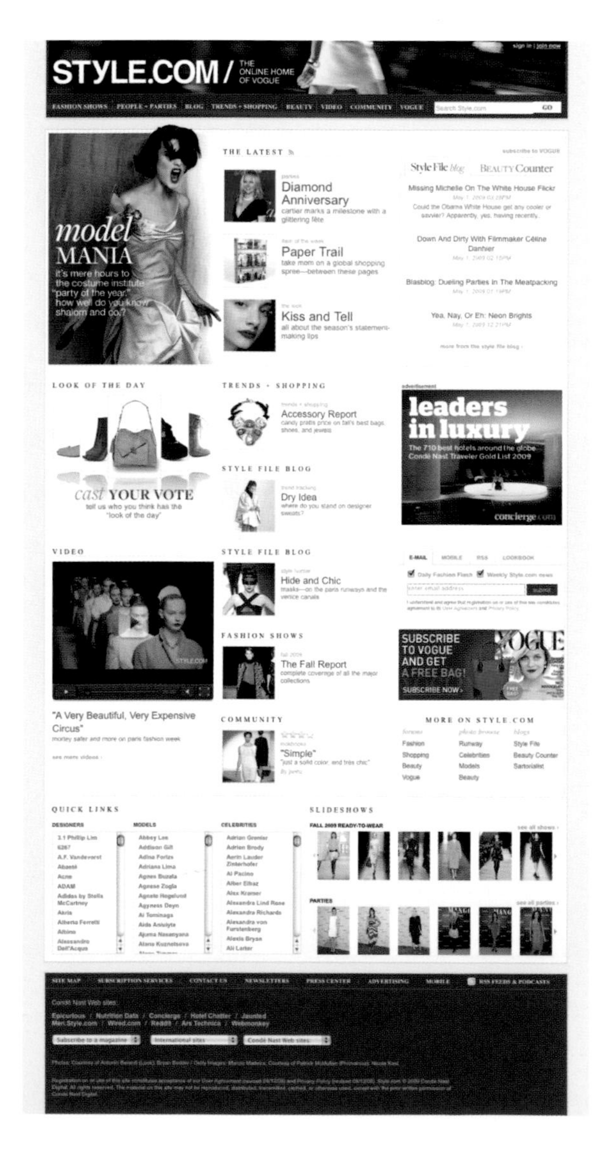

Display

Consumers ultimately determine the success of a textile collection, and their reaction when it reaches the marketplace is decisive for the designer or studio.

Consequently, how a collection is presented or displayed is pivotal as this impacts on the sales of textiles and textile products. Established and new fashion and interior companies invest in retail outlets – often innovative and idiosyncratic environments that capture the spirit of a company and reflect its brand identity – in which to market their latest collections and products. This can result in exterior and interior transformations to existing buildings, and even new ones, using visionary retail store design and display methods.

Two progressive examples in this arena are Liberty and Issey Miyake. Liberty's launch in 2008 of the Liberty of London store with its highly decorative, opulent and modern environment hailed a new era for the company. Designed by creative director Tamara Salman and Paris architects Pierre Beucler and Jean-Christophe Poggioli, Liberty of London captures the essence of the edgy, luxurious and British designs created by its design team and their creative collaborators. One of the objectives was to make a lasting impression on customers, ensuring they remembered the store once they had left it.

Tamara Salman, Creative Director of Liberty Fabric, outside the new Liberty of London store in 2008.

Totally different in aesthetics and atmosphere is the visionary Issey Miyake Tribecca flagship store in downtown Manhattan. A Frank Gehry titanium sculpture winds through a space that is also a creative venue for exhibitions, events and collaborations between artists, echoing Miyake's long-standing commitment to the exploration of form and structure in his fashion garments.

Like retail stores, designers' websites are increasingly inventive in the way they display designs, as are those of clothing and furnishing retail companies like Agnes B. With advances in digital design, virtual shopping is a real prospect for consumers: even now, virtual figures, with personality traits, that represent users can go shopping and buy things in virtual shops.

Above and opposite
The Issey Miyake Tribecca flagship store in New York (2001) incorporates a unique feature: a rippling titanium sculpture by Frank Gehry that weaves its way through the interior space.

Summary

There is, perhaps, no foolproof way to design, but nurturing and cultivating decision-making skills can enhance opportunities for innovation. And while it is true that there is never only one design that is right for a particular purpose, some designs may be better than others in certain textile markets.

The future for design in general, and textile design in particular, seems bright: increasingly, industrialists and politicians are recognizing that good design can provide economic benefits for manufacturing companies and regional economies. It is likely that design in general is set to accelerate as a multifaceted field that impacts on all walks of life. Textile designers already play, and will continue to play, an important role in shaping the material world. This position of responsibility requires intelligent designs that can raise awareness and implement, in varying degrees, responses to ethical, environmental, sustainable and fair trade issues. Only through building aspects of these concerns into a design brief and integrating them into the design process is it possible to provide effective and relevant design solutions. In the creative designs of Sheona Quenby and Ed Forster, discussed in chapter 2, intelligent visual responses to global issues are shown in the use of low-impact digital textile-printing technology. For many companies, it is essential that ethical factors are considered during the textile design process: the public are aware of global issues and want to play their part by being responsible consumers of textile commodities.

7.

Education and employment

Textile design influences the aesthetic and material world, whether through clothing, interior furnishings or other textile products. It can generate new lifestyles and types of design, or it can follow traditions and social norms. Its aesthetic and functional qualities can therefore be unique and idiosyncratic or reflect established styles. All of which can depend on what the textile will be used for.

While some of the new designers who will serve these needs come from regions or families that traditionally specialize in textile design, most of them learn about it at a university or college of art and design. Textile design departments throughout the world offer individual perspectives on the subject while providing basic knowledge and skills. This chapter discusses degree courses and looks at possible career paths with reference to textile design products and markets introduced earlier in the book.

The entry experience

To gain a place on a textile design degree course an applicant typically presents a portfolio of work at an interview where university or college staff determine his or her abilities and decide whether they are suitable for the course. It may be acceptable for an overseas applicant simply to submit a conventional portfolio of design work or CD-ROM portfolio by post and forgo the interview. All will need the appropriate qualifications; in the United Kingdom these are usually an art foundation diploma and A Levels, and similar criteria apply in other parts of the world.

Interviewers look at an applicant's potential to develop skills in research, drawing and the use of colour and pattern. Evidence in a portfolio of a developing understanding of the design process will also be important. Interviewers will look for signs of a genuine interest in textile design, evidenced by the use of textile media in the portfolio and through the enthusiasm and passion for the subject conveyed at interview. Showing good potential in the areas of communication and presentation, writing skills and an interest in historical, cultural and contemporary art and design are all important.

The degree course

A textile design degree course nurtures many of the qualities outlined above in an environment that supports a student's professional development, and ensures that after graduation they have the appropriate creative and professional qualities to participate in the world of textiles.

The first year

The first year introduces students to the potential of textile design and includes workshops in a number of disciplines, the most common of which are printed, mixed media and woven textile design. Typically, they rotate through a series of workshops that introduce techniques, materials and processes within these three areas. At the same time, they are encouraged to develop creatively, a process that culminates in their producing fabric samples that have both technical and aesthetic merit. They may also learn about the basics of colour and pattern.

Students are normally introduced to the computer-aided design (CAD) software relevant to textile designing; like the other subjects this is built on incrementally in the years that follow. At the end of this period of study, although there may be scope for working in two textile disciplines most students focus on only one. This can be beneficial as even within a single discipline a significant amount of knowledge has to be amassed in order to gain quality results, and depth of knowledge in a specific area can enhance employability. Working in two disciplines can encourage innovation through blending ideas and techniques, and may be helpful later in getting a job in a design studio.

The second year

In the second year students continue to develop their knowledge and skills in either one or two disciplines. This part of the course provides a period of sustained creative and technical development that continues into the third year, and a variety of learning experiences, such as exposure to live projects from industry, competitions, work placements/internships and study trips make it a challenging and potentially rewarding time. These experiences may start at the end of the first year and could spill over into the third.

The live project

A live project may take the form of a project brief developed in consultation with a university or college's partner in the textile industry and could culminate in students presenting finished designs to the partner. Universities offering textile design as an undergraduate course develop industry links and contacts to help prepare students for the industry. The partnership may be long-standing and run annually or it might be a one-off partnership for a single project. In some cases the live project might be a group project involving students from other courses, such as furniture or fashion design, too. Usually, however, students work individually with the benefit of seminar discussions to share ideas as the project develops. Successful designs may be taken forward and manufactured commercially and a student may be paid. Alternatively, he or she may be awarded a work placement with the partner. Live projects can be mutually beneficial: students gain insight into how the textile industry works and the partner gains new designs. The range and gravitas of projects varies depending on their profile and the partner.

The location of the university or college can influence the project. For example, if it is on a coast there may be an inclination towards designing textiles for surfwear. This has been a natural choice at the University College Falmouth in Cornwall in England. In the past they have collaborated with the

Above
Printed textile design students on the balcony of the Tate St Ives get feedback on their designs from staff of Mambo surfwear, the industry partner for this 2007 project.

Left
Winning flag designs by Helen Stark were displayed on the promenade in Penzance, Cornwall, following the industry-sponsored Hampshire flag project, 2008.

innovative Australian surfwear manufacturer Mambo on projects that culminated in students' designs being presented to at the Tate St Ives. In another UCF project, sponsored by the Hampshire Flag Company, individual students designed a collection of flags for a specified coastal site. The most successful designs were digitally printed and manufactured by the Hampshire Flag Company, and the flags were displayed in consultation with the local council's arts co-ordinator. While both projects were regionally based the partners were international companies.

The design fibres department at the Savannah College of Art and Design in the United States has a similar industry-linked educational approach. An example is a project set by Northwest Carpets which required students to develop pattern designs for carpets in a four-or five-star hotel. The three winning designs were presented to the company on its exhibition stand at the HD Expo in Las Vegas, and the students were awarded scholarships worth more than $3000.

International industry-linked projects open to all university textile design departments are another option. The Como Texprint project is an example. In 2008, silk printers in Como in Italy, recognizing the wealth of creative potential in printed textile design students at universities in the United

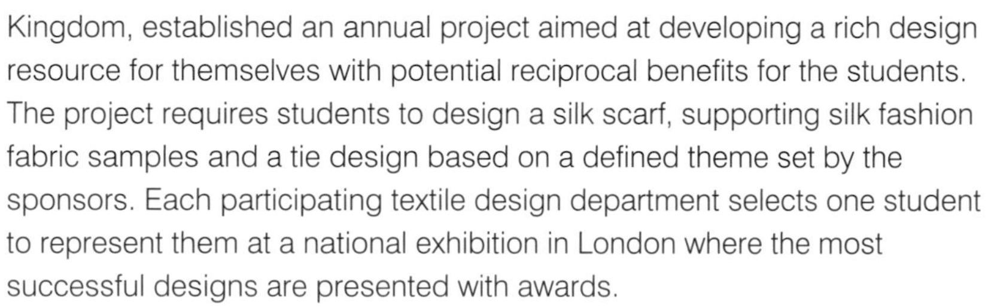

Kingdom, established an annual project aimed at developing a rich design resource for themselves with potential reciprocal benefits for the students. The project requires students to design a silk scarf, supporting silk fashion fabric samples and a tie design based on a defined theme set by the sponsors. Each participating textile design department selects one student to represent them at a national exhibition in London where the most successful designs are presented with awards.

The embroidery competition set by the company Hand and Lock, with sponsorship from companies and organizations ranging from Twistedthread and Madeira to the Powerhouse Museum in Sydney, Australia, is highly regarded. The first prize is $10,000 and the work of the highest placed Australian entry is exhibited in the Powerhouse Museum.

Student competitions

Similar to the Hand and Lock embroidery competition are student competitions set by institutions and organizations that promote design in general and textile design in particular. In the United States, these include the Surface Design Association, the American Association of Textile Chemists and Colorists, and the International Textile Market Association. In the United Kingdom, institutions that provide a similar range of competitions, with industry sponsorship, include the Royal Society of Arts, the Bradford Textile Society and the Society of Dyers and Colourists, whose Global Design competition attracts submissions from as far afield as Australia, China, Pakistan, South Africa and the United States. The final presentations to the winning designers are held in locations like Goa in India. All the competitions enable students to work on well-conceived textile design projects, with financial rewards and work-placement opportunities for the winners. Similar competitions are held in other parts of the world.

Above, left
Como Texprint judges view the designs for scarves (2008).

Top
Members of the Como Texprint hanging committee select student submissions for exhibition and final judging in the gallery at Chelsea College of Art and Design, University of the Arts, London (2008).

Above
Paolo Noseda and Guido Iettamanti with the winners of Como Textprint's scarf project: Helen Greensmith (2008).

Polly Bell: Living Off the Land

Polly Bell was an innovative winner of the annual textile competition set by the Royal Society of Arts in 2007/08. The society is a catalyst for nurturing enlightenment, thinking and social progress in the arts and Bell's textile project embodied this philosophy. Her textile collection was inspired by transition towns, and focused particularly on communities, self-sufficiency, co-operation and permaculture, and in particular explored the notion of Living off the Land.

This intriguing concept was Bell's inspiration and consequent source of imagery, which she developed as drawings and collages. She then developed this visual research into textile designs, using a combination of new technologies in print and weave that took sustainable textile issues into consideration. The digital jacquard loom and digital printer enabled Bell to manufacture her designs efficiently and with limited environmental impact as both technologies produce limited waste. She used earth-based colours and textural fabrics to reflect her original source of inspiration. The market context for the collection was a new restaurant/café in Jubilee Wharf, Penryn, a state of the art sustainable development project. Bell received two prestigious awards: the Eddie Squires Bursary for Outstanding Contemporary Printed Furnishing Fabric Design and the Sir Frank Warner and Sir Ernest Goodale Memorial Award.

She will use the award money to study traditional block printing at the Anokhi textile printing company in Jaipur, India, where there is a focus on traditional textile skills and conservation.

Top and opposite
Barn House (top) and Double Chicken Repeat (opposite), illustrative digital print samples by Polly Bell, winner of the Royal Society of Arts Fashion/Interiors competition in 2008.

Above
Jubilee Wharf in Penryn, Cornwall, by Bill Dunster Architects ZEDfactory Ltd, the location for Polly Bell's printed textile designs (2008).

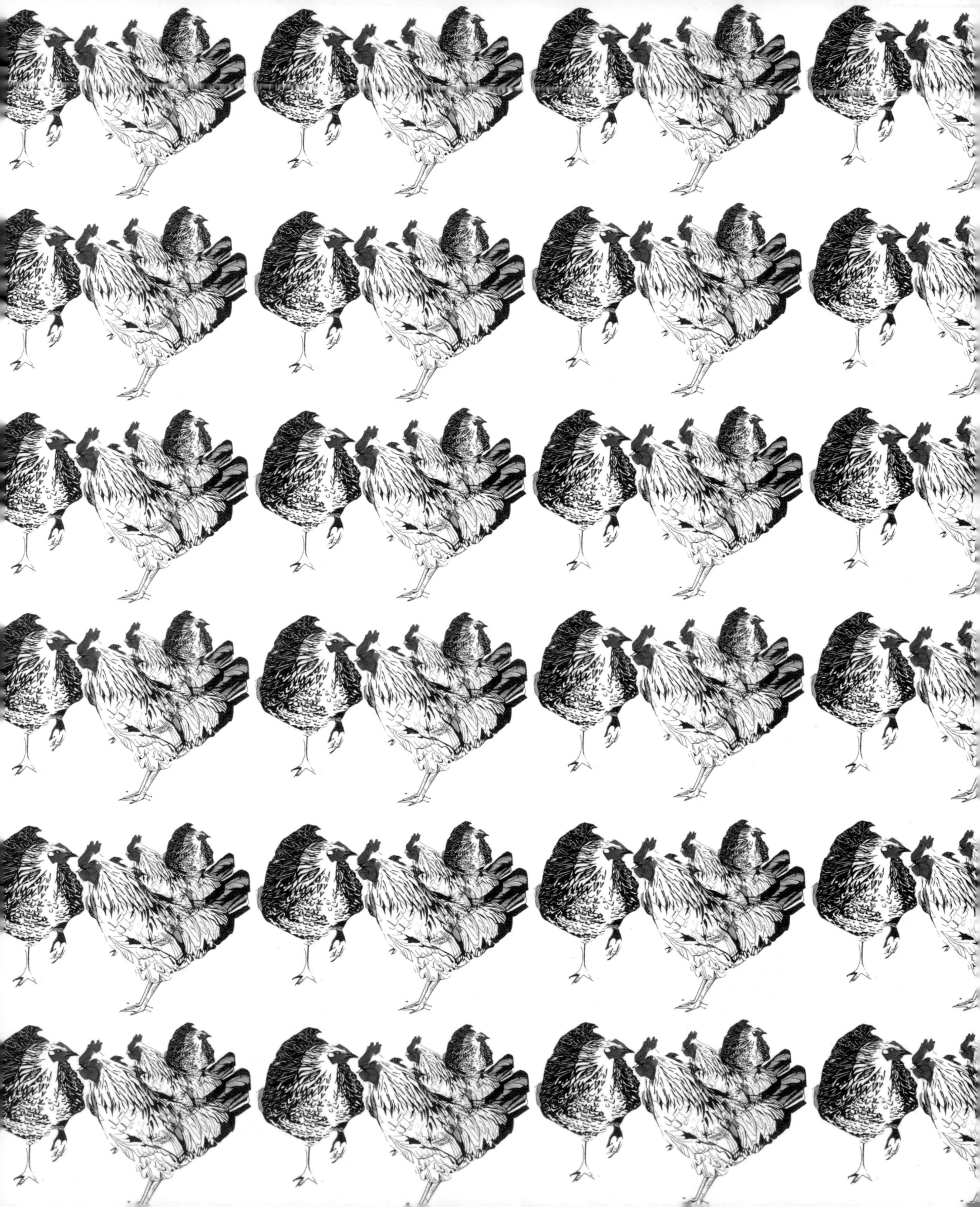

Work placements and internships

A work placement can be in the country where a student is studying or in another part of the world, and provides valuable experience and insight into the textile design industry. Students who opt for working abroad may do so to align the placement with the design discipline that interests them. Its duration can vary from one week to two months on a three-year course depending on the company, the student and the university or college. Students may undertake longer placements so that they can work throughout the full development of a collection, benefiting both themselves and the company. Shorter placements may be undertaken so that they don't impinge on other aspects of a busy textile curriculum, or because the design studio can more comfortably accommodate a student for a shorter length of time.

Assisting with production, design, marketing, promotion and sales activities are some of the professional tasks interns might be involved with. Work experience is definitely beneficial for most students; it helps them to find employment when they graduate – and may lead to a job with the work-placement company.

The study trip

Study trips familiarize students with the textile industry and how it works. For example, attending or even participating in an international textile trade fair gives students an insight into the commercial aspects of textile design, and enables them to get information about design studios and companies. Some textile design departments exhibit at trade fairs, which gives students the opportunity to promote and sell their designs to the industry – and can establish valuable contacts for student and university alike.

New York, London, Paris, Milan and Frankfurt are popular destinations because they host textile trade fairs and are culturally vibrant. A study trip may incorporate visits to design studios and factories as well as museums and galleries, and, for the more adventurous, India and China are rich in textile culture as well as being major manufacturers of textiles.

The third year

At the start of the third year students develop a proposal that sets out what they want to achieve in their final year of undergraduate study. It is similar to a design brief in the textile industry, and it may be modified to allow for unexpected opportunities to be seized. The development of a body of work for exhibition, and a design portfolio, are the main objectives of this final year, but there are other requirements, including: a dissertation, which will need to demonstrate knowledge in a particular field of art and design history and theory; a professional practice requirement showing a student's awareness of their consumer market, demonstrated through market and product research and in the final designs; professional presentation of the final body of design work together with promotional material. At the end of the year there is the final exhibition at the university or college.

Above and opposite
Ruth Summerfield drew her inspiration for these digital print designs for urban fashion from animal and insect camouflage patterns (2009). Interpretations of colour from the natural world were dynamically transformed by her use of oil pastels for her initial studies. The studies were then scanned into the computer and developed into vibrant repeat patterns using Photoshop and Aleph-Step-And-Repeat software packages. The designs were then digitally printed using the Mimaki TX-2 digital printer.

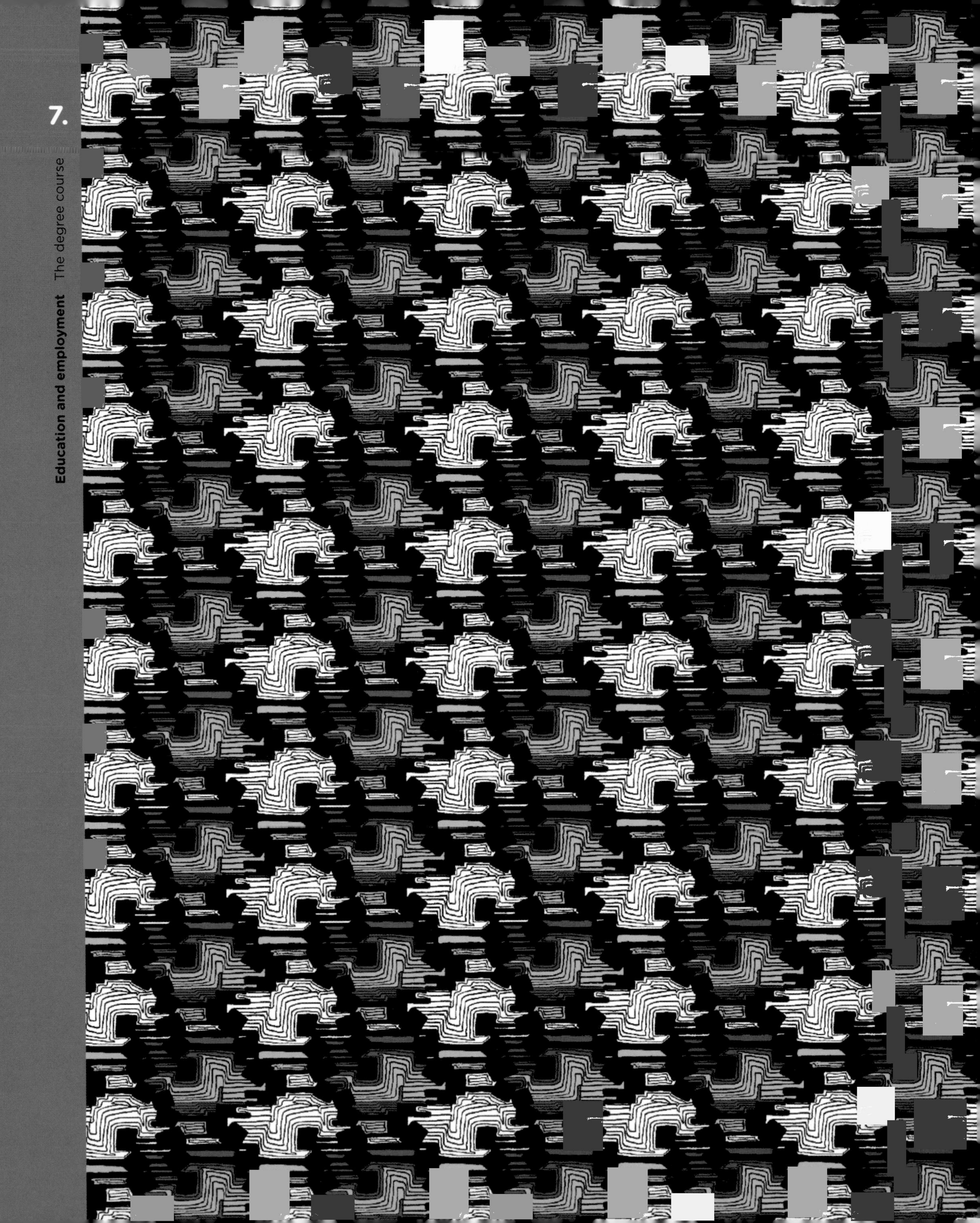

CRAGSTAN

Exhibitions

A number of exhibitions may be held during a degree course, depending upon the projects and the university or college, but the final degree show is a definitive moment as it marks the end of a year of study that will have involved students developing major design projects. With effective marketing and promotion, it can create positive interest in the textile industry and in the press and other media.

In addition to the degree show, textile design departments and their students exhibit their work at graduate fairs. An example of these is New Designers in London, which the textile industry recognizes as a forum that provides an opportunity to engage with new design talent. It benefits regional universities as it attracts companies from around the world, and is a unique venue where textile design graduates can showcase their collections, sell designs and network.

The degree show exhibition celebrates three years of study and is an opportunity to show the design world new, creative and professional design ideas from a new generation of designers. Planning is crucial, and a floor plan for the total space indicating the layout of display boards and allocation of spaces is essential. Lighting and other specific display requirements, such as power points for computers, need to be factored into the plan so that the work that is displayed is seen at its best. The extent of the display space allocated to individual students varies depending on the size and amount of their work. A printed-textile design student who has produced display lengths of fabric and upholstered a piece of furniture requires more space than one who has designed embroidery samples for fashion. The critical factor is to ensure that individual students show their best representative pieces and that the overall exhibition display is aesthetically considered as a whole – for example, by considering how designs by different students will best work in close proximity to each other.

Lengths of fabric can be pinned or stapled to the exhibition display boards, or attached to a ceiling fixture so that they hang in a space away from them. A selection of representative fabric samples from a student's collection, and contextual visualizations, can be pinned on to the boards. Actual products, such as garments and furniture, need to be carefully sited to enhance the exhibition. A minimal aesthetic is generally a more successful display strategy than the bazaar approach, although this is not always the case. When setting up a space it is a good idea to prepare a tool kit beforehand so that any problems can be solved immediately.

Detail is important, and portfolio display stands, tables with portfolios of design collections, catalogues, business cards and sales information need to be considered. Organizing the private viewing of the show and opening it up to the public involves ensuring that all enquiries and sales of design work are professionally managed: this kind of professionalism is as important as the quality of the design work in establishing long-standing business relationships and employment in the industry.

Above and opposite
Printed-textile design samples for fashion from a collection by Anna Glover that depict a journey through a whimsical, surreal world: Flight Across Crystal Stars (above) and Robot Fish Sea (opposite, both 2009). There is no sense of time or space, allowing the viewer's imagination to complete the details of the journey. Detailed drawing and collaged imagery combined with a strong sense of colour and composition are important design elements. Glover's designs were influenced by the formal aesthetic of 19th-century Japanese postcards and the surreal comic-style art of Henry Darger. They were developed in Photoshop and subsequently digitally printed on the Mimaki TX-2.

The portfolio

The contents of a portfolio and the professional way in which it is organized are crucially important when attending interviews or presenting work to a client, and in marketing and promoting work. For this reason, although putting one together echoes much of what was discussed in chapter 6, such as designing, developing and presenting a textile collection, these subjects are revisited and developed here.

The size of a portfolio can vary and is influenced by practical considerations, including how easily it can be carried, in some cases when travelling abroad. A1 (24 × 33.9 inches) would be required to accommodate A2 (16.9 × 24-inch) fabric samples mounted on A1 white card. If the textiles are for a fashion collection this scale would make it possible to show them within garment shape templates, giving the potential customer a good sense of the fabric and its design content. This size would also be appropriate for printed textile designers and for a woven or mixed media collection. However, the most commonly used portfolio is A2 with A3 (16.9 × 12 inches) samples mounted on A2 white card. This is a good choice for printed, woven and mixed media textiles as the samples are big enough to have an impact. An A3 or A4 (8.5 × 12-inch) portfolio may be appropriate if the samples are small – for example, for a mixed media embroidery range. Ultimately, the size is determined by the scale and quantity of the designs and the designer's preference, bearing in mind the customer's needs. A portfolio without a central spiral binding is best. In addition to the samples a portfolio could contain visualizations of the designs in a product context and, especially in the case of printed textiles, examples of the colourways for some of them. A concept statement to support the collection is helpful.

Double-sided tape can be used to mount a sample on card, and is usually applied only to its top edge to enable the customer to handle the fabric easily. An alternative, discussed in chapter 6, is to use a header – a folded piece of card that is attached to the top edge of the design – which also makes for easier handling. Whether card or a header is used, a fabric sample usually needs to be tidied up before it is mounted. This may involve ironing it and trimming its edge with scissors to remove fraying fibres and make sure it is a uniform shape. Some designers run a clear tape along the four edges, on the back of the sample, to prevent further fraying.

Labels are usually typed and are attached to the back of the fabric samples, or of the cards or headers on which they are mounted, typically give the design number for each design, possibly a design name, the name of the collection and the name of the designer; the techniques and materials used to produce the design may also be included.

A collection may consist of more than 40 designs, within which there may be smaller ranges and groupings of designs related to particular themes within the overarching concept. The order in which the samples are shown is therefore of real importance and should have a creative logic that will keep the customer intrigued and interested in the collection. Increasingly, a disk with

Opposite
This portfolio collection by Emma Sheldon explores the concept of Morse code to create individual mixed-media textile samples (2009).

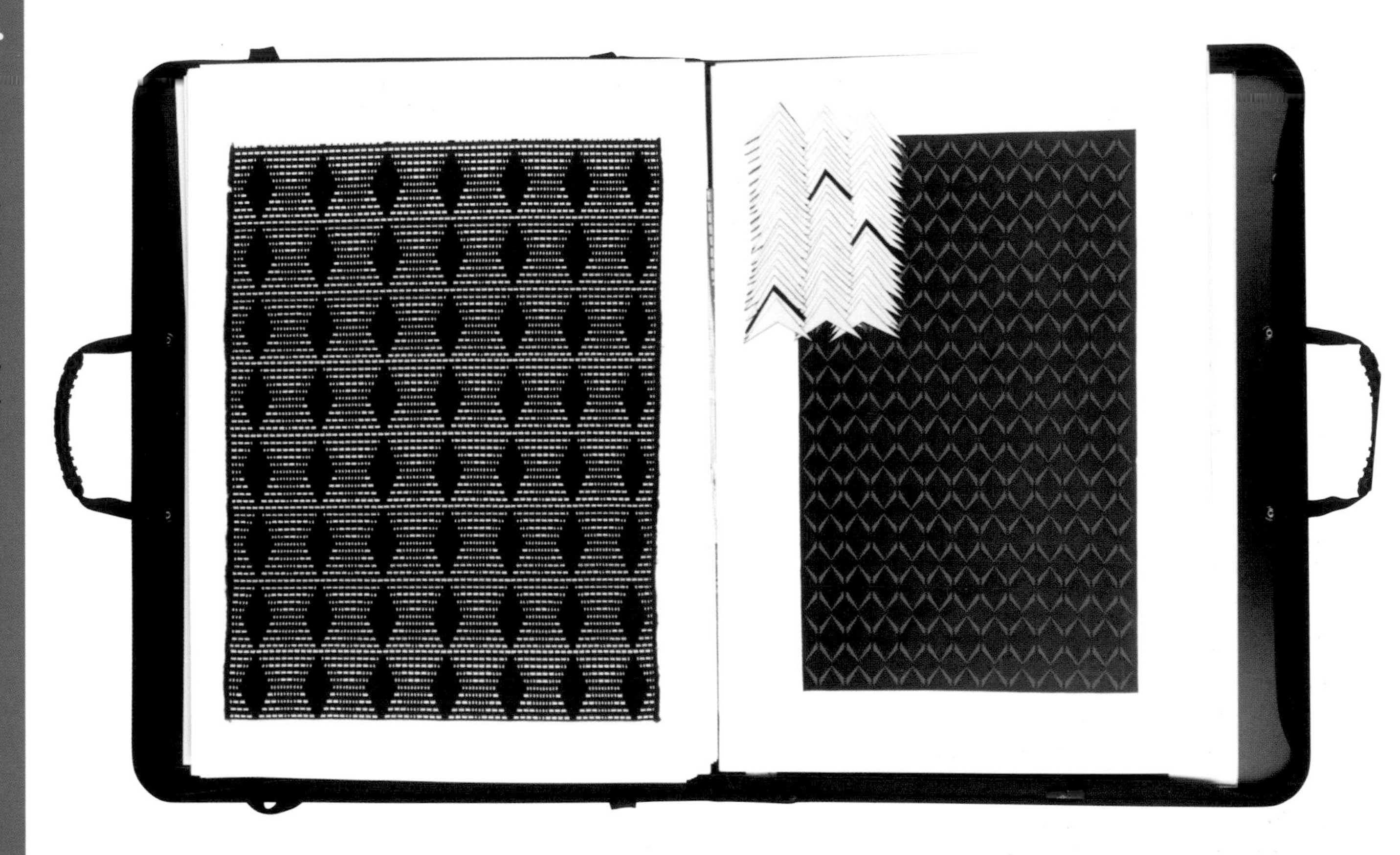

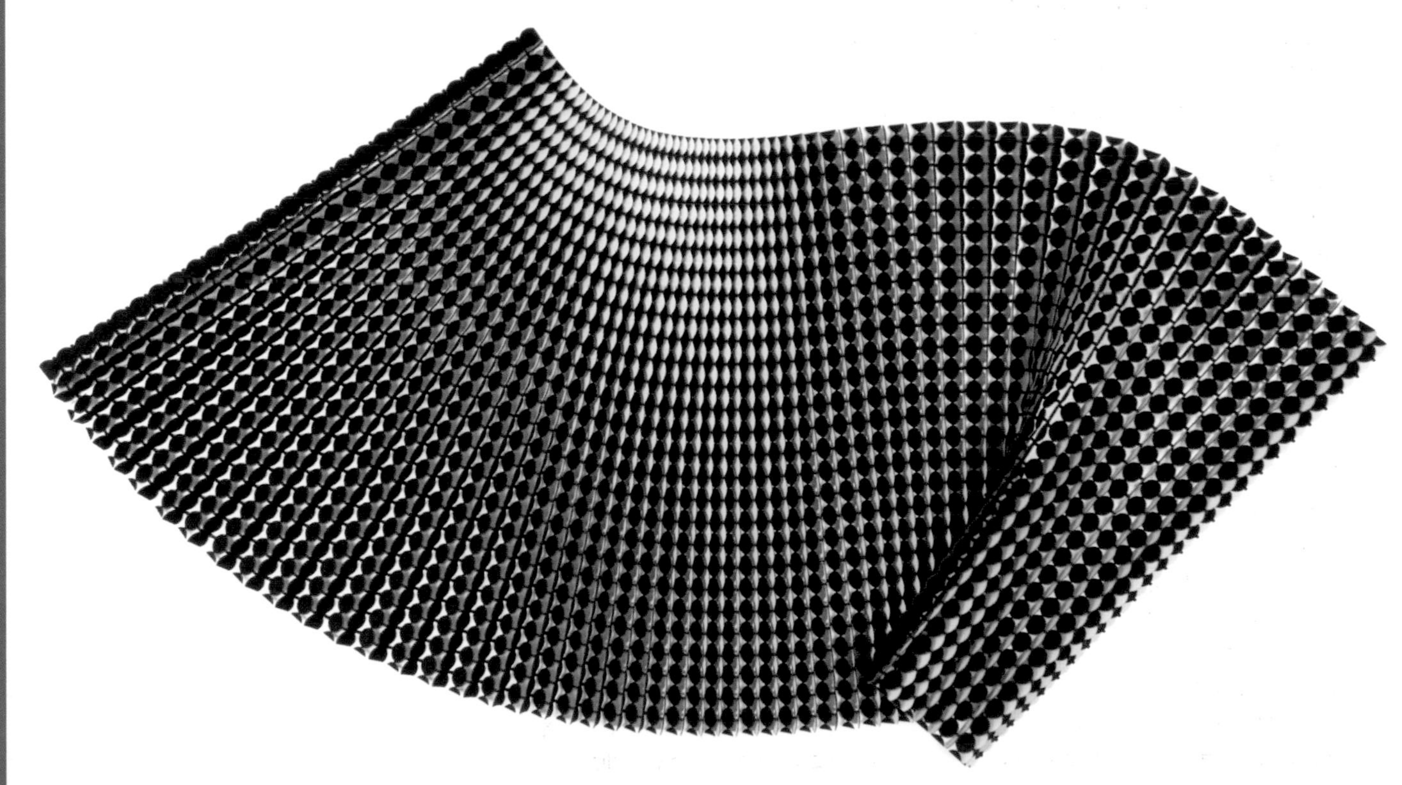

the design is provided along with digitally printed textile samples as it is helpful in preparing a design for manufacture. A CD portfolio is very compact and can be a useful addition to the traditional one. Similarly, a design collection on an external hard drive is also a possibility. Both options are worth considering for situations where it is difficult to travel with a large portfolio, and when the designs are virtual textiles rather than fabric samples. The downside is that the handling and visual experience of the textile is lost. Perhaps future virtual reality collections will give potential customers a sense of the textile in its product context, while at the same time accurately replicating all its design characteristics, with options to see the textile in complex forms, movements and settings, and including considerations such as the effects of wind and light sources.

Distance learning

While the most common method of obtaining a degree in textile design is to attend a university or a college of art and design, it is possible to study at degree level through distance learning. Normally under the wing of a university, this type of course can be very dynamic as it provides flexible methods of teaching and learning within a prescribed structure. Distance learning attracts leading authorities in textile design to act as tutors and an international body of students.

Postgraduate study

Studying at postgraduate level gives recent graduates and textile professionals the opportunity to extend, explore and develop their textile expertise or cultivate new skills. An applicant normally provides a university or college with a research proposal that outlines the areas of investigation that will form a key aspect of their postgraduate study. The main postgraduate

Below left, top and bottom
The multi-storey car park for Debenhams department store in London (designed in 1970 by Michael Blampied) and other car parks, formed the basis for a selection of textile pieces by Sophie Tarbuck.

Below right
This hand screen-printed textile piece (2009) is one outcome of Tarbuck's research into multi-storey car parks and her subsequent development of the ideas it generated.

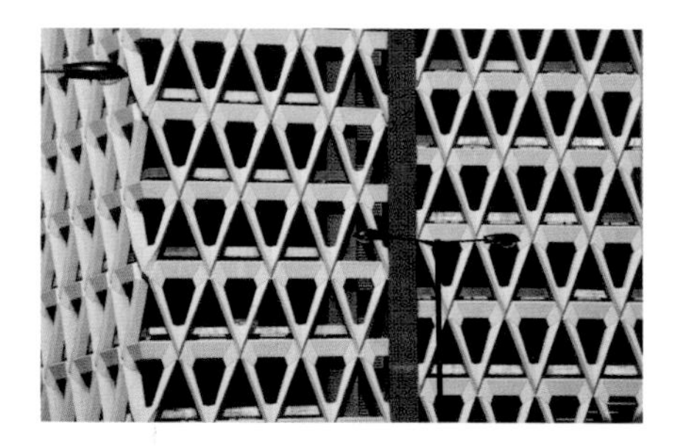

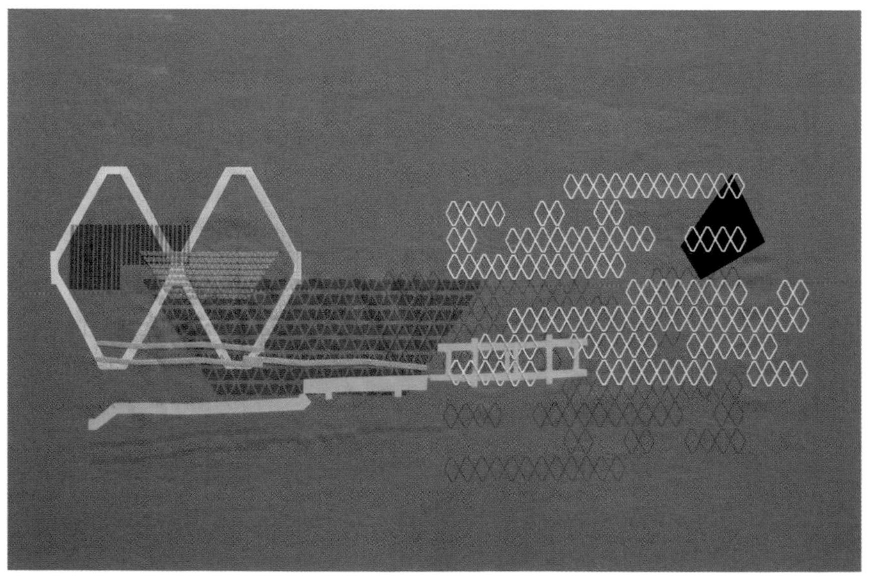

Falling Leaf Dress ref 8443-03 by Claire Armitage (fabric and dress) was first showcased at the Milan Design Exhibition in 2009. 8443-03 is a reference to a delicate 1920s bridesmaid's dress in the Helston Folk Museum, Cornwall. Fusing old and new technologies, the dress consists of three screen- and digitally printed layers: the digitally printed cotton lawn underlayer is shown here.

degrees in textile design are Master of Arts (MA), Master of Design (MDes) Master of Fine Arts (MFA) and, in some cases, Master of Science (MSc), which includes technology in its programme of study. The length of the Masters programme varies from one university to another, and ranges from full-time two-year courses like the one at the Royal College of Art, London to others that run for one year. Part-time options are readily available and differ in length.

Research opportunities can follow on from a period of study at Masters level, and may involve fitting into a specified project or putting forward a proposal for Master of Philosophy (MPhil) or Doctor of Philosophy (PhD) research. At this level there is genuine scope for interdisciplinary, multidisciplinary and transdisciplinary projects. For example, research into a cultural textile may require developing further knowledge in textile design but will also involve learning new research methods for fields such as anthropology and material culture.

Finding a job

In some circumstances students secure employment before graduation, by way of their work placement or by word of mouth – for instance, through a former graduate of the same course who is working in the textile industry and whose employer is looking for a young designer. Getting a job in textile design demands commitment and motivation, and perhaps a willingness to take every opportunity to get a foot in the door. This can be prudent, as experience as a design assistant can make it easier for a new designer to achieve their ideal position within the textile world.

A small percentage of new graduates go on to become the celebrity designers of tomorrow through their individuality, idealism and vision. Others succeed by setting up a design studio and workshop for a particular market. And yet others opt for the security of working for established textile companies, where employment terms vary depending on the new graduate's experience and skills. Relatively new design companies, and even those with high public profiles, may offer only part-time work or temporary contracts, little financial return and limited job security. However, there are also new and innovative companies that provide graduates with both a secure future and a competitive salary that reflects their experience.

Employment possibilities

Throughout this book a variety of textile and product designers, artists, architects and craftsmen have been discussed in relation to how they have created textiles and applied them to products whose contexts range from fashion and interiors to art and craft pieces for exhibition or installation. These are all potential markets that provide opportunities for a graduate either to work within a company or set up a new business for a specific textile market.

The product and market range in textile design is broad and can accommodate a variety of aesthetics and innovations. Marimekko, Maharam and Moroso are examples of international textile companies who have both in-house and freelance designers, and are open to new ideas from recent graduates as well as relying on their established designers. Innovators like Tokojin Yoshioka and Patricia Urquiola have contributed to both product and textile design, highlighting that it is possible for individual designers to succeed.

Fashion provides similar possibilities. Established companies like Liberty Fabric and Linton Tweed offer work placements that may lead to jobs, while innovators like Hussein Chalayan and Alexander McQueen draw on the skills of graduates as well as those of experienced design assistants.

Companies such as Timorous Beasties, Eley Kishimoto and Basso & Brooke prove it is possible to set up a successful textile business, while artists and craftsmen who are involved in large installation projects or are engaged in multiple projects need help. And textile graduates can be well suited to certain site-specific projects, for example, the types of projects designer Petra

Blaisse has been involved in, such as the red-smocked theatre curtain for the Hackney Empire, and those of Christo and Jeanne-Claude, such as wrapped tree and Pont Neuf (see page 136).

There are many other employment possibilities in the textile industry, some of which have courses tailor-made for them. Some of these integrate textile design with technology, which plays a major part in many aspects of the textile industry and requires specialist knowledge to support the design and production process, and lead to a science rather than an arts degree. Business management is another example. This could lead subsequently to a career overseeing the manufacturing process from the initiation of a textile collection to supplying the finished fabrics to the customer. Textile Design, Fashion and Management PhD, MPhil and MSc courses and specific courses in textile technology and textile management and marketing provide preparatory experiences for future employment into these areas.

There are many associated professions intrinsic to the success of the textile industry. These professions include journalism, the media and publishing, magazines like *Vogue*, and *Bloom* exemplifying the rich range of media employment prospects available. Museum curation, archiving and conservation are other options within specialized textile museums and collections ranging from the Cooper Hewitt Museum and the Metropolitan Museum of Art in New York to the Victoria and Albert Museum and British Museum in London.

Potential employers, who may use in-house or freelance textile designers, include manufacturing and processing companies that make clothing, soft furnishings and other textile-based products, as well as fashion and clothing retailers like Top Shop, Marks and Spencer and Gap. Interior design and decoration is another area that is worth exploring.

The curriculum vitae

In the same way that it is essential for a new graduate to get his or her design portfolio right, it is necessary to have a curriculum vitae (CV) that shows the full range of what they have accomplished at university or college, as well as any relevant work experience. A CV should be succinct and compelling, and summarize education, skills and achievements: its purpose is to entice a potential employer to invite its author to an interview. It should be complemented by a concise and relevant covering letter.

The CV must be typed in a basic font so that the information is clear, and details about education and employment should be listed in reverse chronological order. The types of information and topic headings that should be included are; name, date of birth, education, work placements (providing information on activities and experience) competitions and awards, exhibitions, conferences (attended or participated in) and previous employment (relevant to the position if possible, indicating role and responsibilities). Also a contact address, relevant telephone contact numbers, email and a website address if relevant. It may be useful to include relevant

A pleated digital print by Helen Stark, the 2008 winner of the Texprint Breaking New Ground Prize donated by WGSN.

Texprint

Texprint mentors the United Kingdom's most innovative new graduate textile designers and promotes them to the textile world at First View, an event hosted in London and at Première Vision in Paris. Executives from leading textile companies, design buyers and journalists from all over the world are invited to view the new designers' work. This exposure results in invaluable contacts and in sales, commissions, work placements and job offers. The graduates are selected from British colleges and universities because of their high degree of creativity and professionalism in print, weave, mixed media, embroidery or knit.

Texprint also organizes special prizes presented at First View – the categories include print, weave, mixed media and knit, as well as interior fashion and breaking new ground. The winners receive money and the opportunity to exhibit at the trade fair Interstoff Essential Asia in Hong Kong.

The selection and prize-judging panels are made up of invited industry professionals, international artists and designers such as Grayson Perry, and Giles Deacon, creative director of Donna Karan. High-profile designers like Sir Paul Smith have presented the special prizes.

Above, left
Paolo Ingegnoli, Chief Executive of Leggiuno SpA, at Texprint 'First View'.

Above, centre
Sir Paul Smith and Peter Ring Lefevre discuss designs by Hannah Jefferies, winner of the 2008 Texprint Print Prize, at Première Vision.

Above, right
Victoria Shepherd, winner of the 2008 Texprint Interior Fashion Prize donated by Holland & Sherry Interiors.

information such as fluency in a language or languages, computer training and the possession of a driving licence. Avoid personal details like religion, ethnicity or marital status. The CV's basic template should be modified to reflect differing job applications – and it is essential to make sure the CV is sent to the appropriate member of staff in a company. It may be useful to include a single page of images. A covering letter is also a good idea, as is a follow-up telephone call, perhaps two weeks after posting or emailing the CV. References can be provided upon request.

Websites

Designing your own website could be relevant for a number of graduates and is definitely worth considering if you want to work as a freelance designer or plan to set up your own textile design business/studio. Its style and content should echo the design characteristics in the portfolio. Website design is increasingly being taught to third-year students as a component in professional practice.

The interview

It is crucial to prepare for a job interview by researching the history, products and markets associated with a particular company. It is also important to think about possible questions so that answers are readily available – and prepare questions about the job and company.

Personal presentation has an impact in an interview and this applies particularly in design, where clothing or an accessory may have been designed by the applicant. This can create an interesting talking point and is a good ice-breaker.

Honesty about knowledge, skills and experience is always the best policy, and these qualities should be self-evident in the work contained in the applicant's portfolio. If specialist skills are required these can sometimes be provided once the designer is working for the company, for example there might be opportunites to develop skills in project management or fabric sourcing. Specific CAD software packages, different to those used at university, may also be learned once on the job. So there is no need to worry if all a potential employer's criteria are not met. However, what is fundamentally important is to be confident and friendly, and to maintain eye contact with the interviewer and to be positive.

The questions asked at an interview may differ slightly from one design studio to another, and will also depend on the tasks and responsibilities associated with a particular position. A general strategy is to make the applicant feel relaxed at the outset of an interview then ask classic questions, such as why they have applied for the position. The interviewer may seek to draw out the applicant's motivation, communication, teamwork and problem-solving skills. Educational background and work experience are likely lines of questioning, and specific questions will vary depending on whether the applicant will be dealing with a weave, printed, mixed media or other type of

textile. The purpose of these questions is to judge the level of his or her subject-specific knowledge particularly in relation to aesthetic, technical, manufacturing and market contexts. The portfolio will be discussed at some point during the interview, which provides the applicant with the opportunity to display a range of qualities like motivation and communication skills, their knowledge of the design process, and their aesthetic and technical abilities.

If aspects of the position, such as working hours, line managers or career prospects, are unclear it is important to ensure they are clarified. Similarly, a salary should always be discussed before a position is accepted. However, the interviewer must get the impression that the applicant really wants the job.

Above
Hussein Chalayan describes Inertia, his 2009 spring/summer ready-to-wear collection as being about 'the speed in our lives and how it can result in a crash'. The print designs contain motifs of number plates, car handles and fenders taken from photographs of car graves. Chalayan exemplifies all that is experimental and innovative in design – qualities that should be understood and pursued by the next generation of young designers.

Below
Whitechapel Gallery, Prototype Conference Room (2009), a collaboration between artist Liam Gillick and Kvadrat.

Summary

This chapter provides a window into how textile designers are educated and the career options available to them when they graduate. While it is true that there is no concrete formula for securing employment, by engaging fully in all aspects of study and seizing all opportunities, the likelihood of new designers doing what they want to do after graduation is optimized.

Textile design is a persistently challenging industry, and the more aware graduates are of this, and the more they adjust to its demands, the more likely they are to gain employment. And once in the industry the job satisfaction of seeing designs they have worked on or created going into production and on to the catwalk, into retail outlets or displayed at exhibitions, and featured in journals and books, can be immense. Textile designers respond to and inform consumer tastes, and contribute to the material and visual world. This is a major cultural responsibility and if done well is a significant achievement as it enhances the world in which we live.

Glossary

acid dye A textile dye effective in the dyeing of protein-based fibres such as wool and silk.

actuation The technology that enables intelligent textiles to move in response to stimuli, adapting their structures or properties to suit particular environments.

air-jet loom A loom that carries the yarn through the shed by a jet of air.

appliqué The stitching of different fabrics on to a background cloth.

azo dye (see direct dye)

backing cloth In printed textiles, this is an absorbent cotton cloth applied to the print table before printing lightweight fabrics such as silk and Lycra, which reduces smudging and lack of adhesion during printing. In appliqué, small pieces of fabric are stitched on to the backing cloth.

batik A traditional wax-resist dyeing technique.

batting (see wadding)

beadwork The generic term for the design and technical skills employed in the application of beads and sequins to cloth and similar substrates.

beaver cloth A heavy-weight woollen cloth produced through the process of heavy felting with the aim of imitating the properties of natural beaver skin.

binder The catalyst used for the transfer of pigment ink on to cloth in printing.

blind edge Used in appliqué when a decorative sewn edge is not required around the edge of a cut motif. Instead, an allowance around the cut motif is folded under and pressed on to the background fabric and then usually sewn with a tight blind stitch.

block printing A technique in which ink is applied to a chiselled wood-cut design on a wooden block and then applied to the fabric.

blotch screen A blotch screen is used when the ground surface area of a printed textile design is printed rather than dyed. The blotch screen is printed last, because a lot of ink or dye paste will be applied to the cloth resulting in the potential loss of fabric adhesion to the print table.

bobbin The spool onto which weft threads are wound, and which is then placed into the shuttle for weaving on the loom.

border pattern A border pattern features along one, two or four edges of the cloth in a step-and-repeat pattern. It is an established design element in scarf and shawl designs.

braided A twill weave in which the resulting pattern creates a plaited effect due to the diagonal directional changes from one twill repeat section to the next.

brand A particular overarching identity associated with a designer, design studio or company. Marimekko, for instance, has a distinct brand look through its use of bold motifs and bright colours. It may also refer to the identity of a particular seasonal collection.

brief Determined by the client, agent or design studio director, the brief defines a design project's requirements.

carbon paper An ink-coated and waxed paper which, when applied ink-side down on to the fabric and drawn on, transfers the drawing on to the fabric.

catalyst A chemical agent that instigates a reaction between two or more other chemicals.

cellulosic fibres Plant-based fibres such as cotton and hemp.

chiffon A lightweight, transparent fabric made from silk or similar type of crêpe.

chintz A brightly coloured printed fabric with floral, plant, bird and small animal motifs.

colour boards In the development of a collection, the compilation of colour boards is inspired by the concept. They inform the colour palette for each respective story in a collection.

colour-matching This enables the designer to specify exactly the colours to be used. In textile design and manufacturing this is achieved through colour charts issued by companies such as Pantone who provide accurate colour cross-referencing between different substrates such as paper and cloth.

colour separations The separation of colours in a design for application to individual films and screens for printing.

colourway One of several colour solutions for a design.

computer-aided design (CAD) Dedicated design software used partially or wholly by the textile designer in the generation of a design.

computer-aided manufacture (CAM) Computer-driven textile production processes such as digital inkjet printing.

cone winder A cone winder machine transfers dyed hanks on to cones in preparation for weaving the weft.

contextualization The placing or representation of a textile design applied to its ultimate use of context (see also visualization).

cording Stitching of cord into a cloth to create linear forms and firmness. Often used in quilting.

crêpe de Chine A silk or similar type of fabric with a crinkled or crêpe-like finish due to the twisted weft of the yarn used in the weaving of the cloth. It has properties similar to those of chiffon.

croquis An initial design that requires further technical development; this may involve refining the pattern into a true repeat.

cut-through A freely drawn line that divides a design horizontally or vertically with minimal aesthetic disturbance, for example by confinement to the ground colour, in order to camouflage the repeat joins to maintain continuity and rhythm.

definition In digital design and digital inkjet printing this term refers to the graphics file data, which determines the quality of the translation of the design on to the cloth. The definition and file size need to be factored into the design development at the outset. The digital inkjet printer will be set at a specific definition, normally 320 dots per inch (dpi), but can be adjusted according to requirements.

denting plan (see reed plan)

design stories Particular themes within a design collection that have a common source of inspiration in the basic concept.

devoré From the French meaning devoured, this printing technique uses a chemical paste that reacts with cellulosic fibres to burn them away when subjected to dry heat. Devoré is particularly effective with blended fabrics such as silk/viscose velvet where the cellulosic viscose velvet is burnt away to reveal the silk underneath, and also in conjunction with double dyeing techniques.

digital inkjet printing A digitally driven print technology that sprays droplets of ink on to cloth through inkjet heads. It produces far less waste than conventional printing and provides flexibility in production output.

direct dye An inexpensive dye that is effective in the dyeing of cellulosic (plant-based) fibres.

discharge printing Bleaching an area of dyed cloth and simultaneously replacing it with new colour. The method enables contrasting or bright colours to appear together on a printed cloth.

disperse dye A dye that is effective in the dyeing of synthetic fibres, for instance polyester and nylon.

distress An effect created during laser cutting which changes the patina of the surface of the cloth but which does not cut right through it.

dobby loom A loom that can operate manually (using a treadle) or electronically. The dobby mechanism is a chain of bars into which pegs are inserted in order to select which shaft is moved on the loom. Up to fifty bars can be used, enabling the creation of complex weave structures.

doeskin A fine woollen warp cloth, which is felted, raised and dress-face finished. It is similar to beaver cloth but much lighter.

dots per inch (dpi) The dpi value is a gauge of image quality in the printing of computer-generated imagery and is determined by the number of individual dots printed within one square inch.

double cloth weave A two-layered cloth produced by the interconnection of two or more sets of warps and one or more sets of weft yarns.

draft plan (see notation system)

drape How a cloth hangs or falls.

dye Concentrate colour in powder form until mixed with the appropriate catalyst such as a print paste for use in printing interior and fashion fabrics.

eco-textile designers Designers who take into consideration environmental impact of manufacturing and other factors such as recycling at the end of the textile's first life.

eco-textiles Textiles appropriately sourced and manufactured with minimal energy and environmental impact.

elastane (see **spandex**)

embossing A three-dimensional relief design embedded into the cloth, achieved through extreme pressure, heating and baking.

embroidery frame (see **embroidery hoop**)

embroidery hoop Two concentric circles made of wood or plastic with a tightening mechanism to secure the fabric and hold it taught for embroidery.

end (see **warp end**)

engineered design A non-repeating design, often digitally generated and printed, conceived in relation to the shape and form of the product to which it will be applied.

Expandex A print paste that reacts when heated to produce a relief surface on the cloth.

fabric handle How a particular type of fabric feels and responds to the touch as a consequence of the weave and textile finish.

fancy yarn Produced to have novel form and colour characteristics to achieve a distinct aesthetic in the weave.

feed dog The component of a sewing machine that moves and controls the fabric and stitch length under the presser foot.

felting (see **fulling**)

fieldwork Visual research gathered for a design project by conducting primary research on or at the location of the research subject area.

filament yarn (see **yarn**)

filling threads Another name for weft threads, woven across the warp threads to create the cloth.

flatbed screen-printing (see **screen printing**)

float A thread that passes over two or more crosswise threads.

flocking The application of suede or velvet motifs to a fabric surface through adhesive or electrostatic methods.

flying shuttle (see also **shuttle**) Invented by John Kay in 1773, this significantly increased weave productivity on a loom. It incorporated pulleys and cords and a box at each end of the shuttle that enabled a single weaver to cause the shuttle to move back and forth across the loom.

foiling The application of a metallic foil motif to a fabric surface using adhesive.

foulard From the French word for scarf or necktie, foulard is characterized by a pattern of small motifs repeated at measured intervals.

fray The separation of threads on the edge of a piece of fabric.

fulling Popularly known as felting, this is a permanent finish used in woollen fabrics involving a carefully controlled scouring and laundering process that includes shrinkage to create a smoother more compact cloth. Blanket cloth is one example of fulling.

fusible web A synthetic fabric which, when heated, will bond two fabrics together. Popular in appliqué work.

gathering The edge of a piece of fabric collected into small folds by bunching together on a thread.

ghost image This can occur in hand screen-printing if the screen picks up a trace of wet ink from a previously printed area and puts the trace back on to the fabric.

gingham A plain weave of fine to medium cotton coloured yarns designed in stripes or checks.

glover A large needle with a sharp point for sewing on to leather.

ground The colour of the cloth before printing, normally an integral part of the design.

ground fabric The fabric area between the stitched motifs in embroidery.

gum arabic Tapped from the gum tree in Africa and Asia, it is widely used in a number of contexts. It can be crushed and combined with chalk powder and methylated spirit, then passed through a pin-pricked design on paper to provide a marker on a piece of cloth as the guide for stitching.

half-drop repeat (see also **repeat**) The most common form of repeat structure in which the motif is repeated halfway down alongside itself. It requires accurate measurements when drawing in the repeat grid.

hand screen-printing (see **screen printing**)

hank A length of yarn reeled together in preparation for dyeing.

hank winder A machine for reeling together lengths of yarn into hanks in preparation for dyeing.

haptic sensing Relates to touch rather than sight in digital textile technology, and is an important area in the development of intelligent textiles.

heat photogram A photographic processing method that can be applied to synthetic fabrics for fashion and accessories. The process has low environmental impact as inks vaporize when exposed to heat.

heat-transfer printing A technique developed for printing on to synthetic and man-made fabrics using disperse dyes. Dyes are printed or painted on to the surface of a non-absorbent paper, which is then applied to the fabric and subjected to heat and pressure by a heat transfer press or iron. This causes the dyes to vaporize and condense on to the surface of the fabric.

heddle A component of a loom, this is a long, needle-like cord or metal device with a central opening called an eye through which the warp threads are passed to separate them for weaving with the weft.

hem A cut fabric edge that is folded and sewn down.

herringbone A popular twill-weave structure characterized by a V-shaped pattern.

honeycomb weave Created by a twill weave structure, it forms a relief surface on the fabric of raised areas with deepened centres.

hue The exact identification or name of a colour based on its position on the colour spectrum.

interfacing An unseen fabric, ironed or sewn on to the underside of another fabric to add structure. In appliqué it may be ironed on to a cut-out fabric shape to prevent fraying. It comes in a variety of different weights.

jacquard controller The interface between the computer and loom, which converts the digital data into a weave.

jacquard loom Invented in France in 1801 by Joseph Jacquard, it enabled more complex patterns to be created through the controlled use of a series of punchcards attached to the top of the loom. This machine was further developed into a loop system to create repeat patterns. Contemporary jacquard looms are now capable of producing highly complex weaves with the assistance of computer-aided design.

kanga Rectangular printed cloth from Eastern Africa, particularly popular on the Swahili coast. Usually worn in pairs, with one piece worn around the upper part of the body and the other around the lower part of the body.

kente A cloth from Ghana, constructed from strips of woven fabric that are sewn together.

Kevlar A synthetic fabric of significant tensile strength commonly used in the fashion industry and in niche markets such as the manufacture of balloons.

Kuba cloth A patterned woven cloth which incorporates appliqué and embroidery techniques, designed and produced by a confederacy of tribal groups generally known as the Kuba from the Kasai region of the Congo.

lacquer A traditional medium used to make the stencil in hand screen-printing.

lags A dobby mechanism on the side of the loom consisting of a chain of bars into which pegs are inserted in order to select which shaft is moved on the loom, which in turn determines the weave pattern of the cloth.

laser cutting A computer-directed cutting process using laser-beam technology that can cut intricate designs on a range of materials from fine silk to leather.

layout The variety of ways in which motifs can be organized to create a textile design.

leno weave A method in which the weft threads are held in place by the crossing and twisting of the warp threads over the weft picks. This method can be applied to interior and fashion contexts.

lift (see **float**)

lifting plan The specified order in which the shafts are lifted.

lining The bottom fabric used in quilting.

Lycra Elastic polyurethane fibre developed by du Pont for underwear and sportswear.

melton A heavy woollen cloth with a close-cut nap achieved through felting; used in overcoats and jackets.

microfibre yarn A filament yarn, such as polyester, with a fineness less than 1 decitex (1 gram per 10,000 metres).

mirroring A symmetrical reflection of a motif, both subsequently repeated.

moire A rippled or watermarked effect in the finish of the cloth. Taffeta and other lightweight fabrics are often finished in this way.

monoprinting A once-only process in which the screen is painted with Procion™ dye. This is then transferred on to the cloth by passing a dye paste through the screen, which takes the Procion™ dye with it. Fixation of the dye to the cloth requires steaming after printing. Washing is necessary to remove the remaining paste in order to restore the fabric handle to the cloth.

mounting In the context of appliqué, this refers to leaving a fabric allowance around the edge of the backing cloth for the purpose of presentation.

mule Invented by Samuel Compton in 1779, the mule was a hybrid spinning invention that combined roller drafting and running twist manufacturing methods.

multipass printing This is a standard method of digital printing in which an inkjet head passes over a specified area of a design a number of times. Single-pass printing is almost never used in the industry as there is a high risk that errors in printing will show; multipass printing reduces this risk and has no detrimental impact on the colour.

needle plate The metal plate on a sewing machine that encompasses the hole through which the needle passes.

negative space Areas in a design that lie between key motifs or design elements. In some designs it is difficult to discern key motifs and negative space because the whole surface area of a design is actively interrelated.

neoprene A synthetic rubber used in the manufacture of wetsuits.

netting A beadwork method in which beads are sewn together in net-type layouts.

notation system A framework mapped out by the designer to describe the weave structure.

nylon A generic term for strong, lightweight, heat-resistant, synthetic man-made fibres composed of linear polyamide molecules.

ogee A symmetrical onion-shaped layout, much used by William Morris in his designs; popular in interior textile prints.

organza A plain weave, sheer cloth.

origami The Japanese art of paper folding.

overprinting The layering of two colours to make a third colour.

pattern generation The process of making a pattern in computer-aided design.

peg plan (see lifting plan)

peyote stitch A hand-stitching technique to create a solid, flexible fabric of beads.

photogravure A mechanized etching technique that can create photographic quality prints.

pick (see weft pick)

piece dyeing The dyeing of the woven fabric rather than dyeing the yarn before weaving.

pigment Concentrated liquid colours combined with a binder catalyst for screen printing; popular in the manufacture of interior textile prints and some fashion contexts. As pigments have become increasingly refined, they are now used in digital inkjet printing.

pile A raised surface on the top side of a fabric, the pile can be looped weft or warp thread, depending on the weave structure. Velvet is a short pile whereas carpet can be a long pile. The loop may or may not be cut depending upon the desired result.

pile weave Achieved through the use of additional warps or extra fillings to form loops on the surface of the cloth, which are either cut or left uncut. Corduroy is a filling pile cloth with cut loops whereas velvet is a warp pile fabric with cut loops. Rugs are commonly produced using this weave.

plain weave A basic weave in which the warp and weft threads interlace alternatively.

pleat A secured fold in a fabric that can be ironed to fall as a sharp crease or left to fall as a softer fold. A pleat sewn in place along its entire length is called a tuck.

polyester Any long-chain polymer containing 85 per cent esters in its main chain. Most synthetic polyesters are not biodegradable.

poplin Commonly associated with cotton and blended cotton/polyester shirts and quality garments, this a strong, tight, plain weave, originally with a heavy filling yarn, such as wool, and a light warp yarn, such as silk. Poplin has more warp yarns than weft filling yarns.

power looms Mechanized versions of the hand loom.

primary colours Red, yellow and blue. In pigment and dyes their equivalents are magenta (red), yellow and cyan (blue).

primary visual research Research material observed and recorded first-hand from the real world, whether from a cultural field trip, museum display cabinet, or original figurative, landscape or still-life art.

Procion™ dye A reactive dye that is effective on natural fibres, particularly cellulosic (plant-based) fibres. On protein-based fibres it may achieve less consistent results.

protein fibres Animal-based fibres such as wool and silk.

quilting A stitching technique that fastens three layers of cloth together: the top cloth, the middle cloth (wadding) and the bottom cloth (lining).

raffia A fibre from palm leaves used in roofing and the production of natural-fibre ropes.

rayon Man-made fibre made from regenerated cellulose.

reed plan Refers to how the warp threads are threaded through the spaces, or dents, in the reed, a comb-like device that keeps the warp threads correctly spaced.

registration The accurate alignment of a design's colour elements on to films and screens to be applied to the cloth.

relief Raised surface details or patterns.

repeat The unit of a pattern that recurs to produce the whole.

repeat cross A marker on a print design that serves the following functions: a registration marker for the alignment of the colour elements for printing; the marker from which the design's repeat depth is measured; the point from which the repeat stops in flatbed screen-printing are calculated.

repeat stops In flatbed screen-printing these mark the distance from one repeat to the next. During the printing process the screen bracket will be rested against the stop.

rhythm The frequency, sequence or flow of a repeat pattern.

roller drafting The use of rollers to draw out the thread in spinning, as used in the water frame invented by Richard Arkwright in 1771.

roller printing Developed early in the Industrial Revolution, roller printing superseded engraved copperplate printing because it enables high-volume, multicolour printing through the use of engraved rollers. Pioneered by Thomas Bell in 1783 and patented in 1785, it became particularly effective following repeat registration modifications by Adam Parkinson.

rotary screen-printing (see screen printing)

rotation Movement of a motif around a 360-degree axis.

ruffle A strip of fabric that is reduced in length by gathering or pleating, resulting in folds that make up a floating edge that hangs down, stands up or extends sideways. Ruffles are a popular structural decoration at the edge of a garment.

running twist The continuous twisting of fibres into yarn in a process pioneered by James Hargreaves through his invention of the spinning jenny in 1764.

sample In the development of a printed fabric design, the production of samples enables the refinement of motif, pattern and colour. This refinement will be considered in relation to the fabric, printing method and other media to be used as well as the design's eventual context and use.

satin weave Threads not raised consecutively, with a tendency towards long floats in either warp or weft. Silk and rayon are produced by satin weave techniques. Satin weave fabrics are not as strong as plain or twill weaves.

scale The relative size or extent of something. In textile design, the size of a motif in a repeat pattern influences the level of visual impact and may be informed by its context.

screen A component common to both flatbed and rotary screen-printing. Flatbed screens are usually made of a metal frame and a polyester mesh. Rotary screens are composed of end rings on to which a micro-perforated nickel mesh is attached.

screen printing A technique in which a squeegee is used to push printing ink or dye through a screen mesh on to the cloth.

seam The join between two pieces of fabric that have been sewn together.

secondary colours Composed of two primaries: orange (red and yellow), green (yellow and blue) and violet (blue and red).

secondary visual research Research material from publications and similar sources that would otherwise be unavailable to the designer. When used for inspiration, the reinterpretation of this type of source material is vital for copyright reasons.

selvedge edge The finished woven edge of a cloth that runs parallel to the warp and prevents the cloth from unravelling.

sett Defines the spacing of the weft and warp threads in a woven cloth.

shaft On a loom, the heddles are attached to two rods and together they form the shaft.

shed The opening created in the warp threads as the shafts move up and down during weaving, through which the shuttle is passed.

shuttle In the weaving process, the shuttle carries the weft thread, which is wound on to a bobbin, through the shed.

silk georgette A sheer luxury silk fabric that looks translucent when printed. It is similar to crêpe de Chine but not as soft or lustrous.

slub A nub of yarn that can appear due to twisting during spinning. This can be either an unintentional defect or a deliberate feature.

smart textiles Textiles with woven-in nanotechnologies that enable interaction with the environment and microcomputers; used predominantly for performance sportswear and military clothing.

smocking A hand-stitching technique used to secure and adjust the folds in a finely pleated area of cloth.

spandex A synthetic yarn known for its elasticity and strength. It revolutionized the garment industry and continues to have a major impact, particularly in the areas of swimwear and high-performance sportswear.

spun yarn (see **yarn**)

squeegee The component in screen and rotary printing that pushes the printing ink or dye paste through the screen mesh on to the cloth. It has a horizontal blade-like edge that can vary in flexibility and type of finish according to the ink or dye paste consistency and fabric type.

stab stitch A simple stitch in which the needle is stabbed into the front of the fabric and then pulled through from the back.

steaming Printed dyes are affixed to the fabric by steaming. The moisture and rapid heating of the steamer transfers the dye molecules from the thickener paste to the fabric fibres.

stencil In screen printing, the stencil is applied to the screen through which the ink or dye is passed using a squeegee to create the design on the cloth. Stencils can be produced either industrially as a film to be applied to a screen coated with photosensitive emulsion that is then exposed to ultra-violet light, or by digitally wax-spraying the design directly on to the screen.

stitch The movement of a threaded needle from the back of a cloth to the front and then back again. The smallest motif in embroidery.

stuffing Used in quilting to create a relief surface by developing and cutting out a motif from the stuffing material and then sewing it between the quilting fabrics.

substrate setting This determines the positioning of the inkjet heads for digital printing, and needs to be adjusted according to the specific fabric type to be printed. For a fine fabric such as silk the digital inkjet heads are closer to the fabric than for a thick pile fabric such as velvet.

tambour beading Produced on a transparent fabric attached to an embroidery frame, this technique involves sewing chains of beads on to the fabric using a tambour hook and chain stitch.

tertiary colours A primary colour mixed with a secondary colour creates a tertiary colour.

textile finishing A generic term for all subsequent treatments applied to a finished woven cloth, such as inks and dyes as well as starch and flame-retardant treatments.

toile de Jouy An illustrative style of printed design, sometimes narrative-based, usually printed in a single colour on a pale ground. It originated in the town of Jouy-en-Josas, near Paris.

top cloth The upper layer of the three sewn fabrics in quilting that carries the design.

treadle loom The precursor to the modern hand- and industrial loom, it has long pedals that are operated by the weaver's feet and are tied to one or more shafts to raise and lower warp threads in selected combinations. It allows weavers to keep their hands free to manipulate the shuttle.

trend forecast An indicator of fashion, creative and technical developments in the market.

turned-edge appliqué A basic technique that involves turning the edge of a cut fabric shape, requiring a seam allowance with small cuts around the edge of the shape, which is then turned under, ironed and pinned down. A small stitch is used to secure the shape around the edge of the fold.

tweed A rough-surfaced cloth made in plain or twill weave in two or three colours to create check or plaid patterns. Originally from Scotland.

undulating twill weave Produced by varying the diagonal angle of the twill pattern, how hard the weft yarns are packed together, or the tensions of the stretched warp yarns.

variegated pattern A textile design motif or pattern without symmetry or consistency caused by shape or colour variations.

velour A plush woven cloth created through felting, similar to velvet; widely used in millinery.

viscose Cellulose xanthate combined with sodium hydroxide creates the spinning solution viscose, which is used to make the cloth viscose rayon. The raw material is wood pulp or cotton linters.

visualization Digitally mapped, photographic or hand-drawn rendering of a textile design in product context, for example on a piece of furniture or in garment form.

wadding The middle cloth used in quilting.

waffle weave A weave that has a recessed square repeat pattern with raised edges around it.

warp Tensioned threads attached lengthwise or vertically to the loom to support the weft threads. A single warp thread is known as a warp end.

warp end A single warp thread.

warping mill A mechanism used in the preparation of warps for weaving.

water-jet loom A loom that carries the yarn through the shed by a jet of water.

watermark (see **moiré**)

wax-resist printing A technique popular both in the West and in Africa, wax-resist printed fabrics are produced industrially using a resin resist, to mimic the aesthetic of batik.

weft Horizontal filling threads in weaving that run from one selvedge to the other. A single weft thread is known as a weft pick.

weft pick A single weft thread.

yarn Falls into two main categories: spun yarns composed of relatively short lengths of fibre that are mechanically twisted or spun; and filament yarn composed of continuous strands of fibre, such as silk.

yarn dyeing The dyeing of yarn before weaving, rather than piece-dyeing the finished cloth.

yarn palette A working area for yarns that can be added to a design, which comes from a library of yarn files within computer software for weaving.

Further reading and additional resources

Introduction

Books

Sarah E. Braddock Clarke and Marie O'Mahony, *Techno Textiles 2, Revolutionary Fabrics for Fashion and Design*, Thames & Hudson, 2005.
Bradley Quinn, *Textile Futures: Fashion, Design and Technology*, Berg, 2010.

Journals, magazines and websites

Collezioni donna haute couture – logos.info
Dazed & Confused magazine (fashion, art, film, music and ideas) – dazeddigital.com/

Chapter 1 - Context

Books

Hazel Clark, David Brody, *Design Studies, A Reader*, Berg, 2009.
Kate Fletcher, *Sustainable Fashion and Textiles: Design Journeys*, Earthscan publishers, 2008.
John Gillow and Bryan Sentance, *World Textiles: A Visual Guide to Traditional Techniques*, Thames & Hudson, 1999.
Mary Schoeser, *World Textiles, A Concise History*, Thames & Hudson, 2003.

Journals, magazines and websites

European Textile Network – etn-net.org/
Text: For the Study of Textile Art, Design and History, The Textile Society – textilesociety.org.uk/
Textile: The Journal of Cloth & Culture, Berg Publishers.

Chapter 2 - Printed textile design

Books

Melanie Bowles and Ceri Isaac, *Digital Textile Design; Portfolio Skills Fashion and Textiles*, Laurence King Publishing, 2009.
Nadine Coleno, *The Hermès Scarf: History and Mystique*, Thames & Hudson, 2009.
Leslie W. C. Miles, *Textile Printing*, The Society of Dyers and Colourists, 1994.
Susan Mellor and Joost Elffers, *Textile Design: 200 Years of Patterns for Printed Fabrics Arranged by Motif, Colour, Period and Design*, Thames & Hudson, 2002.
Alex Newman and Hardy Blechman (eds), *DPM, Disruptive Pattern Material. An Encylopaedia of Camouflage: Nature, Military, Culture*. DPM Ltd, 2004.

Journals, magazines and websites

American Association of Textile Chemists and Colorists – aatcc.org/
R A Smart: digital printing, screen printing and jacquard weaving – rasmart.co.uk/
Texitura, Printing Design Magazine, Circulo Textil – texitura.es/

Chapter 3 - Woven textile design

Books

Anni Albers, *On Weaving*, Dover Publications, 1993.
Chapurukha M. Kusimba, J. Claire Odland and Bennet Bronson (eds), *Unwrapping the Textile Traditions of Madagascar*, University of California Press, 2004.
Michael Maharam, *Maharam Agenda*, Birkhauser, 2010.
William Watson, *Textile Design and Colour*, Ariel Books, 1996.

Journals, magazines and websites

The Ann Sutton Foundation – theannsuttonfoundation.org/
The Journal for Weavers, Spinners and Dyers, The Association of Guilds of Weavers, Spinners and Dyers – wsd.org.uk
The Worshipful Company of Weavers – weavers.org.uk/

Chapter 4 - Mixed media textile design

Books

Brooke Hodge, *Skin and Bones, Parallel Practices in Fashion and Architecture*, Thames & Hudson, 2006.
Sheila Paine, *Embroidered Textiles: A World Guide to Traditional Patterns*, Thames & Hudson, 2008.
Francoise Tellier-Loumagne, *The Art of Embroidery: Inspirational Stitches, Textures and Surfaces*, Thames & Hudson, 2006.
Colette Wolff, *The Art of Manipulating Fabric*, Krause Publications, 1996.

Journals, magazines and websites

Embroidery, Embroiderers' Guild – embroiderersguild.com/
Hand & Lock Embroidery – handembroidery.com/
Madeira Embroidery Threads – madeira.co.uk/

Chapter 5 - Design principles

Books

Allen C. Cohen, Ingrid Johnson and Joesph Pizzutto, *Fabric of Science*, 9th edition, Fairchild Books, 2009.
Clive Edwards, *How to Read Pattern: A Crash Course in Textile Design*, A&C Black, 2009.
Barbara Glasner, Petra Schmidt and Ursula Schondeling (eds), *Patterns 2. Design, Art and Architecture*, Birkhauser, 2008.
Johannes Itten, *Itten: The Elements of Colour, A Treatise on the Colour System of Johannes Itten*, John Wiley & Sons, 1970.

Journals, magazines and websites

Frame, Peter Huiberts publishing – framemag.com/
Lectra, CAD/CAM software for fashion, accessories, footwear, furniture, automotive, marine or industrial contexts – lectra.com/
Pantone, international authority on colour – Pantone.com
Textile View Magazine, Metropolitan Publishing BV – viewpublications.com/

Chapter 6 - Creating a collection

Books

Sandy Black, *Fashioning Fabrics: Contemporary Textiles and Fabrics*, Black Dog Publishing, 2006.
Joachim Kobuss, Alexander Bretz and Arian Hassani, *Become a Successful Designer: Protect and Manage Your Design Rights Internationally*, Birkhauser, 2010.
Bradley Quinn, *Textile Designers at the Cutting Edge*, Laurence King Publishing, 2009.
Angeli Sachs, *Nature Design: From Inspiration to Innovation*, Lars Muller Publishers, 2007.

Journals, magazines and websites

Heimtextil Trade Fair, Frankfurt – heimtextil.messefrankfurt.com
Première Vision Trade Fair, Paris – premierevision.fr
Style.com/the online home of Vogue – style.com
Vogue – vogue.co.uk
WGSN, trend forecasting – wgsn.com

Chapter 7 - Education and employment

Books

Caroline Evans, *Fashion at the Edge: Spectacle, Modernity and Deathliness*, Yale University Press, 2003.

Journals, magazines and websites

Bradford Textile Society – www.bradfordtextilesociety.org.uk
British Fashion Council – britishfashioncouncil.com/
Design Council – designcouncil.org.uk/
Society of Dyers and Colourists – sdc.org.uk
The Textile Institute – texi.org/
Texprint (promoting new textile designers) – texprint.org.uk/

Textile museums and galleries

USA
Metropolitan Museum of Art, New York
www.metmuseum.org

Cooper Hewitt, National Design Museum, New York
www.cooperhewitt.org

Textile Museum, Washington, D.C.
www.textilemuseum.org

UK
Victoria and Albert Museum, London
www.vam.ac.uk

Whitworth Art Gallery, University of Manchester
www.whitworth.manchester.ac.uk

Design Museum, London
www.designmuseum.org

Italy
Museo del Tessuto, Prato
www.museodeltessuto.it

Design Gallery Milano
www.designgallerymilano.com

France
Musée des Arts de la Mode et du Textile, Paris
www.lesartsdecoratifs.fr

Musée d'Art Moderne, Paris
www.mam.paris.fr

Musées des Tissus et des Arts Décoratifs, Lyon
www.musee-des-tissus.com

Toile de Jouy Museum, Jouy-en-Josas
www.museedelatoiledejouy.fr

Netherlands
Nederlands Textielmuseum
www.textielmuseum.nl

Centraal Museum, Utrecht
www.centraalmuseum.nl

Germany
Bauhaus-Archiv, Berlin
www.bauhaus.de

Museum fur Kunsthandwerk, Frankfurt-Am-Main
www.angewandtekunst-frankfurt.de

Denmark
Oksnehallen, Copenhagen
www.dgi-byen.dk/oeksnehallen

India
The Calico Museum of Textiles and the Sarabhai Foundation Collections, Gujarat
www.calicomuseum.com

Australia
The Powerhouse, Museum of Applied Arts and Sciences, Sydney
www.powerhousemuseum.com

Canada
Textile Museum of Canada, Ontario
www.textilemuseum.ca

Selected textile design departments and schools

UK
Royal College of Art, www.rca.ac.uk

Central Saint Martins, University of the Arts
www.csm.arts.ac.uk

Chelsea College of Art and Design, University of the Arts, www.chelsea.arts.ac.uk

London College of Fashion, University of the Arts
www.fashion.arts.ac.uk

University College Falmouth www.falmouth.ac.uk

Birmingham Institute of Art and Design
Birmingham City University, www.biad.bcu.ac.uk

Winchester School of Art
University of Southampton, www.wsa.soton.ac.uk

Manchester School of Art
Manchester Metropolitan University
www.art.mmu.ac.uk

Glasgow School of Art, www.gsa.ac.uk

USA
Cranbrook Academy Department of Fibers
www.cranbrookart.edu

Philadelphia University
School of Engineering and Textiles
www.philau.edu/engineeringandtextiles

School of the Art Institute of Chicago
Department of Fiber and Material Studies
www.saic.edu

Savannah College of Art and Design
School of Design, Department of Fibers
www.scad.edu

North Carolina State University
College of Textiles, www.tx.ncsu.edu

Italy
Nuova Accademia di Belle Arti Milano
Academy of Fine Arts and Design
www.italian-design-academy.com

France
École Nationale Supérieure des Arts Décoratifs
www.ensad.fr

Netherlands
Design Academy Eindhoven
www.designacademy.nl

Japan
Kobe Design University
School of Design, Department of Fashion and Textile Design, www.kobe-du.ac.jp

Hong Kong
The Hong Kong Polytechnic University
The Institute of Textiles and Clothing
www.itc.polyu.edu.hk

New Zealand
Massey University College of Creative Arts
www.creative.massey.ac.nz

Textile trade fairs

Textile trade fairs provide a variety of products including basic fabrics, novelty fabrics, fibres and yarns, eco-textiles, textile design resources, trend forecasts and CAD/CAM and styling services.

Textile Trade Fairs are visited by a variety of customers ranging from designers, garment and textile manufacturers, trading companies, garment and textile buying agents, buyers for department- and chain-stores, mail-order company representatives, wholesalers and retailers. The main international fairs are listed below.

Première Vision, Paris

February: spring/summer collections
September: autumn/winter collections
(Also showcased in New York, Moscow, Tokyo and Beijing)
Incorporates: First vision, Expofil Fashion, Indigo Fashion
Fashion: fabrics, textile design, fibres, yarns and threads, trend forecasts, textile innovation

Pitti Imagine, Florence

January: spring/summer collections
Fashion: fibres and yarns, fabrics, garments, textile design, trend forecasts, textile innovation

Interstoff, Hong Kong

March: spring/summer collections
Fashion: fabrics, fibres and yarns, garments, textile design, trend forecasts, textile innovation

Heimtextil, Frankfurt

January: home and contract textiles: fabrics, textile design, tend forecasts, textile innovation

Index

Page numbers in *italics* refer to picture captions

Picture credits Agent Provocateur/Photo: Tim Bret-Day 20 (left); akg-Images/Erich Lessing 11 (bottom); Alamy 133; Alamy/© Picture Contact/Jochem Wijnands 105, 117; © Ed Alcock 108 (bottom); Ancient Art and Architecture 79; © AOYAMA Satoru/Property of Microsoft Art Collection courtesy Mizuma Art Gallery/Photo: Keizo Kioku 114; Claire Armitage 209; The Art Archive/© ADAGP, Paris and DACS, London 2009. 24 (top right); Courtesy of Artifort. 181 (bottom); Arup 102, 103 (top); Courtesy of John Baldessari/marian goodman gallery, New York 147 (right); Cecil Balmond/Arup photo Alex Fradkin 103 (bottom left and right); Ed Barber 85 (top left); Basso & Brooke/Spring Summer 2009 Catwalk images © Fernanda Calfat 64; 184, 185; Polly Bell, 50, 173, 200 (top), 201; With thanks to: Bernina Sewing Machines Bogod & Company Ltd www.bernina.co.uk 115 (top and bottom); Ozwald Boateng 104; Sarah Bone 73; Carlo Borlenghi/SEASEE.COM 30 (top right); The Bridgeman Art Library © The Potteries Museum and Art Gallery, Stoke-on-Trent, UK/© Trustees of the Paolozzi Foundation, Licensed by DACS 2009 151; The Bridgeman Art Library/© The Design Library, New York, USA 38 (left), 57 (right); The Bridgeman Art Library/© Ashmolean Museum, University of Oxford, UK/Robert Shaw Collection 85 (bottom); The Bridgeman Art Library/Private Collection/© Philip Mould Ltd, London 16 (top left); The Bridgeman Art Library/Private Collection/Photo © Bonhams, London/Sofa Compact (473) © Eames Office, LLC (eamesoffice.com) 28 (bottom left and bottom centre); The Bridgeman Art Library/Royal Botanical Gardens, Kew, London, UK 149 (bottom); CA2M/Shigeru Ban Architects Europe & Jean de Gastines/Artefactory 103 (centre, left and right); J.R. Campbell 68 (top and bottom right); Catwalking 6 (right), 83 (top), 109 (top), 121, 127 (top), 128 (bottom), 132 (top), 157 (left), 170 (top); Hussein Chalayan 214 (top); © Christo 1998 (top) and 1985 (bottom) 136 Photo: Wolfgang Volz; Simon Clarke 67, 139, 164 (bottom); Simon Clarke/RA Smart 164 (top); Classic Chevy – © Chuck Close/Courtesy Jay Jopling/White Cube (London) 96 (top); © Annie Collinge 191; Como Textprint 199; Lia Cook 21 (left); Corbis 12 (top), 16 (top right), 17, 32, 38 (top right), 38 (bottom right), 78 (top), 80, 128 (top); Corbis/Conde Nast 20 (right), 30 (top left); Corbis/Girard folk art collection at the Museum of International Folk Art in Santa Fe, New Mexico 28 (bottom right); Shirely Craven/Private Collection. Photo: Ferens Art Gallery, Hull Museums 152; Création Baumann, CH-Langenthal, www.creationbaumann.com 88; Ana de la Cueva 134; Nathalie Du Pasquier/Memphis Milano 155 (bottom right), 168; Rebecca Earley 72 (left and centre); eBoy © 2006 76 (top); © Eggleston Artistic Trust Courtesy Cheim & Read, New York 147 (left); Courtesy of Eley Kishimoto Apparel Ltd Photographer: Kumi Saito 37, 45, 145 (right); Ulrika Erdes/© DACS 2009 132 (bottom); Etro 162; Mary Evans Picture Library 116; © 2007 Lillian Farag 61; Ian Finch for Strangelove 54; Ed Forster 69; Fowler Museum at UCLA/Photo: Don Cole 126; Jonathan Fuller 66; Aleksandra Gaca 156; Courtesy Gee's Bend 122; Getty 19, 106 (top right), 120, 127 (bottom); Liam Gillick, *Prototype Conference Room* (2002/09) Photo: Richard Bryant 214 (bottom); Anna Glover 1, 5, 204, 205; Zaha Hadid Architects 150; Designer Jane Harris, 2003/04 'Potential Beauty', 3D Computer Graphic Animation, Mike Dawson, Performer, Ruth Gibson Supported by: Central Saint Martins Research, University of the Arts London & The Arts and Humanities Research Council; Messe Frankfurt Exhibition GmbH / Helmut Stettin 186 left, Petra Welzel 186 right ; Eric J Heller 6/1993 161 (right); howies® "The Wheel" designed by Ollie Wolf www.howies.co.uk 33 (bottom); Inside Outside 129; Itten/© DACS 2009 144, 145, 146 (top); Jan Jansen Shoes/Photo: Joost Guntenaar 76 (bottom); Anna Keck 125; Embroidered by the Women of the villages Hamburg, Bodiam, Bell in Eastern Cape, south Africa/Keiskamma Org. 118, 119; Wendy Kotenko 85 (top right); Kvadrat 93 (top and bottom right); Kvadrat/Ronan and Erwan Bouroullec 8; Collection of the Kyoto Costume Institute, Photo by Takashi Hatakeyama 157 (top and bottom right); Nico Laan 21 (top right); Makeba Lewis 100 (top); By permission of Liberty PLC 35, 38 (centre), 41, 46, 47, 48/49; Linton Tweeds Limited 83 (bottom); LKP 14; Maharam, 2007 Inox Structure 92 (top); 2005 (The Story of my Life by Maria Kalman) 92 (bottom right), Design 9297 by Josef Hoffmann 2007 92 (bottom left), A4 Studio for Maharam 94 (top), 95; Copyright © Marimekko Corporation, Puusepänkatu 4, 00880 Helsinki, Finland. All rights reserved 31 (top right), 31 (left), 39, 167, 171, 182; Andrew Meredith 188, 189; Jason Miller 166; The Minneapolis Institute of Arts 34; Moroso Photo: Alessandro Paderni 7, 123 (top); © Paul Morrison. Courtesy Alison Jacques Gallery, London 170 (bottom); NedGraphics 96 bottom: Hettie Nettheim 174, 175; Rupert Newman 59; Rupert Newman and Simon Clarke 55, 56 ; © Karen Nicol 113; © NOWHERE CO., LTD. All rights reserved. 1993/2009 62 (top); NUNO photo: Sue McNab 28 (top left and top right), 78 (bottom left); Seaplane - Designed for Pacific Clothing Inc. Honolulu, Hawaii by Marlo Fabrics, Honolulu, Hawaii, 179 (centre right); Wooden Boat – Pacific Clothing Company. Inc. Honolulu Hawaii by Hoffman California Fabrics, Mission Vieio, California 179 (bottom left); Woodie – Designed for Pacific Clothing Company. Inc. Honolulu, Hawaii by Trans Pacific Textiles Honolulu, Hawaii 179 (bottom right) Cadillac Cruising – Designed for Pacific Clothing Company, Inc. Honolulu, Hawaii by Marlo Fabrics, Honolulu, Hawaii. Print design licensed by General Motors. 179 (top left) Designed for Pacific Clothing Company, Inc. Honolulu, Hawaii by Marlo Fabrics, Honolulu, Hawaii. Print design licensed by General Motors. 179 (top right), Marlin – Designed by Pacific Clothing Company. Inc. Honolulu, Hawaii 179 (centre left); © Desiree Palmen/Photography Desiree Palmen & Risk Hazekamp/www.desireepalmen.nl 26; © Panton Design, CH-Basel 25; Images extracted from Peclers Paris fabric review A/W 09/10 (textile manufacturer KBC, ULYSSE PILA, FPP Cotonnades, ULYSSE PILA, FPP Cotonnades, Hokkoh). 141 (top left); Images extracted from Peclers Paris fabric review A/W 09/10 (textile manufacturer from top down Henitex, KBC, KBC, Trouillet). 141 (top right); Images extracted from Peclers Paris fabric review A/W 09/10 (textile manufacturer from top down Hokkoh, JCR, KBC, Textiles en Biais, KBC). 141 (bottom left); Images extracted from Peclers Paris fabric review A/W 09/10 (Textile Manufacturer from top down Henitex, Tiss et Teint, ACD Maille, Tailor, Tiss et Teint). 141 (bottom right); © Grayson Perry/Courtesy: The Collection Art and Archaeology of Lincolnshire and Victoria Miro Gallery, 2006 109 (bottom); Kay Politowicz 72 (right); Courtesy of Prada 74; © Première Vision 187; Promostyl Creative Staff (team) 142; Sheona Quenby 42, 68 (bottom centre); Karim Rashid, Inc. 94 (bottom); Tom Ray 160; C.E.B. Reas Image courtesy bitforms gallery nyc 137, 161 (left); Rex Features 106 (bottom); Vibeke Riisberg 33 (top left and right); Ismini Samanidou 98; Scala, Florence/©2009. DeAgostini Picture Library/© DACS 2009 163; Scala/© ARS, NY and DACS, London 2009 23; Scala/© DACS 2009 146 (bottom); Scala/MoMa, New York/©DACS 2009 22; Courtesy of Jakob Schlaepfer/Photo: Rudy Facchin von Steidl 130; Courtesy of Jakop Schlaepfer 131; © William Scott Foundation 2010/Fermanagh County Museum/Northern Ireland Museums Council/Photo: Bryan Rutledge 153; ScotWeave.com 84, 89 (bottom), 90, 97, 99 Courtesy of Casper Sejersen and Kvadrat A/S 77, 93 (top left and top centre); Emma Sheldon 172, 207; Showroom Dummies/Abigail with Fly Sky print. Hackney Wick, London. Photo: Coco Amardeil, 2003 75; RA Smart, Macclesfield 65; Sottsass Associati/Image concept and photo montage studio: Rethinkinggroup.com 155 (top); Steve Speller 135; Kay Stanley 27; Helen Stark 198 (left), 212 (top); © Norma Starszakowna/Photographer: Andy Taylor 52; © Mary Steiglitz 68 (top and bottom left); Studio Tord Boontje 106 (top left); Style.com 190; Ruth Summerfield, Textile Designer 195, 202, 203; Tanu Kanga 12 (bottom); Sophie Tarbuck 208; © Tate, London 2009/© Bridget Riley 2009. All rights reserved. Courtesy Karsten Schubert London 154 (left); © Tate, London 2009/Courtesy Jim Lambie 154 (right); Sarah Taylor 101; Texprint ® Photograph by James McCauley 212 (bottom left), Texprint ® Photograph by Nicola Gleichauf (bottom centre & right); Photograph: The St Ives Times & Echo. 198 (right); Timorous Beasties, Alistair McAuley and Paul Simmons. www.timorousbeasties.com 36, 58; Topfoto 13 (bottom); Anne Townley 111; Hitoshi Ujiie 71; University College Falmouth 96, 115: Urafiki 13 (top left); Patricia Uriquiola 123 (bottom); © V&A Images, Victoria and Albert Museum 9, 18, photo© Curtis Moffat/© L & M SERVICES B.V. The Hague 20090707 24 (top left), 29, 60, 108 (top); Dries Van Noten 6 (left); Eugène van Veldhoven 70; © Alec Walker/Penlee House Gallery and Museum, Penzance/© The Artist's Estate 51; Marcel Wanders/Moroso 181 (top); © Paul Warchol 192, 193; Werner Foreman Archive 10, 11 (top), 15; Photo: Stephen White/Courtesy Jay Jopling/White Cube (London) © Tracey Emin. All rights reserved, DACS 2009 107; Matthew Williamson AW09 Look 21 21 (top left); © Grethe Wittrock/Photographer: Anders Sune Berg 53; zedfactory.com 200 (bottom).